JOURNAL FOR THE STUDY OF THE PSEUDEPIGRAPHA SUPPLEMENT SERIES

38

Sheffield Academic Press

On Scrolls, Artefacts and Intellectual Property

edited by

Timothy H. Lim
Hector L. MacQueen
Calum M. Carmichael

Journal for the Study of the Pseudepigrapha
Supplement Series 38

Published by Sheffield Academic Press Ltd
Mansion House
19 Kingfield Road
Sheffield S11 9AS
England
www.SheffieldAcademicPress.com

Typeset by Sheffield Academic Press
and
Printed on acid-free paper in Great Britain
by MPG Books Ltd
Bodmin, Cornwall

British Library Cataloguing-in-Publication Data

A catalogue record for this book is available
from the British Library

ISBN 1-84127-212-4

CONTENTS

Part IV
SCHOLARLY ENTERPRISE AND INDIVIDUAL PROPERTY RIGHTS

Appendix
THE SUPREME COURT JUDGMENT

ABBREVIATIONS

AP	Associated Press
BAR	*Biblical Archaeology Review*
BCIA	Berne Convention Implementation Act 1988
BSAJ	*British School of Archaeology in Jerusalem*
CA	Copyright Act 1976
CBRL	Council for British Research in the Levant
CDPA	Copyright, Designs and Patents Act 1988
CIL	*Corpus inscriptionum iudaicarum*
DJD	Discoveries in the Judaean Desert
EIPR	European Intellectual Property Review
FARMS	The Foundation for Ancient Research and Mormon Studies
Fe Supp	Federal Supplement
GRUR	Gewerblicher Rechtsschutz und Urheberrecht. Internationale Teil
IAA	Israel Antiques Authority
Inc.	Incorporated
INS	International News Service
JJS	*Journal of Jewish Studies*
JRS	*Journal of Roman Studies*
MMT	Miqṣat Ma'aśe ha-Torah
n.	footnote
PAM	Palestine Archaeological Museum
S.C.	Supreme Court
TR	Teacher of Righteousness
USC	United States Code

Abbreviation in Case Citations:

A.C.	Appeal Court
C.L.R.	Commonwealth Law Reports
E.C.R.	European Court Reports
F.S.R.	Fleet Street Reports
W.L.R.	Weekly Law Reports

Refs to Acts, etc.

Art.	Article (in European Directives)
para.	paragraph
reg.	regulation
Sch.	Schedule

List of Contributors

Professor Calum Carmichael, Cornell University
Professor Cindy Alberts Carson, Whittier Law School
Justice Dalia Dorner, Supreme Court of Israel
Professor Wojciech Kowlaski, University of Silesia
Dr Timothy H. Lim, University of Edinburgh
Professor Hector MacQueen, University of Edinburgh
Professor David Nimmer, Irell & Manella and UCLA School of Law
Dr Kay Prag, Manchester Museum
Professor John Richardson, University of Edinburgh
Rt Hon Lord Rodger of Earlsferry, Court of Session
Mr Hershel Shanks, Biblical Archaeology Society
Professor John Strugnell, Harvard University
Dr Paul L.C. Torremans, University of Leicester
Professor Emmanuel Tov, Hebrew University of Jerusalem
Professor Geza Vermes, University of Oxford

INTRODUCTION

Timothy H. Lim

Are modern editors to be considered as 'authors' of the ancient manuscripts that they edit? Do archaeologists have special claims to the artefacts that they dig up, record and interpret? Can curators claim copyright for the work that they restore? What are the principles underlying the claim to intellectual property and how are they formulated in international copyright laws?

Eight of the thirteen papers published in this volume were read at a one-day symposium held on 19 May 1999 at New College, Edinburgh. Sponsored by the two University of Edinburgh Faculties of Divinity and Law, the Shepherd & Wedderburn Centre for Research in Intellectual Property and Technology, and Cornell Law School, the gathering sought to address the interdisciplinary issue of the intellectual property rights of archaeologists, principal text editors and curators in the study, publication and preservation of artefacts.

The symposium focused on issues arising out of the law suit undertaken by Elisha Qimron and the 20 March 1993 judgment by the District Court of Jerusalem against Hershel Shanks, Biblical Archaeology Society, Robert Eisenman and James Robinson on the publication of the composite text of 4QMMT (a text of the Dead Sea Scrolls from Cave 4 called *miqṣat ma'aśe ha-torah* or 'some precepts of the Torah'). The defendants had appealed to the Supreme Court of Israel and the decision, upholding the District Court ruling, was handed down on 20 August 2000.

For the symposium, the speakers were asked to address its wider ramifications rather than the case itself. Thus, Kay Prag and John Richardson were invited to speak about and reflect on analogous issues involving the publication of the Kenyon Excavations of Jerusalem and Greek and Latin inscriptions respectively. John Strugnell and Geza Vermes were asked to discuss the history of the publication of the Dead Sea Scrolls generally and not on MMT in particular. Vermes, of course, is the one who had coined the frequently quoted sound bite, 'the academic scandal *par excellence* of the twentieth century', to describe the pre-1977 publication process of the scrolls, although he and others have also extended this battle cry for the subsequent period up to 1991. In the paper, he writes about his 50 years of personal experience of access or the lack of it to the unpublished material. Strugnell's paper describes the history of the publication of the scrolls from the perspective of an insider and former Editor-in-Chief. He describes the formation of the original team and the informal and gentlemanly agreements that were operative before responding to criticisms about the speed of the publication project by comparing the work on the Scrolls to six other projects. Whether these projects are comparable to the Scrolls is, of course, debatable. An invitation sent to the editors of the Oxyrhynchus papyri was turned down, because they did not feel that their work was relevant to the Scrolls controversy. Emanuel Tov, the present Editor-in-Chief, provides an authoritative report on the present state of Scrolls publication projects and estimates that there have been some 50 conferences devoted to the Scrolls.

Immediately before, during and after the symposium, it became evident that the case involving 4QMMT must be addressed directly. Hershel Shanks was invited to discuss the ramifications of the MMT case for the Biblical Archaeology Society's work in the popular dissemination of archaeological findings generally. Instead, he spoke primarily about the MMT case. Elisha Qimron, misunderstanding the aims of the symposium and concerned that this meeting might be misappropriated by Shanks, complained that he too should have been invited to speak about the case and to present his side. But the symposium was an academic conference and not a trial. There was a range of opinions expressed in the papers presented there and in this volume. For example, Hector MacQueen, a co-editor and co-organizer of the symposium, provides a British perspective on the MMT case, broadly supporting Dorner's ruling and concluding that the copyright protection is conferred on the right kind of skill and labour. Cindy Carson, on the other hand, disagrees with Dorner's judgment and argues that copyright is conferred on 'originality' and not labour, of which Qimron's text editing is an example.

Following the symposium and after a protracted discussion among the editors, it was decided that the MMT case must be addressed directly in the proceedings. This was primarily due to the wider audience/readership for which the volume was intended. Not every interested reader would know about the details of the case. To this end, it was decided to publish Justice Dalia Dorner's judgment in an accurate English translation. Qimron was also invited to contribute to the volume. Having accepted the invitation, he withdrew without giving a reason.

Paul Torremans of the University of Leicester was invited to contribute a piece on the issue of choice of law in the MMT case and Wojciech Kowalski of the University of Silesia another on the international guidelines for publishing cultural artefacts. Both these papers bolster the legal section of the volume beyond the original programme of the symposium and address important issues about which law, American or Israeli, should have been used in the trial and what legal, cultural and international rights and guidelines are to be considered in the publication of the Scrolls.

Weeks after the papers were submitted to the publishers, the appeal panel of the Supreme Court of Israel, consisting of Chief Justice Barak, Justice Türkel and Justice Beinish, handed down their decision. Subsequent activity, both on the Internet and elsewhere, brought us together with David Nimmer, who had represented a 'Committee of Concerned Intellectual Property Educators' in its *amicus curiae* ('friend of the court') petition which was denied by the Supreme Court. Nimmer has written a book entitled *Copyright in the Dead Sea Scrolls* and had commissioned an English translation of the decision of the Supreme Court by Ms. Yoninah Hoffman, an advocate of the appellant. Nimmer was invited to contribute a piece, based on a chapter from his book,[1] that analyses the judicial decision on Qimron's originality. Hoffman's translation of the decision is included in this volume.

Many individuals and institutions are to be thanked for contributing to the symposium and the publication of this volume. The Rt Hon. Lord Rodger of Earlsferry took time out of swearing in the ministers of the new Scottish Parliament to open our symposium with remarks that appear as the Foreword in this volume. Lord Sutherland, Principal of the University of Edinburgh, welcomed the participants of the symposium to Scotland's capital. The Faculty Group of Arts, Divinity and Music, and the Provost, Frances Dow, once again supported research on the scrolls in Edinburgh with a conference grant. Financial subvention

1. *Houston Law Review* 38 (2001).

was also received from the Shepherd & Wedderburn Centre for Reseach in Intellectual Property and Technology, of which Hector MacQueen is the Director. David Johnstone, then Regius Professor of Civil Law at the University of Cambridge, at short notice stepped in for Russell Osgood, then Dean of the Cornell Law School but about to take up an appointment as President of Grinnell College. Jeremy Phillips, Visiting Professor in Intellectual Property Law at the University of Alicante, University College London and Bournemouth University, and consultant to Slaughter & May, treated the participants of the symposium to a highly entertaining after dinner speech. Calum Carmichel, co-organizer and co-editor, and Professor of Comparative Literature and Adjunct Professor of Law at Cornell University, was instrumental in establishing contacts in the United States. Larry Hurtado, a colleague in Divinity and Professor of New Testament, kindly read John Strugnell's paper when it became evident that the latter would be unable to travel from Harvard. The paper was followed by a conference telephone call during which time Strugnell participated in the discussion. Graeme Auld, another colleague in Divinity, Professor of Hebrew Bible and Head of the Graduate School, has been supportive in every aspect of the symposium. Lydia Lawson, a secretary in the Faculty of Law, handled the practical matters of the running of the symposium with great expertise. We especially thank her. Many thanks to Michael Birnhack of the Faculty of Law, University of Haifa, who, having translated the Supreme Court decision and published this on the Internet, lent his expertise in revising my translation of Dorner's Judgment. Dr Peretz Segal of the Israel Ministry of Justice kindly had copies of the district court judgment and Supreme Court decision sent to me. And thanks to Philip Davies and Sheffield Academic Press for flexibility and accommodation in the publication of this volume.

A few points call for clarification. First, the text for which Elisha Qimron has been given copyright is referred to as 'the composite text' (*ha-text ha-merchav*) by Dorner in her judgment (section 6), but the Supreme Court decision calls it 'the deciphered text' (*ha-text ha-mephua'nach*; see 'Background'). Second, in section 22 of Dorner's Judgment, it states that Strugnell believed that the sentences were nine lines long and he therefore assembled them *vertically*, but that Qimron thought that they were 18 lines long and assembled them *horizontally*. Although the specific texts and fragments in question are not mentioned, they may well have been the reverse.

Finally, the original idea for the symposium came quite incidentally. Responding to a call for papers for a previous conference on the Scrolls in Edinburgh in 1998, now published as *The Dead Sea Scrolls in their Historical Context* (Edinburgh: T. & T. Clark, 2000), Cindy Carson had offered to read a paper on 'Raiders of the Lost Scrolls', the same title as the article that she had previously published in the *Michigan Journal of International Law*. The organizer, however, did not think that the topic was appropriate for that conference, but was so intrigued by the issues raised in the publication as to make plans for a second conference on the Scrolls in the following year.

OPENING REMARKS TO THE SYMPOSIUM ON INTELLECTUAL PROPERTY AND CULTURAL ARTEFACTS

Rt Hon. Lord Rodger of Earlsferry

It is my honour as Lord President of the Court of Session to say a brief word of welcome to all the participants in this symposium. It is in fact not only an honour but also a pleasure since the theme of your symposium is one which I find intensely interesting.

Nor is this surprising since, perhaps like nearly all Western lawyers, I am an inheritor of the Roman Law tradition, one part of which begins, according to legend, with the embezzlement of a cultural artefact. The cultural artefact in question was the collection of legal formulae kept by the pontifical college. We are told that around the beginning of the third century BCE Cn. Flavius, the freedman of Appius Claudius Caecus, published an unauthorized copy of these formulae and so made this procedural information freely available to the people of Rome. Up until that period, so the story goes, these formulae had been a closely guarded secret of the college of pontiffs and their publication can be represented as a blow for freedom of information and a blow against the power of an élite based upon the careful hoarding of information. In fact, modern scholars dismiss this interesting story as pure invention. As one German authority puts it, 'Sensational events have no place in the history of Roman legal science.' However many times I have read that sentence, both in the original German and in the English translation, I have never been quite able to decide whether it was intended to be humorous or not.

Although the general public might find it hard to believe, your scholarly fields of study have been the scenes of events which can indeed be described as 'sensational'. The stories which appear from time to time, even in the general press, about the disputes over the control of the Dead Sea Scrolls are sufficient proof of that. In my own area of interest, Roman law, many recent advances have been made possible by the activities of anonymous and mysterious figures with metal detectors who have eventually sold huge bronze plates of legal texts on the black market—thereby raising questions about where exactly the objects were found. But even though I have been aware of these romantic tales, I confess that—like most people, I suspect—I had not seen them as raising acute legal issues. In particular, it had not really occurred to me that the disputes about the delays in publishing the Dead Sea Scrolls could be seen as giving rise to *legal* issues about the ownership and exploitation of the material. I have mentioned the discoveries of important bronze plates containing Roman legal texts. When word of the discoveries in Spain first got out and years then went by during which one could not see the texts but merely read articles based upon them—carefully written so as not to reveal anything of what the texts actually contained—I, like many others, found the delays frustrating in the extreme. But I know of no-one who ever thought of bringing legal proceedings to force those who had the texts to reveal their contents.

Doubtless, there are many reasons for this. Legal proceedings, especially in foreign countries, are expensive and not something which even the most frustrated textual scholar can contemplate lightly. Moreover, I confess that I would have doubts about what kind of action I would bring against the scholars with the texts. And I am too much instilled with the spirit of the classical Roman lawyers to avoid feeling that, if I cannot think of an appropriate action, then I probably do not have any right recognized by the law. But, having read some of the material which Hector MacQueen sent me in connexion with your deliberations today, I realise that this may well have been a simplistic view and that concepts such as 'cultural property'—hitherto unknown to me—have been developed by those dealing with these matters. Though how one would define the cultural group which would have a legal right to see the ancient Roman law texts, I find it hard to determine. Would a scholar from a civil law country, such as France, have more rights than a scholar from a common law country such as Australia on the basis that Roman law played a greater part in shaping the modern civil law systems? One cannot also help wondering what real connexion there is between an official text dictated in ancient Rome and a spot in the far distant province of Spain where the copy of that text sent there for publication has been excavated almost two thousand years later. And yet, for many reasons, scholars and others may choose to represent the text as part of the culture of that region of Spain. The law being developed to deal with these issues is clearly very complex.

But I suspect that my failure to recognize the legal significance of these questions springs from a somewhat deeper cause. Those who are interested in ancient texts and other cultural artefacts have tended to think of them in terms of scholarship rather than in terms of property. They are therefore something to be shared, rather than to be kept to oneself. Perhaps the fact that we have now to consider these legal implications reminds us that the world of scholarship itself has changed. When Niebuhr discovered the manuscript of Gaius's Institutes in the cathedral library in Verona in 1816, he was an envoy from the Prussian government breaking his journey en route to negotiations in Rome. He sent word to Savigny, a professor of substantial wealth, who soon published an account of the discovery in a German scholarly journal. Men such as these were subject to very different pressures from those which bear down on scholars today. No worries for them about hoarding scholarly treasure against the need to produce articles to meet the demands of the official Research Assessment Exercise upon which the university's funding may depend. No worries about promotions either. Today, by contrast, scholarly treasures can be used to build careers and to establish and maintain university departments. They therefore have not only intellectual but economic value. Perhaps for that reason they are that much more likely to become the subject matter, not merely of jealousy, but of actual legal dispute.

But it would be wrong for a judge of the Court of Session to pretend that disputes over cultural artefacts are exclusively the product of this very modern academic world, for, as Professor MacQueen could tell you better than I, just over 40 years ago a great treasure comprising brooches, bowls and other objects dating from about the eighth century CE was found by archaeologists from Aberdeen University excavating an ancient church on St Ninian's Isle in Shetland. The university claimed the treasure on the basis of the ancient udal law which was said to apply in that part of the Kingdom. Their claim was disputed by the Lord Advocate who argued that the treasure belonged to the Crown. A famous case followed in the Court of Session in which Professor Smith, then the professor of civil law in this university and formerly a professor at Aberdeen, represented the university. Despite his efforts the Crown eventually won. The result is that the treasure came to be housed in a museum here in Edinburgh rather than in the university in

Aberdeen. I do not venture an opinion as to whether this was from all points of view the ideal solution, but it does mean that those of you who have the time can see that particular part of our cultural heritage carefully preserved in the Museum of Scotland less than a mile from here.

I must not, however, distract you, for you have a most fascinating programme ahead in the symposium. I wish you every success in your discussions.

19 May 1999

Part I

THE CASE OF 4QMMT

THE JUDGMENT*

Dalia Dorner

In the District Court in Jerusalem

Before Justice D. Dorner

Elisha Qimron

v.

Hershel Shanks
Robert H. Eisenman
James M. Robinson
Biblical Archaeology Society

Advs. Y. Molcho, J. Melcer, Y. Langer argued for the Plaintiff
Advs. D. Frimer and Y. Gelman argued for Defendants 1, 3, 4
Adv. A. Hausner argued for Defendant 2.

The Judgment

The Factual Background

1. This is a suit about the infringement of copyright with regard to the deciphering of one of the Dead Sea Scrolls.

2. The Plaintiff, Elisha Qimron, is Professor of Hebrew Language at the University of Ben-Gurion in Beer Sheva. Before he joined the academic faculty of the University in 1981, the Plaintiff worked for 12 years in the Academy of Hebrew Language. He is engaged in philological research and his research specialization is the ancient scrolls that were found in the caves of Qumran which are situated in the Judaean Desert.

* Translated by Timothy H. Lim. Many thanks to Michael Birnhack and Hector MacQueen for revising the translation and advising me on legal terminology, both in Hebrew and in English.

3. For 11 years the Plaintiff has been engaged in the research and decipherment of one of the most important of the 800 Dead Sea Scrolls (hereafter 'the Scroll'). He named it 'some precepts of the Torah' (MMT), having discovered that its language is earlier than the language of the Mishnah and that it appears to be a letter from the leader of the sect of the Judaean Desert (who in other scrolls is entitled 'the Teacher of Righteousness') written to the leader of the people in Jerusalem (who in other scrolls is designated 'the Wicked Priest'; the widely held view is that he was Jonathan the Hasmonaean) (the Plaintiff, *Trial Transcript*, pp. 174-55). The Plaintiff saw in this work his life's endeavour, gave up the additional income for lectures which is the accepted practice among his colleagues, and devoted all his attention to research on the Scroll. Professor Ya'acov Sussmann, a well-known talmudic scholar with whom the Plaintiff consulted, recounted:

> My recollection was that sometimes the Devil had taken hold of him. That is to say, for years this was the subject that had interested him and this was the subject that engaged him. And it seemed to me that he did not read nor was interested in anything else, but that which could somehow bring him nearer to the issues connected with the Scroll (*Trial Transcript*, p. 63).

The Plaintiff expected that his name would be associated with the Scroll; he also expected to be its first editor and gain renown and academic recognition.

4. Torn remains of the Scroll were found at the beginning of the 1950s in one of the caves of Qumran (Cave 4), in which 15,000 fragments of different scrolls were discovered. The Government of Jordan, under whose rule the area was at the time, safeguarded the scrolls in the Rockefeller Museum in Jerusalem in the hands of a small international team. Access to the scrolls was restricted only to researchers who participated in this team. Professor Strugnell of Harvard University was one of these researchers. Strugnell, who was then one of the youngest of the researchers, was given the task of identifying the fragments of the Scroll and their decipherment. Two of the researchers senior to him—Milik and Cross—assisted him in the identification of a few of the fragments that were part of the Scroll, but most of the identification was done by him.

During the 1950s Strugnell identified 100 fragments, a portion of which were tiny pieces containing one letter or even parts of a letter. The fragments were assigned to six copies of the Scroll in different scribal hands; some of them were written on parchment and others on papyrus (Magen Broshi, Curator of the Dead Sea Scrolls and Director of the Shrine of the Book in the Israel Museum, *Trial Transcript*, p. 8; the Plaintiff, *Trial Transcript*, p. 163). The scholars submitted that the Scroll was written in the period of the Mishnah and it was referred to as 'mishnaic'. Strugnell drew up transcriptions of the fragments and joined them to one another according to the shape of the fragment. As a result, the number of separate fragments was reduced to between 60 and 70 (the Plaintiff, *Trial Transcript*, pp. 164-66). At this stage the work of decipherment 'was stuck'.

5. The continuation of the decipherment needed the filling out of missing pieces in the Scroll. This could not be done without expertise in Jewish Law. Strugnell, who is not Jewish, was a stranger to Halakha, and according to the words of Broshi 'he came up against a brick wall' (*Trial Transcript*, p. 9).

   In 1967 the scrolls were transferred to the authority of Israel, and their care was handed over to the Israel Antiquities Authority (then called the Department of Antiquities). The [Israel Antiquities] Authority did not change anything as regards the arrangement of the research procedures; it did not open up the scrolls to the study of the scientific community generally, and the same international team, with changes caused by the death of researchers, continued its work.

6. In 1980, Broshi brought together Strugnell and the Plaintiff, who in addition to his expertise in the Dead Sea Scrolls, knew the talmudic literature. From then on, the two of them worked together. Strugnell, whose research extended over many areas and whose contribution over the years was also reduced to virtually nothing for both physical and mental reasons, left the majority of the work to the Plaintiff. As mentioned, the Plaintiff was aided by the advice of Professor Sussmann. Sussmann had refused Strugnell's proposal to work in partnership with him in his efforts to decipher the Scroll, but agreed to advise the Plaintiff. The Plaintiff assembled, from the 60 to 70 fragments of the six copies, a composite text of 121 lines

(hereafter the composite text). Forty per cent of this version was lacking in the original (the Plaintiff, *Trial Transcript*, p. 175). In assembling the fragments there was no physical match, and the filling in of the missing part required linguistic and Halakhic research. The research lasted several years, and the version changed its content from time to time according to the advancement of the research (Sussmann, *Trial Transcript*, p. 81; the Plaintiff, *Trial Transcript*, p. 171).

7. In the course of the years the Plaintiff lectured on his findings at international conferences and published scholarly articles.

8. This wide-ranging work stood close to completion. In 1990, it was agreed in principle with the English Oxford University Press, which had published interpretative books about other scrolls, that it would publish the joint work of Strugnell and the Plaintiff. Within the context of this publication it was agreed to include photographs of the Scroll, the composite text (in its final version), its translation into English, and also the exegetical notes and commentary. But then in December 1990, one Dr Kapera of Krakow, Poland, published one of the drafts of the composite text in the journal *The Qumran Chronicle* (Exhibit 4), with a note that the source was anonymous. It turns out that one of the researchers who had received the draft had anonymously circulated it by post. One of the recipients, Professor Norman Nahum Golb of the University of Chicago, testified that this was indeed so. It appears that this is how the composite text came into Kapera's hands. As mentioned, the latter published it, with the editorial caveat that readers were requested not to copy and circulate it to other people, and that it was possible that this was a hoax and that if so then the matter 'will be a great laugh for us'. Kapera sent a copy of the aforementioned journal to the Plaintiff. The Plaintiff sought the intervention of the Israel Antiquities Authority. The Director of the Authority, Amir Drori, on 12 March 1991 sent a warning letter to Kapera (Exhibit 5), in which he stated that for years Professor Strugnell and the Plaintiff had been engaged in the decipherment of the Scroll and in research upon it, that in this work they had invested much toil, that it had been completed, and that their work was about to be published. He insisted that Kapera stop the distribution of his bulletin.

Also, in an international conference which took place in Spain the participants attacked Kapera for infringing the Plaintiff and Strugnell's copyright. Kapera wrote a letter of apology to Drori (Exhibit 6). He explained that he had circulated only a few copies in which he had asked that they should not be further distributed to other people and that he promised to stop the circulation.

Shanks, editor of *BAR* [=*Biblical Archaeology Review*], was one of the recipients of Kapera's journal. *BAR* is a journal for biblical archaeology, which is published in the United States. Shanks, prior to pursuing his interest in archaeology, was a lawyer and graduate of Harvard Law School. *BAR* is known both for the stature of the people whose work it publishes and also for its popularity. According to Shanks, it has a circulation of 185,000 copies and reaches more than half a million readers in many countries, Israel among them (Shanks, *Trial Transcript*, p. 254). For many years Shanks has led from the pages of *BAR* an obstinate and polemical struggle to open up the study of the Dead Sea Scrolls to all who are interested. He testified that he served as the voice of all those who were left out of the research cartel. He thought that the pressure which was exerted on Kapera to cease distribution of the composite text was illegitimate, and encouraged readers of his own journal (Exhibit 13) interested in studying the Scroll to purchase Kapera's journal.

9. In November 1991, Shanks published in the United States under the publication aegis of Defendant 4 *A Facsimile Edition of the Dead Sea Scrolls* (Exhibit 14), a book in two volumes containing photographs of many hundreds of fragments of scrolls, and included among them fragments of the Scroll that were hitherto available only to designated researchers. The book included one deciphered scroll and this was the composite version which appeared in Kapera's book. The Plaintiff's name was not noted. The photographs came to Shanks through the mediation of Professor Robert Eisenman who is engaged in research on the Scrolls. Eisenman and an additional researcher, Dr James Robinson, prepared an Index of the photographs and an Introduction, but in neither of the Volumes was the composite text acknowledged. Shanks added a 'Publisher's Foreword' in which he attacked the Israel Antiquities Authority in a sharp, polemical way. He dealt especially with the composite version, which he called 'a transcription', and which, according to

what was previously said, had been done by Strugnell, and he did not mention the Plaintiff's name.

10. Before publication, Shanks sent the aforementioned introduction to Robinson and Eisenman, without attaching the composite text. They were against its publication on account of its polemical style, but Shanks did not take heed of their advice. On the title page of the book is written:

A Facsimile Edition of the Dead Sea Scrolls
Prepared with
an Introduction and Index
by
Robert H. Eisenman
and
James M. Robinson

11. Shortly after Shanks's book was published the composite text appeared in two additional books, neither of which mentioned the Plaintiff's name: one in Poland by Dombroski under Kapera's imprint (Exhibit 18), and the second in the United States by Eisenman and another researcher, Michael Wise (Exhibit 19). In the Introduction to the book by Eisenman and Wise, it was noted that the transcription was the fruit of the authors' own labour and that they were not aided by anyone. In this Introduction it was noted that the decipherment had taken only six weeks (Exhibit 19, p. 9). However, while the published version of Exhibit 19 included specific changes, it seemed in essence to be the composite text, including errors that had crept into it (the Plaintiff's testimony, *Trial Transcript*, pp. 180-81, 188-89). Norman Nahum Golb, Professor at the University of Chicago who testified for Eisenman, admitted that the composite text was in the authors' hands (*Trial Transcript*, p. 402), but according to him they did not rely upon it. He explained that the errors in the composite text were indelibly impressed in their memory and that they had committed the same errors quite apart from copying it (*Trial Transcript*, pp. 384-85).

This does not seem to me an adequate explanation. In any case, his explanation does not account for the fact that while this decipherment of Exhibit 19 is essentially identical to the composite text, another part of the Scroll (the calendar), which the Plaintiff had deciphered but did not published, is completely different from the decipherment of Exhibit 19 (Golb, *Trial Transcript*, p. 414).

12. When the Plaintiff learned about the publication of Shanks' book, he was shocked. His dream of becoming the first publisher of the Scroll had vanished. He felt that his life's work was stolen from him and that his world had crumbled around him. He was afraid of the Defendants, whom he regarded as rich and with much influence, against whom a suit would entangle him in a heavy financial burden. However, he resolved that he must bring a suit against them 'to save his honour' (*Trial Transcript*, p. 207) and he did so.

13. Shanks too was amazed. He had not anticipated that the Plaintiff, a shy and diffident person, would challenge him. In his own words (*Trial Transcript*, p. 336): 'He was quiet and shy…it was a total surprise, I was shocked.' Shanks wrote to Robert Arnold, Chairman of the Board of Trustees of Ben-Gurion University, saying that the University was liable to suffer as a result of the litigation (Exhibit 26). Meanwhile, he had also written to Eisenman and Robinson (D/B/8/A; D/B/9) that he would take upon himself the liability in full if they should lose the suit. Nevertheless, he noted that in his opinion it would be possible to force the Plaintiff to settle out of Court, both by filing a suit against him in the United States, whither he was said to be going for a sabbatical year (and such a suit was indeed filed), and through Ben-Gurion University. Concerning this matter, Shanks wrote the following words: 'At some point, I think Qimron will be willing to talk to me. He is going to look very bad in the next *BAR* and the authorities at his school…cannot be very happy with him.'

The Legal Proceedings

14. On 14 January 1992, the Plaintiff brought a suit in this Court against Shanks, owner of *BAR*, Eisenman and Robinson, complaining of infringement of copyright, material and moral. In this suit, he sought an injunction and also damages in the amount of NIS 472,500.

    On 21 January 1992 an interlocutory injunction was issued *ex parte* and also a permission to serve the suit upon the Defendants outside the jurisdiction. A request from the Defendants to nullify the permission, both on technical grounds and arguing that the Court in Israel is not the appropriate forum [*forum non-conveniens*] for trying the suit, was rejected (Motion 238/92). The continuation of the discussion was halted by agreement so as to allow a decision on the appeal over this matter. However, the appeal that had been filed was withdrawn, the Defendants having accepted the judgment, and they no longer contest the jurisdiction of this Court.

The Claims

16. Neither Robinson nor Eisenman has appeared in the Court nor have they provided testimonies. Their defence, as presented by their lawyers, was that they were not responsible for the publication of the composite text. They did not serve as editors of the book and they had no knowledge that Shanks was going to publish the composite text. Their contribution was confined to the preparation of the Index and Introduction, and in addition they were against the publication of the Foreword that Shanks had written. Shanks on his side testified at length. The essence of his claim is that the copyright belonged to 'the Teacher of Righteousness'. It was he who wrote the Scroll. Copying it, even though it involved labour, did not attract copyright protection for the copyist. Also, he claimed that he did not know that the Plaintiff contributed to the editing of the copy. He thought that the work was essentially done by Strugnell. In any case, he had not given much thought to it: in his own expression, 'I just didn't focus' (*Trial Transcript*, p. 307). Was not the composite text in any case already in the hands of colleagues in the profession? But later on, he admitted that the composite text would have been published even if he had known that the Plaintiff had edited the reconstruction and had invested years of great labour in it (*Trial Transcript*, p. 322).

17. On the basis of this factual version, Defendants 1 and 4 put forward these arguments: (1) American law applies to the suit, but it has not been proved. Since a property right is at stake, the presumption of equivalence of the laws cannot be made and the United States' Copyright Act should be applied; (2) the work which the Plaintiff had done is not protected by the Copyright Act since it was a reproduction which, though difficult, was not creative, and moral rights, according to their meaning in law, do not arise. (3) No

damage was proved. Since this is so, it is also impossible to accord statutory damages, which are conditional upon proving harm. (4) The copyright does not belong to the Plaintiff but to the Israel Antiquities Authority, which by force of its right to supervise the work is considered to be the employer for the purpose of acquiring copyright. The Authority in truth had given the Plaintiff a confirmation that the copyright belonged to him, but the retroactive transfer of copyright is invalid. Alternatively, copyright belongs to Strugnell and to other researchers who have done most of the reconstruction. (5) From the time when the composite text was published by Kapera, the Defendants were entitled, according to the accepted conventions of the academic community, to publish it without the permission of the Plaintiff. (6) Alternatively, the publication was done in good faith, and on this matter Shanks' testimony is to be accepted.

Defendants 2 and 3 claimed that they were not liable at all for the publication. Eisenman also claims, alternatively, that in apportioning liability between him and between Defendants 1 and 4 his portion comes to naught.

The Normative Framework

18. The copyright on literary and artistic works is protected in Israel under the English Copyright Act of 1911 (hereafter the Act), that applies in Israel by force of the Word of the King on the law of copyright 1911 (its imposition on the land of Israel), 1924, and subject to alterations made by the Ordinance of Copyright 1924 (hereafter: the Ordinance), in order to adapt it to the local framework. In 1949, the State of Israel joined the Berne Convention for the Protection of Literary and Artistic Works, and the said laws were altered in order to adapt them to the main requirements of the Berne Convention (A Bill for the Amendment of the Copyright Ordinance, 1953, H.H. 38). In 1981, the Act of Amendment of the Copyright Ordinance (Amendment no. 4) incorporated the concept of 'moral right' (*droit moral*) into Israeli law. Moral rights are protected by the Berne Convention, where the right of the author to pecuniary rewards from the fruit of his creation was supplemented with 'the moral right' that the creation be attributed to his name and published with fidelity to the original, without distortion or falsification. It was further determined that the infringement of this

right is a civil wrong under the Ordinance of Torts [New Version]. The amending Act also adopted the procedure followed by the United States (Copyright Act 1976, 17 U.S.C., Sec. 504 [C]) with regard to statutorial compensation where the damages are not proven (Bill for the Amendment of the Copyright Ordinance. [Amendment no. 4] 1981,).

19. All agree that the suit is governed by the law of the place of infringement, that is, the laws of the USA (W.A. Copinger and J. Skone, *On Copyright* [London: Sweet & Maxwell, 12th edition, 1980], p. 450). It is also undisputed that this law has not been proved. The question is whether the presumption of the equivalence of laws applies to the suit, bringing us back to Israeli law.

The presumption of identity of the laws, recognized by international private law, is based upon the premise that the laws of enlightened states are identical (C.A. 51/49 *Yazdi v. Yazdi* 4 P.D. 762, at p. 767). This presumption does not apply to all branches of the law. So, case law tends toward the view that, in face of the uniqueness of laws concerning personal status in Israel, there is no place for relying on the presumption of equivalence of the laws in matters of personal status (C.A. 37/49 *Rapaport v. Feldverovski* 4 P.D. 645, at pp. 647-48).

The Defendants sought to rely upon a test that was suggested by Professor Levontin: on questions concerning local issues (status and property) that are anchored in a specific legal system, it behoves the Plaintiff to prove the foreign law, whereas in transitorial suits (contracts and torts) there should be no deviation from the laws of the place of jurisdiction, except if the other party raises a defence based upon the foreign law (A. Levontin, *Choice of Law in International Contracts* [Jerusalem: Israel Academy of Sciences, 1969] III, p. 201, n. 238). According to the Defendants, the suit against them was proprietary, and therefore the Plaintiff should have proved the foreign law.

20. Case law has not taken a stance in relation to this test. Only lately has the Supreme Court depended upon the presumption of the equivalence of the laws with regard to a suit concerning property rights of partners (C.A. 755/85 *The estate of the late Salem Shaman v. The estate of the late Sa'ada Shaman et al.*, 42(4) P.D. 103, at p. 107).

In any event, it is important that, again according to Professor Levontin, the presumption of equivalence of the laws applies to the issue before me.

First, even though copyright is proprietary, a suit for infringement is tortious by nature. The Act establishes that the infringement of moral rights is a tort according to the Torts Ordinance [New Version]. The Torts Ordinance complements the special instructions for copyright which are established in the Copyright Act (Y. Weismann, 'The Personal Right [Droit Moral] in Copyright Law', 7 *Inquiries in Law* 51 [1989] at 54).

Second, the test which Professor Levontin suggested is not based upon a mechanical classification of the law into branches. The determining factor is whether the said issue is or is not implicated in the local law specific to the place of jurisdiction. Property law and status were mentioned as examples of such locality. The law of copyright in Israel is not local, and laws comparable to them are accepted in the enlightened world.

In any case, in our subject the presumption of equivalence of the laws is not fictitious at all. As was previously said, in Israel the English law was absorbed, from which also American law has developed. On a particular matter (statutory damages) the procedure in Israel follows the procedure adopted in the written American law. The entire legislation has been adapted to an international treaty.

Finally, the presumption of equivalence of laws applies, and accordingly the Defendants bear the burden of proving an affirmative defence according to American law. This they have not done.

After the completion of argument, the Defendants brought in additional authorities. In this context they charged for the first time that 'there is no *droit moral* according to the laws of the United States (apart from six states)...'. They have not depended upon American judicial sources but upon S. Presanty's book, *Copyright Laws* II (1992), pp. 497-98, 504-507. The author points out that *droit moral* applies in six states in the United States, without detailing their names. Later on, she adds that the law exists in five states in the USA: New York, California, New Jersey, Maine and Rhode Island.

This argument which, for whatever reason, was raised after the completion of the debate, is insubstantial. First, the principle is this:

a foreign law is considered as a fact, for which proof by means of experts is necessary (Eliahu Harnon, *Evidence Law*, vol. 2 [Jerusalem: Harry Sacher Institute, 1985], pp. 52-54). The Defendants have so argued themselves when they sought to have the suit dismissed on the grounds that the Plaintiff has not proved American law. Second, going beyond what was argued, the book in question in the suit (Exhibit 14) was published in Washington, DC and Defendants' authority has not proved that the said right is unprotected in the place of the book's publication (i.e. whether *droit moral* is the law in Washington, DC. From a positive standpoint it is improper, [to conclude] that moral rights are not protected by the laws of the states whose names have not been detailed.

The result is that the whole suit, including the suit dependent upon moral rights, has to be decided by the law operative in Israel.

Originality of the Composite Text

21. The protected copyright is defined in section 1 of the Act, in which it is determined:

> copyright shall subsist throughout…in every original literary, dramatic, musical and artistic work.

In the official translation of the laws of the land of Israel, the requirement of originality was omitted. But the determinative formulation is the English version. English and American case law holds that the accepted meaning of 'originality' is not to be ascribed to the term, that is, inventiveness, but as Justice Netanyahu stated in C.A. 360/83 *Strossky Ltd et al. v. Weisman Ice Cream* 40(3) P.D. 340, at 346: 'all that is required is that the work was not copied from another work, that its origin will be in its creator, in its author'. Neither is there a practical difference whether the material used in the work was copied. It is enough that effort was expended, modest though it may be, in compiling, arranging and editing the material (C.A. 136/71 *supra*, at p. 347; C.A. 360/83, *supra*, at p. 347). This is also the law in the United States (M.B. Nimmer, *On Copyright* [New York: Matthew Bender, 1963], pp. 2-85). This ruling is clearly summed up in the American case, *Gelles Widner Company v. Milton Bradley Company* 313 F 2d 143 (1963):

> …almost any ingenuity in selection, combination or expression, no matter how crude, humble or obvious, will be sufficient.

Therefore, copyright will subsist in assembling and editing copied material. As against this, [mere] copying [itself], even if much work [labour] was expended on it, is not protected. According to this test, a suit for copyright in a regional telephone book, in which the material was copied from a national telephone book, failed: *Feist Publications Inc. v. Rural Telephone Services Co., Inc.* 18 USPQ2d 1275. It was also determined that illustrations which have been copied from ancient illustrations whose colour has faded are not protected by law, and even though this required great labour to restore the original colour (*Hearn v. Meyer*, 664 F. Supp. 832, [1987]).

22. On the case in question, Broshi and Sussmann defined the deciphering work as 'creative' (Broshi, *Trial Transcript*, p. 7, Sussmann, *Trial Transcript*, p. 65). Strugnell, in response to a leading question of the Plaintiff's lawyer, agreed with what was said about the work being 'creative' (*Trial Transcript*, p. 157, Testimony of Strugnell in the United States: hereafter: Strugnell's *Trial Transcript*). However, later on in his testimony he expressed reservations. He explained that innovation and inventiveness are required for decipherment, and therefore could be referred to as 'a creative work' (Strugnell's *Trial Transcript*, p. 165). However, on his part he did not use this expression but preferred to define the work of deciphering as 'reconstruction', which gives meaning to the material that is deciphered (Strugnell, *Trial Transcript*, pp. 161, 162, 165). Golb was even more extreme. In his opinion, the argument that the decipherment was a creative work was absurd (*Trial Transcript*, p. 409).

However, the present question for decision does not depend upon how scholars define the work, but upon the meaning of the expression 'original' in the Act as interpreted in case law. The Defendants believe that the decisions on the matter of copying the telephone book and the illustrations are authorities that apply to this case. According to them, our subject also involved reconstruction of an original work in which the effort has not contributed to the results of the content.

Certainly, according to the criteria which emerge in case law, copying of an original, even if it is difficult and complex and requires skill, does not attract copyright. It is also true that in the case before me, the goal of the person who deciphers is to reconstruct the original Scroll. However, the original Scroll was not found intact. The tens of fragments which were discovered relate to different copies; there was no physical match between a considerable portion of the fragments, and even after assembling all of them together the missing portion amounts to about half of what had been written. As was said, it was not possible to join the fragments, one to another, and to fill in the gaps without research into the language and Halakha. In any case, it was impossible to arrive at a uniform reconstruction, because the way of reconstructing and filling in the gaps depended upon the results of the research. These, for the most part, are not uniform, because disagreements arise among scholars. As an example of what I have said, the Plaintiff provided two disagreements between himself and Strugnell: (1) Strugnell believed that in particular fragments the sentences were nine lines long; and he therefore assembled them vertically. The Plaintiff arrived at the opinion, after research, that in the relevant fragment the sentence was of eighteen lines, and therefore it was necessary to assemble the fragments horizontally. Of course, the different assemblage has substantially affected the content of the Scroll (the Plaintiff, *Trial Transcript*, pp. 184-90); (2) one section is composed of six tiny fragments, and the Plaintiff explained that the entire method of relating them together is a speculation (*Trial Transcript*, p. 194). It depended upon the question of whether one missing letter should be filled by the letter *aleph*, as Strugnell thought, so that the word would read *orot* ('lights'), or should be completed by the letter *ayin*, so that the word would read *orot* ('hides'). After Halakhic research into the matter of purification of hides in the aforementioned period, the Plaintiff arrived at the opinion that the text is concerned with *orot* ('hides') (*Trial Transcript*, p. 181). He assembled the section depending upon this assumption, and of course the content was definitely different from the content which would have been accepted had he assembled the fragments on the basis of the assumption that the word under discussion was *orot* ('lights'). There is no substantive similarity between the work of the Plaintiff, in which creative and original elements were found, and the cases under discussion in the case law upon which the Defendants depended, which concerned, as was said previously, the copying of a telephone book and of illustrations.

From all that has been said, it appears that in editing the transcription and the combination of the fragments that are physically matched one to another no originality is required. In contrast to this, the assembly of the composite text depended upon Halakhic research and linguistic research from an original, and constitutes an original creation.

Based on all this, the composite text is protected by law.

The Copyright Owner of the Composite Text

23. From the Defendants' arguments during the debate it appears that according to their opinion the only one, among those who had worked on the decipherment, who is not a copyright owner of the composite text (if it were possible to obtain copyright at all) is the Plaintiff. According to their argument, the right belongs to Strugnell and Milik, who did most of the work of transcription, to the government of Jordan who was the employer of the researchers aforementioned, to the Ben-Gurion University, and to the Israel Antiquities Authority, which was the employer of the Plaintiff. This view is based upon two arguments: (1) the composite text was a collective creation, most of which, that which is identifiable, was authored by Strugnell and Milik. Therefore, there is no copyright for the Plaintiff in the text as a whole; (2) the Plaintiff worked in the service of the Israel Antiquities Authority which oversees the work of the researchers and therefore was the owner of the copyright of the composite text.

24. These arguments are not apparent to me.

As a general matter, the author is the owner of the copyright and moral rights (Article 5[1] of the Act). The moral right remains in his hands for ever, whereas the transfer of the economic right is possible only if done in writing (Article 5[2] of the Act). The law distinguishes between a creation produced by a number of authors, in which it is impossible to separate the portion of one author from those of other authors (section 16 of the Act); and a collective creation written in parts, in which it is possible to attribute each portion to its author (section 35 of the Act). In a joint work, each of the authors is entitled to copyright on the entire work. In contrast to this, in a collective work, each author is entitled to copyright on his portion alone.

25. As was said, the composite text was essentially the fruit of the Plaintiff's labour. He assembled it from the copies which Strugnell and Milik had prepared. The copies which they had prepared, as explained above, are *prima facie* not protected. At the beginning of the work the Plaintiff worked in co-operation with Strugnell, but this joint work is not divisible. In its context Strugnell and the Plaintiff met many times and discussed the suggestions of decipherment that the Plaintiff had advanced (the Plaintiff, *Trial Transcript*, p. 182). This is also deduced from Strugnell's testimony: he estimated that the Plaintiff's portion in the work of decipherment amounted to over 50 per cent, and he also pointed out that he was unable to indicate specifically his own work (Strugnell's *Trial Transcript*, p. 177). It is to be pointed out that Sussmann's recollection was that, beginning in the 80s, Strugnell had removed himself from the work of decipherment and the burden was essentially borne by the Plaintiff (*Trial Transcript*, pp. 60-61).

26. Regarding the rights of the Israel Antiquities Authority, it is clear that the rights of ownership in the Scroll lies with the State of Israel, but the copyright over the fruit of the Plaintiff's labour does not belong to it. The State of Israel was never his employer, and section 5(1) of the Act does not apply to this matter. According to the aforementioned section, in the absence of an agreement, the employer is the first owner of the copyright of a work which an employee produces in the course of his employment by the employer under a contract of service. In the case law it was determined that the only test for determining whether it is concerned with a contract of service is that of authority or control (C.A. 571/68 *Yanai v. Mansfeld* 23[1] P.D. 501, at 504).

In the matter before me, the contract of reward for service between the Plaintiff and the Israel Antiquities Authority has not been established. The Plaintiff did not engage in the work of decipherment at the request of the Authority; instead Strugnell sought his help, just as he had sought Sussmann's assistance. On this matter the Director of the Israel Antiquities Authority, Amir Drori, testified that his connection with the Plaintiff in the matter of the decipherment work of the Scroll was limited to Drori's knowledge that the Plaintiff was attached to Strugnell in the research of the Scroll (*Trial Transcript*, p. 99). However, in essence the relations among the designated researchers and the Israel Antiquities Authority were not relations of authority or control. Broshi explained that the researchers 'were entirely autonomous'; no one intervened in their work. They were 'masters of the work' (*Trial Transcript*, p. 12).

In the cross-examination, Drori confirmed that the Authority had fixed, in accordance with the advice of the Editor-in-Chief, a timetable for publishing the Scroll, and had let the assigned researchers know that it held in its hand the right to take from them the exclusiveness of the research if they did not maintain this timetable (*Trial Transcript*, p. 113). Clearly, this notification does not constitute supervision and control of the research work. Also Strugnell confirmed that there was no supervision of the work of the researchers (Strugnell's *Trial Transcript*, pp. 31, 65, 75, 77).

27. The Israel Antiquities Authority never saw itself as owner of the copyright in the researchers' work. The confirmation in writing concerning this matter (Exhibit 7)—which was issued at the Plaintiff's request after the suit had been filed and as a response to the Defendants' claim that the Plaintiff was not the copyright owner of the composite text—does not constitute a transfer of the rights which would have have a retrospective validity or effect, but an expression of the existing legal relations. And thus it is said in Exhibit 7 which referred to Qimron and Strugnell:

> We wish to clarify that the Israel Antiquities Authority does not dispute that you have full copyright in the decipherment and reconstruction of the 4QMMT Dead Sea Scroll which is the product of your effort.

Under these circumstances, the Defendants are not able to force upon the Israel Antiquities Authority the ownership in the copyright, as the Authority itself has not disputed the fact that the ownership of the copyright in the decipherment of the scrolls and their interpretation belong to the researchers who have done the work.

In summation, it has been proved that the copyright in the Scroll belongs to the Plaintiff.

Publication According to the Academic Community's Convention

28. The Defendants argued, depending upon Magen Broshi's testimony, that according to accepted conventions in the academic

world that strives for a free flow of information there is no restriction in the publication of scholarly material that has already been published, except that the material be attributed to its author. Therefore, it was not an infringement of the Plaintiff's copyright in the publication of the composite text which had become public domain since it had already been published by Kapera and even before that had already circulated among researchers. This argument is unacceptable, on both legal and factual grounds.

The distribution of the composite text among researchers does not constitute publication, neither according to academic custom (the Plaintiff, *Trial Transcript*, p. 37), nor according to the law. Copinger and Skone's book writes on this matter (*On Copyright*, p. 27) the following:

> The writer of a literary work may permit his manuscript to be viewed or read by any number of persons without thereby publishing his work.

And see also Nimmer, *On Copyright*, pp. 4-18.

29. Furthermore the Defendants' argument in the matter of the existence of the said custom lacks evidentiary foundation. Moreover, even if a custom such as this existed, there would be no basis for it in law. Prior publication as such does not negate the copyright. This too is not disputed by the Defendants.

Of course, the law and convention speak as one in not permitting publication of material the publication of which is an infringement of copyright. Moreover, in lawful publication it is not permitted to copy freely the fruit of the author's labour without his authorization or without mentioning his name as has been done in this case. The convention, as explained by Broshi, allows for reliance, in the context of research, upon material that has been published by way of *citation* from it. Thus, Broshi said concerning this matter:

> Once a researcher submits a manuscript to a scientific journal, it lies in the public domain and from that very moment anyone is entitled to quote this—of course not as though he had deciphered or done this… (for example) in an old article by Yadin he referred to an article of a certain Allegro by citing his name… It is usually said, 'as we have seen in the article of Shimon Ben-Levi', then our view is such and such (*Trial Transcript*, pp. 37-38).

In the present case before me, in the book Exhibit 14 the composite text had already been published by Kapera. But this latter publication was itself forbidden. As already noted, Kapera himself apologized for what he has done, and stressed that in the context of prohibited publication he asked readers not to copy it nor to distribute it to others. There is thus no basis for the argument based upon the convention and it should be dismissed.

Bona Fides Protection

30. Section 8 of the Act provides that:

> Exemption of an innocent infringer from liability for monetary damages.
>
> Where proceedings are taken in respect of the infringement of the copyright in any work and the defendant in his defence alleges that he was not aware of the existence of the copyright in the work, the plaintiff shall not be entitled to any remedy other than an injunction or interdict in respect of the infringement if the defendant proves that at the date of the infingement he was not aware and had no reasonable grounds for suspecting that copyright subsisted in the work.

From this, it follows: (1) the burden of proof of bona fides, which is a defence, is placed upon the publisher; (2) a subjective mental state of bona fides is insufficient and the publisher has the burden to prove, according to an objective test, that he could not 'have suspected' the existence of copyright (C.A. 241/55 *Neographica Printing House et al. v. Masada Ltd et al.*, 11 P.D., 890, at 892).

In the matter before me, not only was there no proof of the defence for bona fides but it was proved that the composite text was published with the knowledge that the Plaintiff had copyright in the work.

31. Among the three Defendants, the only one who had argued for bona fides in court was Shanks. His version was: (1) he did not know that the Plaintiff participated in the decipherment, and he assumed that the decipherment was done by Strugnell (*Trial Transcript*, p. 260); (2) the composite text was a copy of the Scroll that had been written by the Teacher of Righteousness (*Trial Transcript*, p. 265).

This testimony is unacceptable to me.

32. As for the Plaintiff's part in the assembly of the composite text, Shanks admitted that he knew that the Plaintiff had assisted

Strugnell in the research of the Scroll (*Trial Transcript*, p. 259) and that in the context of this assistance he had participated in the reconstruction and that this possibly included also the filling in of the missing parts (*Trial Transcript*, p. 296). Not just this, but also Shanks' testimony on this matter of not having known the Plaintiff's part in the decipherment, is contradicted by objective evidence: Drori's letter to Kapera (Exhibit 5) which came into Shanks hands and which he published in the book Exhibit 14 (Figure 9). As previously noted, in this letter Drori stated that Strugnell and the Plaintiff were engaged for years in decipherment of the Scroll. Under these circumstances, Shanks' testimony of not having known has been rebutted and I dismiss it.

As for the argument that Shanks explained that the composite text was a copy of the Scroll: Shanks knew that the Scroll had not been discovered intact, but was in fragments of six different copies which were not joined to a whole version, and that reconstruction required the filling in of missing portions. He also knew that this work required great expertise, competence and aptitude. He admitted this (*Trial Transcript*, pp. 292-93), but he explained that he had not given sufficient thought to it. And thus he said:

> I didn't focus on it. I really didn't think much about this then (*Trial Transcript*, p. 292).

He further emphasized that at the time he did not know that it involved many fragments and many missing sections (*Trial Transcript*, p. 292).

33. It is unnecessary to say that lack of attention is inconsistent with the objective defence of bona fides. However, the entire story is unacceptable to me, because Shanks' knowledge in the matter of the many fragments and the many missing sections has been proved by objective evidence.

34. As for the fragments, in the article D/12/A, which was published in *BAR*, it is written that the six copies that had been discovered were all very fragmentary. Shanks himself, in the Publisher's Foreword which he published in Exhibit 14, in connection with all the photographs of the scrolls that he published and including the Scroll (Plate 213), wrote the following words:

> Anyone perusing these plates, however briefly, cannot help but be struck by the difficulty of making any sense of them. *The best are mere fragments.* Many are simply unintelligible scraps (emphasis added).

Also the extent of the missing sections was known. What had been filled in was inserted into the text in brackets. Shanks observed these brackets. His explanation as to why he also believed that what had been said in the brackets was written by the Teacher of Righteousness is curious, and I will cite it in his own words:

> In this case I believe some of the brackets did not end, there was a beginning but no end. So I knew that even if it's a reconstruction, it's a precise word of the ancient author (*Trial Transcript*, p. 292).

The substance of the matter regarding his explanation in the matter of brackets—that they were not closed bracketed—lacks a basis in the composite text, but on occasion the filled-in section extended over a number of lines. As was said, the extent of the filling-in was approximately half of the text and this can be observed without difficulty.

A summation of the issues: it has been proved that Shanks knew that the Plaintiff had participated in the assembly of the composite text and that the text was not a copy of the Scroll, but was rather a pastiche of fragments from a number of copies, in which even then there remained extensive 'holes' which the aforementioned researchers filled in.

35. Shanks is a lawyer by profession. Therefore it is improbable that before he published the composite text he did not give adequate thought to its copyright. Not just this, but also he knew that there were claims to the copyright in the composite text and that the intervention of the Israel Antiquities Authority had prevented the continuation of the distribution of Kapera's publication. In the Publisher's Foreword in Exhibit 14, Shanks referred to this matter when he cited from Drori's letter (Exhibit 5), which saw in the publication of the composite text by Kapera 'an infringement of the rights of your colleagues' (Strugnell and the Plaintiff). Indeed, in the course of his testimony, Shanks admitted that he had deliberated upon whether copyright existed in the composite text, but he explained his conclusion that copyright existed only in the translation of the composite text to English, while in the text itself copyright belongs to no-one (*Trial Transcript*, p. 291). However, it is

inconceivable, given the facts known to him, that he honestly thought so. Therefore, he also denied that he knew the aforementioned facts. But as already stated this denial, to me, is unacceptable. From the sum of evidence, it can be deduced that Shanks, after deliberation, arrived at the conclusion that it was unlikely that he would be sued for an infringement of copyright, either by the illness-ridden Strugnell (and in this he was right), or by the diffident and modest Plaintiff, not least because he lived in Israel. As Shanks said, he was stricken with shock when the suit was made known to him.

36. Concerning Robinson and Eisenman, as already stated, they abstained from testifying, and there is no factual version whatever before me that proves their good faith. True, the testimony of their defence, advocate William Cox, was that Eisenman was surprised and angered by the inclusion of the composite text in the book (*Trial Transcript*, p. 437). However, from the sum of the evidence that proves Eisenman's knowledge of Shanks' intention to include the composite text in the book, Cox's testimony in the matter of the surprise cannot be accepted.

Eisenman's lawyer, advocate Hausner, argued that his client could have understood from the Publisher's Foreword, in which the composite text was referred to as a 'copy', that it concerned a work of copying in which copyright does not subsist.

It seems to me that Shanks' use of the expression 'a copy' as such is insufficient evidential base to prove the defence of bona fides. In parenthesis I will add that Shanks testified that after the suit had been filed Eisenman had argued in his presence that he had not read, in the Publisher's Foreword that he had sent to him, the part relating to the composite text (*Trial Transcript*, p. 277). However, the whole argument is negated by objective evidence. Robinson and Eisenman edited the Index of the facsimiles in Exhibit 14. Therefore, they knew what the fragments of the Scroll looked like (facsimile 213). A quick look at the aforementioned facsimile will show that one could not decipher the Scroll by transcription alone. Moreover, in the Introduction it was written that the book was publishing the text that Kapera had published, and they both had seen Kapera's publication (thus Shanks testified, *Trial Transcript*, p. 278). Therefore they were able to know by a glance at the composite text that it was not a work of transcription.

Finally, Eisenman made use of the composite text in the book Exhibit 19. True, in the Introduction to Exhibit 19 it was claimed that the work of decipherment was done by the authors alone (Eisenman and Wise) without anyone else's help. But, as already mentioned, Golb confirmed that the composite text was in their possession, whereas the Plaintiff and Broshi had testified that in Exhibit 19 the composite text had been copied (Broshi, *Trial Transcript*, p. 26; the Plaintiff, Exhibit 11, *Trial Transcript*, p. 179).

However this may have been, in the book, Exhibit 19, in which the composite text was included, copyright was claimed. It was written thus on the title page:

> All rights reserved.
> *No part* of this book may be reproduced in any form or by any means, electronic or mechanical, without permission in writing from the Publishers (emphasis added).

These words prove that Eisenman knew that copyright did exist in the decipherment work of the Scroll, and contradict the argument that he thought that the composite text was a work of transcription to which the Copyright Act does not apply.

In summation of the matter, the argument in the matter of bona fides is dismissed.

Droit moral—its Extent

37. Article 4a of the Copyright Ordinance lays down:

> 1) An author is entitled to his name being mentioned in his work in the accepted extent and measure.
> 2) An author has a right that no distortion, whether in defect or other changes, is done to his work, or that any other action is done to it that might depreciate the value of this very work and be liable to harm the reputation or name of an author.
> 3) A violation of the rights according to this section constitutes a civil wrong, and the directives of the Torts Ordinance [New Version] shall apply to it.
> 4) An author's right according to this section will not depend upon his material right in the same work, and will continue to exist for him even after this right, in whole or part, has been transferred to another.
> 5) In a suit in accordance with this section, the author is entitled to compensation in a sum that the court will determine according to

> the circumstances of the case, even if pecuniary damage has not been proved, this directive will not lessen other court's authority according to Chapter E of the Torts Ordinance [New Version]

In this way the concept of moral rights were integrated into the Copyright Ordinance, but their infringement is defined as a tort according to the Torts Ordinance [New Version]. However, it seems to me that the application of tort law to infringement of copyright does not take its scope beyond the said definition in the aforementioned Article 4a. Its scope, with the differences laid down by the aforementioned definition, is identical in my view to copyright under the Act regarding the determination of the protected works, the bona fides defence and the considerations for an award of remedies. This can be seen from the inclusion of the right in the Copyright Ordinance and from the legislative purpose of the amending Act, which is to supplement the particular directives of the Copyright Act, which protects only pecuniary rights. This conclusion can be supported also from the legislative history of section 4a. In the words of the explanation for the Bill of the Amending Act (H.H. 1981, p. 238):

> An author has two rights in his work. The first is material: the right to financial reward for the fruit of his work. And the second is moral: his right that the work appear under his name, and be published in a form faithful to the original, without distortion or defect. The system of intellectual property laws of the State of Israel today affords the protection of material right alone, but the author's intellectual/moral right has not yet been anchored in law and the Act does not protect them… The Bill before us proposes that Israeli law be amended in line with the spirit of the aforementioned article (Article 6 bis of the Berne Convention).

From these words, it is apparent that the legislature did not seek to create a new right disconnected from existing copyright but to supplement the material copyright with a moral (intellectual) copyright as an additional component, so that the two rights, the material and moral, make up copyright. Professor Weismann, who pointed this out, sought to conclude from the changes of the text in Article 6a that moral right is part of copyright: in the 1948 version of article 6a, it was laid down that moral rights exist 'independently of the author's copyright', but in the version of 1967 the text was corrected to say: 'independently of the author's economic rights'. Professor Weismann's conclusion was that the application of the Torts

Ordinance upon moral copyright does not negate the supposition that personal rights (the moral) are part of the copyright (Weismann, 'Personal Right', pp. 53-54). Ms Presanty arrived at the same conclusion (Presanty, *Copyright Laws*, p. 467).

38. The lawyer representing Defendants 1, 3 and 4 deemed it permissible for them to add, after the conclusion of the trial, arguments on the matter of moral right which were not argued in their pleadings. In these arguments there is no substance, because they show absolute disregard for the directives of section 4a of the Copyright Ordinance which is an original Israeli law. To acccommodate their view, however, I shall relate the essence of these arguments.

Their first argument is that according to English law, 'whoever is considered to be an author for the purpose of the application of the Copyright Act does not have moral right'.

This argument cannot be accepted. According to Article 4a of the Copyright Ordinance the moral right is added to the economic right (Presanty, *Copyright Laws*, II, p. 467, Weisman, 'Personal Right', pp. 53-54).

Their second argument is that the existence of moral rights depends upon explicit assertion by the author. This argument is based upon these points: (1) Article 6a of the Berne Convention that lays down the author's right to claim copyright as an author; (2) an English law enacted after the enactment of the aforementioned Article 4a, that is the Copyright Designs and Patent Act 1988. In section 77 (1) of this Act, it is laid down that the realization of moral rights depends upon the assertion of their existence by the author, in ways detailed in section 78 of the same Act.

In my view, one cannot interpret the words of Article 6a of the Berne Convention defining the right of the author 'to claim authorship' as dependent upon a formal assertion. This also follows from the Israeli case law from before the enactment of the aforementioned Article 4a, in which it was established that publication of a work which the author himself had not yet published (and it is unnecessary to say that he had not asserted his identity upon it in a formal way) and without relating it to its author, constitutes an infringement of moral right as defined in Article 6a of the Berne Convention (C.A. 528/72 *Ettinger v. Almagor et al.*, 29[2] P.D. 116, at 118-119; C.A. 559/69 *Almagor v. Godik et al.*, 24[1] P.D. 825, at 829). Also, Professor Tadesky has defined moral right without any condition whatsoever: 'A right to the author's intellectual paternity of his work is recognized in Article 6a of the Berne Convention as a right when his work is presented or mentioned in publicity, to have it mentioned as his work' (G. Tadesky, 'Intellectual Property and Personal Right', *Jurisprudence* 10 [1980] 392-93).

However this may be, the aforementioned Article 4a is an original Israeli law. Therefore, as was said in the words of explanation to the Bill, it was enacted in the spirit of Article 6a of the Berne Convention, but the legislature did not embrace the aforementioned Article in its own language, but laid down in Article 4a a detailed arrangement, in which the moral right is not dependent on any condition.

Over and above what is required, I will say that in the present case before me copyright was asserted in the letter Exhibit 5 to Kapera.

The Defendant's final argument is that one cannot order compensation for violation of moral right 'except to the extent that actual or special damages have been proved'.

This argument should be dismissed in light of section 4a(5), under which the author is entitled to compensation even if pecuniary damage has not been proved. As already noted, the infringement of moral rights is a tort according to the Torts Ordinance [New Version], and it is clear that non-pecuniary damage can be compensated according to this Ordinance (Y. Engelard, A. Barak, M. Heshin, *Tort Law: General Theory of Torts* [ed. G. Tadesky; 2nd ed, Jerusalem: Magnes Press, 1977], p. 169).

When the defence's argument is rejected the fact remains that the fruit of the Plaintiff's labour, namely the composite text, was published without mentioning his name, and so his moral right has been infringed. The argument that according to accepted convention it was sufficient to mention Strugnell's name alone is refuted in light of the Plaintiff's part in the assembly of the composite text and on this I have already taken my stance (Sections 23-25 of this Judgment).

The Argument in the Matter of Judicial Policy

39. The Defendants argue that even if the law has been violated, the suit should be dismissed on grounds of judicial policy, which

prevails over copyright laws in their precise (petty; specific; detailed) interpretation. In the present case, a liberal judicial policy should be adopted, leading to the unrestricted flow of research work amongst the scholarly community, without restraining it through inflexible laws of copyright.

This argument is to be dismissed. It seems that the defendants confuse the scholar's right to research the Scroll (for which they have struggled), and also to depend in his research upon published works, with the taking of another person's work without his consent and without due acknowledgment to him. The sharp response of the participants of the scholarly conference in Spain towards Kapera's pirated publication, about which the Plaintiff had spoken (*Trial Transcript*, pp. 195-96), shows the academic community's view of such matters.

Even a scholar has copyright in his work, and it is right that judicial policy seeks to protect this right.

The Liability of Shanks and Defendant 4

40. There has been no dispute that the composite text was published on Shanks' initiative, by his hands, and in the publication of Defendant 4. Therefore the two are liable for the infringement of the Plaintiff's copyright.

Robinson and Eisenman's Liability

41. The names of Robinson and Eisenman appear on the title page of the book as those who had prepared it. Eisenman's advocate, Mr Hausner, suggested his own interpretation for what has been written. According to him, the version was put together by Shanks, and one should not read it literally but according to the intention of both sides, as expressed in the memorandum (D/A/11), written on 16 September 1991, between Shanks and Eisenman and Robinson. In Article 2 of the memorandum it is said that:

> The title page of the edition is to state that it is introduced with an index by Robert H. Eisenman and James M. Robinson.

From which it would seem that the word 'prepare' (below) refers to the Index and Introduction alone.

This argument cannot be accepted. In the Introduction, Robinson and Eisenman made clear that, in addition to their work in the preparation of the book, they had written the Introduction and the Index. I will cite their own words:

> Robert H. Eisenman...and James M. Robinson...were engaged not only to help *prepare* this edition but *also* to provide an Introduction and Index (emphasis added).

Indeed, the Introduction bears a date prior to the memorandum (A/1/11), but the authors continued to update it up to the time of publication. This is submitted according to a footnote dated 8 October 1991.

According to the literal sense, the word that is synonymous with the preparation of the book is its editing. Indeed, this is how Broshi sees it, and based upon the written annotations, he emphasized that it is clear that Robinson and Eisenman are the editors of the book Exhibit 14. And thus he said:

> I have no doubt that on the title page of the book (Exhibit 14) is written that this book's editors are Eisenman and Robinson (*Trial Transcript*, p. 58).

Thus also is it inferred from the questionnaire (D/A/10[1]) which advocate Frimer, who at the time represented both Robinson and Eisenman, formulated and presented to the Plaintiff. In question number 19, Mr Frimer defined the book Exhibit 1 thus:

> Facsimile Edition of the Dead Sea Scrolls *by* Robert H. Eisenman and James M. Robinson (emphasis added).

42. The book Exhibit 14 itself, on whose title page the names of Robinson and Eisenman appear, is ostensible proof that the two of them are responsible for its content. The question requiring a decision is whether there is evidence to the contrary before me. As was said, these Defendants have not appeared in the court, have not conveyed any version of events, and have sought to base their defence upon Shanks' testimony and Eisenman's defence, Advocate Cox. Eisenman's lawyer, Mr Hausner, also argued that they had sent a message with his version in a letter to the Editor of *The Jerusalem Post*, after the suit was filed against him (Exhibit 23/c). This letter was presented by the Plaintiff and in this presentation there is an admission of its content.

This argument should be dismissed. Exhibit 23/c of the aforementioned document was presented during Shanks' cross-examination, attached to a copy of Shanks' interview that had been aired in the Foreign Affairs news report of *Kol Israel*. The copy was served to prove that Shanks had published the book Exhibit 14 in Israel. In the interview itself, publications in the press were mentioned, and among them the publication in the newspaper *The Jerusalem Post*. Sections of the above mentioned newspapers, including Exhibit 23/c, were attached to it. The Defendants opposed these press clippings being served. I dismissed their objections, and I explained that I am accepting the aforementioned documents as part of the cross-examination, so that I would know about what he (i.e. Shanks) was being examined (*Trial Transcript*, p. 336).

The argument in the matter of the admission in Eisenman's version in Exhibit 23/c has no substance, and I dismiss it.

43. As for the Cox and Shanks testimonies: Cox, an American lawyer, represents the owner of the photographs published in Exhibit 14. This [anonymous] man sought to publish the photographs and Cox mediated between Shanks, Eisenman and Robinson (testimony of Cox, *Trial Transcript*, p. 440).

Cox testified that, according to his understanding, there was no editor for the book Exhibit 14 (*Trial Transcript*, p. 438) and that it was supposed to include the photographs, the Index and the Introduction alone (*Trial Transcript*, p. 436). Shanks testified that he himself was responsible for the publication of the Publisher's Foreword (*Trial Transcript*, p. 761). However, he emphasized that Robinson and Eisenman did not oppose the publication of the Foreword, but had reservations about its tone (*Trial Transcript*, p. 277). Shanks dismissed the version which Mr Hausner suggested to him, that Eisenman was angered when the inclusion of the composite text in the book was made known to him, and reiterated and explained that Eisenman knew about the publication of the composite text, because he (Shanks) had sent him the Publisher's Foreword in which it was said that the text published at the time by Kapera was included in the book. To be sure, he did not attach the text itself, but Eisenman was familiar with the text that Kapera had published (*Trial Transcript*, p. 278, and see also p. xvi in Exhibit 14).

Shanks also confirmed that he had given Eisenman a draft of the legal arguments (D/B/7/) which he intended to submit to the court, in which it was written that Robinson and Eisenman were not the editors of the book. However, he regarded it as apt to underscore that he had not written in his letter that the two of them were not the editors of the book, but that it only concerned the relaying of the draft arguments (*Trial Transcript*, p. 280).

Thus, Shanks' position was ambivalent. True, he agreed that the two of them had been practically restricted to the arrangement of the photographs, the preparation of the Index and the writing of the Introduction. But Shanks was not prepared to confirm this version of lack of knowledge.

44. However all this may have been, the question that needs to be decided is not how Cox and Shanks have defined Robinson and Eisenman's roles, but what their roles were in practice.

On this matter it has been proved, both by the attribution on the title page and the sum of the evidence that Robinson and Eisenman were engaged in the work of editing, the preparation of the Index being one of the notable characteristics thereof (see A. Even-Shoshan, *The New Hebrew Dictionary* [Jerusalem: Kiryat Sepher, 1968], V, under 'editing').

Indeed, Shanks initiated the inclusion of the composite text in Exhibit 14. He made this intention known by sending the Publisher's Foreword to them both for perusal. As such, the communication points to their position as editors. Their reservations about the tone of the Foreword, which cannot be adequately judged, are irrelevant, because the suit relates to the publication of the composite text itself, and Robinson and Eisenman had no reservations about its publication. The two, who are expert researchers, regarded it as appropriate to give their names consciously to a book in which the fruit of the Plaintiff's labour was included, this without his authorisation or an attribution to him. Thus, they have infringed the Plaintiff's copyright under section 2(1) of the Act, and his moral right under section 4a(1) of the Ordinance.

Proportion of Liability among the Defendants

45. The four Defendants are liable to the Plaintiff, jointly and severally. Each one of them is accountable in full for his damages.

However, in the relations between the Defendants the principles of participation apply: the proportion of liability of each one is established according to the extent of his responsibility for the damage (Barak, 'Theory of General Damages', p. 507). In appropriate cases, one can fix the relative proportion of a wrongdoer up to 100 per cent (Barak, 'Theory of General Damages', p. 509).

In the case before me, Shanks decided to publish the composite text. In his testimony before me and in the writing that he sent to Robinson and Eisenman, he accepted full liability. Seeing that this is his stance, his relative liability as against the two is 100 per cent.

The Injunction

46. On 21 January 1992 a temporary injunction was served, which forbade the Defendants from continuing to distribute the composite text. This injunction was followed. The composite text has been left out of the second edition of the book Exhibit 14. The first edition consisted of 413 copies. Up to the issuing of the restraining order, some 200–300 books had been sold (Shanks's testimony, *Trial Transcript*, p. 270).

Today, the Defendants do not seek the right to publish the composite text. Shanks has testified to this clearly (*Trial Transcript*, p. 271), and also Eisenman's lawyer had already argued, as previously noted, that his client had been opposed to the publication of the composite text from the beginning. The Defendants' lawyer did not respond in any way, in their pleadings, about the Plaintiff's petition for the issuing of an injunction. Under these circumstances—though in light of the position taken by the Defendants the injunction may not have to be issued—and barring forthcoming objections that the Defendants might rightly plead for, this permanent injunction should be issued.

47. The Plaintiff lost the right to publish the composite text first. Graver still than this, since the composite text has been referred to as coming from an unknown source, it was again published without due acknowledgment of the Plaintiff's name. Broshi has explained it in this way:

> Without a note of the name of the decipherer and reader, the text of MMT has turned into an ownerless property (*Trial Transcript*, p. 23).

Even in a critical article relating to the Scroll, the Plaintiff's name was not mentioned (Broshi's testimony, *Trial Transcript*, pp. 24-25). Also, Professor Sussmann has taken a stand on the significance of having lost the right to publish first. To Mr Frimer's question, whether publication of the composite text with accompanying interpretation by the Plaintiff would rectify the damage done to his reputation and earnings, Professor Sussmann replies:

> This depends upon what happens between now and when this text will be published. If this text be known the world over and everyone begins to work on it, and everyone writes whatever he will write and the matter enters into known scholarly editions, who knows what consequences there will be for this, that this will be published in some other place (*Trial Transcript*, p. 85).

This has caused the plaintiff financial damage and mental anguish.

Monetary Damage

48. In section 20 of the Plaintiff's suit, material damages were sought according to the following calculation:

a) Loss of profit and/or publishing royalties…according to the estimated sale of the book of the owner of the copyright totals NIS 350; the Plaintiff's publishing royalties at the rate of 5 per cent; and the reduction of distribution of the book by 5,000 copies…NIS 87,500.
b) Loss of income in the future…according to monthly damage of NIS 1000 each year for 20 years…(according to the rate of 3 per cent per year): NIS 180,000.

The Plaintiff's estimate was based on the view that the publication of the composite text will lessen the sale of the book that he is about to publish, as explained in section 20(a) of the Plaintiff's suit, and that his honoraria from lectures will diminish by the amount detailed in section 20(a) of the Plaintiff's suit.

There is a difficulty: this calculation has no basis in material evidence, and not one of the witnesses was able to ascertain a firm estimate of the effects that the publication of the composite text will have upon sales of the Plaintiff's book and on his lecturing honoraria, and these matters are understandable. One cannot estimate in an objective manner the extent of the effects on the publication of the Plaintiff and Strugnell's book sales and on the Plaintiff's reputation, through which he would be invited to lecture.

The lawyer for the Plaintiff, Mr Molcho, argued that a court of law is entitled to set compensation for future monetary damage, based upon an estimate of probability of less than 50 per cent. But the question before me is not the extent of the proof, but the absence of even a minimum of objective facts, enabling me to consider the damage according to the extent of any probability.

The Plaintiff's suit can be considered in the framework of cases where the damage has not been proved, and for which the court of law is dependent upon the effect of section 3a of the Ordinance in order to determine statutory compensation.

49. In this matter, the Defendants have argued that this authority is applicable only when damage has been caused, but its extent not proved. This argument is irrelevant to the case before me, in which, as was previously said, it has been proved that damage has been caused to the Plaintiff. Beyond the requirement, let me say that according to the explanation given to the aforementioned section 3a in the case law, a Plaintiff whose copyright has been proved to have been infringed is entitled to seek statutory compensation without having proved actual damage, even if he has chosen not to present evidence or if he were to bring evidence, but failed to prove damage (C.A. 592/88 *S. Saggi et al. v. Estate of the late Abraham Ninio et al.*, 46[2] P.D. 254, at 264-65).

50. In the aforementioned section 3a the court is authorized to set statutory compensation at a rate not less than the sum of NIS 10,000, and not more than NIS 20,000. In the aforementioned C.A. 592/88, it was decided that the sum of compensation without proof of damage was to be determined by considerations of both compensation and deterrence. Thus it is said (*id.* p. 271):

> In deciding the amount of compensation without having proven damage, it is the duty of the court to consider the two fundamental aims enshrined in copyright laws: the one—compensation of the copyright owner; the second—the deterrence of infringement and of other potential infringements. On the one hand, the first aim requires that one should not be entirely detached from appraising the actual estimated damage of the Plaintiff, nor should he be unjustly enriched... On the other hand, the second aim justifies the consideration, for the necessity of determining the sum of the compensation, of the mental state of the

> infringer , that is to be less severe with the unwitting infringer and to be more severe with the intentional infringer.

As was said, in the case before me the Plaintiff has lost his right to be first to publish the work, to which he has dedicated many years. The compensatory consideration itself justifies the determination of the higher sum. The precedent upon which Mr Hausner depended (C.A. [District Court Case] 1143/83 *Belbo Film Production v. Monitin Press Co. Ltd et al.*, 1987 [b] P.M. 391, at 396), in which statutory compensation amount to the sum of NIS 250, estimated on 13 January 1983, is comparable to more than NIS 13,000 today, and exemplary of the deserved rate. In the same case, compensation was set for the infringement of copyright in a documentary film in which the person who apprehended Eichman was interviewed. On these matters, it is realized that the great labour that the Plaintiff had invested, and its nature, make it clear that the damages should be set at a higher level than the damage which was caused to the owner of the copyright in the film.

51. As for the aspect of deterrence, the Defendants knowingly published the composite text; it seems that Shanks saw this publication as part of his struggle against the establishment, which had permitted only a certain number of researchers to study the Scrolls. In the Publisher's Foreword he bragged that in contradistinction to Kapera who had submitted to the authorities, he had decided to distribute the text; he was publishing it. In this struggle he was not deterred from infringing the copyright of the Plaintiff, who had no part whatsoever in the restriction of access to the study of the scrolls. It found that the consideration for deterrence also requires a judgment for the maximum statutory damages—NIS 20,000.

Non-pecuniary Damages

52. In section 20(b) of the Plaintiff's suit, the Plaintiff sued for NIS 100,000 for mental distress and injury to reputation. Mr Molcho explained that the composite text was not ripe for publication. This was a draft only. Therefore, publication harms the Plaintiff's reputation among the researchers who could recognize that it is his work.

The argument in the matter of harm to reputation is insufficiently based on facts. It is reasonable to presume that scholars who were well-versed in the field would know that the composite text was the fruit of the Plaintiff's labour. They would also have understood that this was a draft. It is possible to assume that they would know that Strugnell and the Plaintiff were about to publish together the completed work with interpretation. However, there is no doubt that much mental anguish was caused to the Plaintiff. In his testimony the Plaintiff explained how he felt that his world had crumbled around him and his dream of gaining fame had vanished. I will cite him in his own words:

> I was shocked. I was unable to describe this feeling; it was as though someone had come and taken [it] away from me by force, saying 'Who are you?' This belongs to me, the work that I had done… I would not have accepted [the assignment of] an unpublished text and worked on it for so many years had I not been assured that my right to publish first would be protected. Because the Scroll as such or any text for that matter that is published will always be called by the name of its first editor. However many subsequent studies may follow, they will not be editions, reverting always to the principal edition…for years I worked on 'miqsat ma'aseh ha-torah' almost without working on anything else…the whole family lived thriftily…if my wife complained, I would say: 'Look, this is our life, we will become famous. This is perhaps more to be considered than money' (*Trial Transcript*, pp. 207-208).

As was previously said, the Defendants violated the Plaintiff's moral right. In this they have committed a wrong under the Torts Ordinance, and the Plaintiff is entitled to compensation for mental anguish. On the estimate of this damage, the generally accepted guidelines in the Torts Ordinance apply within the ambit of the special principles for compensation in copyright law. As was said, in this matter the court takes into account both the consideration of the compensation and the behaviour of the publisher.

53. The principle assumed as the basis of the theory of torts is 'the restoration to the state in which things were before' (*in statu quo ante*); that is to say: placing the damaged individual in the same state in which he was able to be had he not been harmed by the one who had inflicted injuries against him. Our case concerns emotional harm, which is not open to exact quantification. However, it is still possible to re-establish approximately and in essence restoration *in statu quo*, and this can be done by granting monetary compensation

that recompenses the material harm. The matter has been explained in the aforementioned book (Barak, 'Theory of General Damages', p. 571):

> The monetary compensation that is given to the injured party is intended to enable him to obtain in the future happiness and joy which would counter-balance the suffering and distress he has experienced in the past, in a way that the balance between the two will place him, as far as possible, back in the state in which he would have been had it not been for the wrong done to him.

Together with this, in the theory of torts there is also consideration for the behaviour of the wrongdoer: first, in the estimation of non-pecuniary damage of an emotional harm, one can impose a higher compensation by considering the severity of the violator's behaviour (Barak, 'Theory of General Damages', p. 578); and second, in appropriate cases compensation is imposed in order to punish the wrongdoer for his behaviour (exemplary compensation) (Barak, 'Theory of General Damages', p. 579; C.A.30/72 *Friedman v. Segal* 27 [2], P.D. 225). Although the imposition of exemplary compensation is controversial, in the aforementioned C.A. 30/72 it is noted that the debate has become academic, because the increased compensation includes for the most part almost the entire elements of exemplary compensation.

Therefore, the rate of the compensation to which the Plaintiff is entitled can be affected by the behaviour of the Defendants. That infringement of moral right is also a tort should not take anything away from this.

In this case, and considering the severity of the harm to the Plaintiff's feelings and Shank's behaviour, it seems to me that the suitable compensation for mental anguish is 80,000 NIS.

54. On this basis, I issue an injunction prohibiting the Defendants from publishing the composite text or distributing it in any way. Likewise, I find the Defendants, jointly and severally, liable to pay the Plaintiff NIS 100,000 plus differential indexation and legal interests, from the day of the filing of the suit (14th January 1992) and until the actual payment.

As for legal expenses, as a rule it is fitting to determine liability for expenses in light of the outcome of the case. Moreover, the court is authorized, in appropriate cases, to bring into the calculation additional considerations and in them the trouble that has been caused by the suit (Y. Sussman, *Civil Procedure* [ed. S. Levin; Jerusalem: Aminun, 6th edn, 1991], p. 513). The discussion of this case has been complicated in the extreme. The Plaintiff's lawyer had to fly to the United States to participate in the examination of the defence's witness, Strugnell. As was said, the Defendants are not Israelis and the preparation was extensive. The case itself lasted over several sittings, and the *Trial Transcript* runs to over 600 pages.

In consideration of all that has been said above, I make the Defendants liable to pay the Plaintiff the lawyer's fees in the amount of NIS 50,000 and legal expenses as determined by the registrar of this court. Also this sum will carry the differential indexation and legal interest until the actual payment is made.

Delivered today 30 March 1993.

Intellectual Property Law and the Scholar: Cases I Have Known

Hershel Shanks

> Jarndyce and Jarndyce drones on. This scarecrow of a suit has, in course of time, become so complicated, that no man alive knows what it means. The parties to it understand it least; but it has been observed that no two Chancery lawyers can talk about it for five minutes, without coming to a total disagreement as to all the premises.[1]

One wonders whether Mr Dickens by some prescient sense is writing not of Jarndyce and Jarndyce, but of *Qimron v. Shanks*.

It is not over yet. After seven years, it drones on. In the course of time it has become so complicated that it takes an academic conference to understand it. Lawyers disagree about it. And, to disclose the end at the beginning, the case still lies in the bosom of the Israel Supreme Court. I will tell you later *when* I think it will be decided, but not what the decision will be, only what I would decide if I were the judge.

Let us first have before us the facts. They are simple—or relatively so.

In early 1991 there came into my hands from a source still unknown[2] 1787 photographs of the then-unpublished Dead Sea Scrolls. We promptly published them in a two-volume folio edition to which I wrote a lengthy 'Publisher's Foreword'. My foreword bitingly recounted the refusal of the official Scroll editors to provide access to the unpublished Scrolls. I consciously took a very aggressive stance because, frankly, I was fearful of a lawsuit by the Israel Antiquities

1. Charles Dickens, *Bleak House* (New York: Modern Library, 1985), pp. 7-8.

2. William Cox, Esq., who testified at the trial, represented the person(s) who somehow obtained the photographs. As the court's opinion explained, he mediated on behalf of his unnamed client, among Robert Eisenman, James Robinson and myself. In effect, however, I got the pictures through Eisenman. Who gave them to Eisenman remains unknown.

Authority. It all seems very benign now but, believe me, with the Scroll establishment against me, the possibility of a lawsuit instituted by a sovereign state was no small matter. If the Israel Antiquities Authority was considering a lawsuit, as the director later confirmed to me they were, I wanted them to know I was no patsy.

At one point in my Foreword, I discussed the case of MMT. I wanted to show how hard the establishment was trying to keep things to themselves. A hand-copy of the 120-line text of MMT had circulated widely. Virtually every Scroll scholar had a copy. Seminars were being taught on MMT. Indeed, a copy had even been published in a Polish journal. Yet officially it was unavailable. Moreover, the establishment had bullied the editor of the Polish journal to withhold all undistributed copies of the offending publication, as if somehow the genie could be put back in the bottle.

In recounting these events in my Foreword, I noted that MMT had been assigned to Professor John Strugnell for publication. I should say here that John and I are now friends. I attribute this to his being the consummate gentleman. We talk on the phone. We get together when I am in Boston. Of course it is easy for me to be friendly with him. It is not so easy for him to be friendly with me. Let me just say that I admire him greatly for this (he would say that he is just being Christian). I confess I still regard him as an intellectual anti-Semite, although quite benign if that is possible. But we do not discuss that, so we get on fine. But at one time, John was the chief devil. It was he who was withholding MMT. I knew Elisha Qimron was working with him, but I did not know the extent of his contribution. And I did not want to be critical of a young untenured Israeli scholar, so I wrote, 'With a colleague, Strugnell proceeded to write a 500-page commentary on this 120-line text.'

With that statement I brought down upon myself the wrath of heaven: I did not mention Elisha Qimron's name. I wanted to save Qimron from the criticism I was heaping on John Strugnell, but I ended up offending Qimron beyond redemption.

I also printed as figure 8 to my Foreword a photocopy of the page of the Polish journal containing the Hebrew text of MMT. At my smart-alecky best—or, perhaps more accurately, my smart-alecky *worst*—I sarcastically remarked, 'Outsiders must still await publication of the [MMT] commentary before they can see the text [of MMT] (unless they look at figure 8).'

Qimron never contacted me about the slight that so upset him. Instead he retained counsel, one of Israel's most prominent lawyers, Yitzchak Molcho. Mr Molcho, a member of an old Jerusalem family, is the personal lawyer of the Prime Minister, Benjamin Netanyahu. At present, Molcho also heads the Israeli team that is negotiating a peace agreement with the Palestinians. In short, Molcho is well-connected and knows how to fight a bitter lawsuit. And, to anticipate a bit, he absolutely wiped up the floor with me. There was not one matter of any significance that we won. I hasten to add that, as a lawyer myself, I have nothing but admiration for his skill. If I were in trouble in Israel, I would want him on my side.

Molcho initiated the lawsuit without so much as a letter or a telephone call. Nor did he simply file a complaint. Instead, he went to the judge without me or my lawyer and asked for emergency relief—a worldwide injunction against my distributing the two-volume folio edition of unpublished texts so long as it included the page with MMT in it. When the judge granted him the relief he requested, Molcho faxed the order to me. He not only knew where I was, he had my fax number. He could, of course, have faxed *before* he went to the judge so my attorney could present my side of the dispute, but he did not do that. In the United States, he would have been required to inform the court that he had been unable to locate me to get this kind of emergency *ex parte* relief, but apparently that is not the law in Israel.

This typifies how the case was fought—meanly and bitterly. There was no interest in an apology. It was about money—and lots of it. The object was to cause pain. Once when I was in Jerusalem, Molcho obtained an order—again on an *ex parte* basis, apparently his specialty—forbidding me from leaving the country. The airport and border police were notified. It took a judicial hearing the next day to have the order lifted. Actually, I have always been grateful this happened: I had an extra unplanned evening in Israel that I spent wonderfully with a sick friend who died shortly thereafter.

When I wanted to get the testimony of John Strugnell, which I thought would be somewhat favorable to me (it was), the Israeli court required me to pay for Mr Molcho to come over from Israel.

I mention these things only because they illustrate how a lawsuit vigorously pursued by competent counsel can become something of a monster, regardless of the outcome. As Learned Hand, a great American judge who knew something about litigation, once stated: 'As a litigant, I should dread a lawsuit beyond almost anything else short of sickness and death'.[3]

You may wonder how the Israeli court got jurisdiction over me: Molcho successfully argued that it was sufficient that three copies of the book had been mailed to Israel and that it had also been advertised in *Biblical Archaeology Review*, which was mailed to some subscribers in Israel.

On 1 and 2 February 1993, we had a two-day trial in which some of the most powerful people in Israel testified against me, describing my Foreword as immensely damaging to the plaintiff, both financially and emotionally. The witnesses included the Director of the Israel Antiquities Authority (Amir Drori), the Curator of the Shrine of the Book (Magen Broshi) and a leading professor of Talmud (Ya'akov Sussmann), who testified that scholars were sometimes paid as much as $10,000 for a single lecture. Presumably by printing MMT without his name, I was depriving Professor Qimron of this income.

On 30 March 1993, Judge Dalia Dorner (who has since been elevated to the Israel Supreme Court) rendered her opinion and decision, holding me and the other defendants (the Biblical Archaeology Society, Robert Eisenman and James Robinson) liable, awarding what is reportedly one of the largest judgments ever made in a copyright case in Israel.[4]

As Judge Dorner allowed in her 46-page opinion,[5] this is an 'extremely complex' case. She found the defendants liable on two grounds: (1) copyright infringement; and (2) violation of the plaintiff's *droit moral* because of my failure to name Qimron in connection with the work.

Copyright, as you know, inheres only in an original work of authorship. The work does not have to be at all good; indeed, it can be drivel. But it must be original. Here Qimron was trying to reconstruct an ancient text written by someone else 2000 years ago. To do this

3. 'The Deficiencies of Trials to Reach the Heart of the Matter', *Lectures on Legal Topics 1921–1922*, III (New York: The Macmillan Company, 1926), p. 105.

4. 20,000 shekels, the maximum statutory damages for copyright infringement where damage has not been proved ($7400 at the time); 80,000 shekels for violation of Qimron's *droit moral* ($29,600); and 50,000 shekels in lawyer's fees ($18,500), all plus interest. In addition, the award was 'indexed' to account for the inflation in Israel.

5. I refer to the unofficial English translation.

required great scholarship. But did this make Qimron's work an 'original creation?' Did this make him, for copyright purposes, the author of the composite text which he assembled from approximately 70 fragments? The court held it did. Here are the two sentences in which the court stated its holding:

> Making the transcription and combining the fragments that physically match each other do not constitute the required originality. By contrast, *assembling* [emphasis mine, H.S.] the Composite Text based on *halachic* and linguistic research from an original text does constitute an original creation.

With all due respect, I submit that this paragraph is hardly a model of clarity. Perhaps that is because the translation is bad,[6] but that is all I have. What it seems to say is that *assembling* the disparate fragments (where there is no physical match) is enough to give Qimron a copyright, provided this assembling is based on *halakhic* and linguistic research.

The court gave only one example of the kind of research it was talking about: a single letter was missing from one of the critical words. If that letter were an *aleph*, the word would mean *orot*, 'lights'; if it were an *ayin*, the word would be *orot*, 'hides'. Qimron decided on the basis of his research that it was an *ayin* and this enabled him to place the fragment in the assembled work.

So Qimron's copyright, according to the court, inheres in the *arrangement* of the fragments. It is this that cannot be copied.

Strangely enough, the court does not seem to hold that Qimron's copyright results from the reconstructions themselves, only from assembling the pieces. The court notes Qimron's allegation that he reconstructed 40 per cent of the text. She also states, 'Not all of the assembled fragments were physically matched, and linguistic and *halakhic* research was needed to complete the *missing parts*' [emphasis mine, H.S.]. But nowhere does she follow up on this to find that Qimron held a copyright in these 'missing parts', these reconstructions, perhaps because she recognized that 'the decipherer's purpose was to reconstruct the original scroll'. The only specific reconstruction she refers to in her opinion is the reconstruction of *orot* as hides. I think it

6. [The author used the English translation given to him at the trial and this is not the same as the authorized one included in this volume. Eds].

is clear that reconstructing a single letter could not result in the authorship required for copyright, even if he did this many times.

Inasmuch as Qimron failed to prove any damages from the infringement, the court was limited to so-called statutory damages, the recompense allowed when no damage is proved. In Israel, this is limited to a maximum of 20,000 shekels and she awarded the maximum. But she was clearly unhappy with me and my testimony and was able to find a way around this limit—namely, a violation of the so-called *droit moral.* The *droit moral* is essentially a civil law concept that has received increasing attention in the United States although it is not part of American common law. In Israel, it has been legislatively incorporated into the copyright statute. The *droit moral* accords an author or artist the right to have his name associated with his work and the right to have his work exhibited without distortion or alteration. In other words, even if you own a Picasso, you cannot paint a beard on a beardless man in the painting. And you cannot paint over Picasso's signature.

My violation of Qimron's *droit moral* was based on my failure to mention his name,[7] although of course the wrong was compounded by the fact that my publication of MMT was an unauthorized publication. Without his name, in the words of the court, 'his dream to achieve fame had vanished'. For this she awarded him 80,000 shekels based on the emotional distress this had caused him. He had testified:

> I was shocked. I can't describe the feeling; it's as if someone came and took away the thing I had made by force, telling me: 'Go away! This belongs to me'... The Scroll or any text, when published, will always be called by the name of its first editor. No matter how many editions there are, they will always refer to the first edition... During the years I worked on [MMT], I did almost no other work... The whole family lived very frugally... When my wife complained, I would tell her, 'Look, this is our life, we will achieve fame.'

Lawyers will recognize a tricky question of conflict of laws in this issue. The Israeli court here applied the Israeli law statute regarding *droit moral*. On general conflicts principles, however, the court held that American law was applicable in this case because the infringement had occurred in the United States. But the plaintiff had failed to prove American law. The court nevertheless held that, with some exceptions

7. The court stated: 'The product of Claimant's efforts, namely the Composite Text, has been published without his name being mentioned, and thereby his moral right has been infringed'.

not applicable here, Israeli courts apply a 'presumption of equal laws' in which it is presumed 'that the laws of enlightened countries are identical'. The court applied that presumption here and therefore applied Israeli law as American law. Although we argued that *droit moral* was not part of the common law of the United States, the court held that it was our burden to prove this and we had not met the burden. Therefore, she ruled, 'the entire action, including the argument based on the *droit moral*, must be decided according to Israel law.'

Whether the decision of the lower court will hold up is anyone's guess. I will let the practising lawyers argue about this. I want now to consider only the ramifications of the decision.

The paradoxical nature of this victory—if it is a victory—is that it gives Professor Qimron far greater rights than he ever wanted or even hoped for. Traditionally, scholars assigned to publish an ancient manuscript are given the right of *first* publication. In the case of the Dead Sea Scrolls, we effectively argued for a limitation of this right: 35 years was long enough to wait. But what the court gave Qimron was a copyright, not simply the right of first publication. This means that even now, after the *DJD* publication of MMT,[8] he still owns the copyright and he will have the exclusive right to publish it for his lifetime, after which his heirs will have that right for 50 more years. Remember that his copyright is in the 'assembling of the Composite Text'. That means that no one can copy the arrangement of the pieces as Qimron arranged them without his permission. He holds a copyright in the arrangement of the pieces, or at least the pieces that are not contiguous.

How threatening is that to the scholarly world? I could argue that it would throw a monkey wrench into scholarship. After all, scholarship is made of one scholar standing on the shoulders of his or her forebears. All scholars who publish new editions or translations of MMT, including my friend Geza Vermes, will use Qimron's arrangement and reconstruction to some extent. All such use, however, is a copyright violation—a violation of Qimron's copyright. In fact, Qimron heard of two scholars who were working on MMT with an eye to publishing their own edition. On his behalf, Qimron's lawyer wrote to these scholars, Ben Zion Wacholder and Martin Abegg, as follows:

8. Elisha Qimron and John Strugnell, *Discoveries in the Judean Desert*. X. *Qumran Cave 4*: V. *Miqṣat Ma'aśe Ha-Torah* (Oxford: Clarendon Press, 1994).

> We have been informed that you might be using portions of Professor Qimron's reconstruction in a publication planned by you and [Wacholder/Abegg]. On behalf of Professor Qimron, please accept this letter as notification that any use of Professor Qimron's reconstructed text is a violation of his copyright and Professor Qimron will take all steps available to him under both American and Israeli law to protect that copyright.

Wacholder and Abegg sued Qimron in an American court seeking a declaration that Qimron did not have a copyright in MMT. They eventually withdrew that suit, however. And that may be the critical point I want to make. Although the result in *Qimron v. Shanks* may be very bad law, it may nevertheless as a practical matter be relatively unimportant for the academic community. Wacholder and Abegg withdrew their lawsuit because they became confident that Qimron would not sue them, that he will not sue any scholar who uses his copyrighted text.

In the Fourth Edition (1995) of Geza Vermes' translation of the the scrolls, he refrained from publishing a translation of MMT: 'I have decided to postpone a full translation of MMT until the legal storm has blown over', he wrote. He also noted the 'opinion of most European and American scholars [that] the complaint could and should have been settled out of court'. In the latest edition, Vermes does provide a translation but he carefully notes that he refrained from using Qimron's reconstruction, noting that he found some of the restorations 'conjectural'. He did not even use Qimron's arrangement of the fragments.[9]

In short, the unique circumstances that led Qimron to sue the man standing before you are very unlikely ever to arise again. Even Qimron does not really want a copyright in MMT. Or at least it is fair to say that now that it is published he would not object to any scholar's using it in any way for a new edition.

I want to mention a couple of other cases that did not involve litigation. They are nevertheless part of the continuing struggle between those who control intellectual property and those who want to make use of it.

I recently wrote a book on the archaeology of Jerusalem, published in the United States by Random House.[10] My publisher forwarded a

9. *The Complete Dead Sea Scrolls in English* (London: Penguin Press, 1997), p. 221.

10. *Jerusalem: An Archaeological Biography* (New York: Random House, 1995).

letter to me that it received from the Tower of David Museum in Jerusalem asserting that I had 'violat[ed their] publishing rights'. What had I done? I had printed an aerial photograph of Jaffa Gate taken by a professional photographer that included the museum building and I had neither obtained the museum's permission to publish the picture nor paid them for it. The Qimron syndrome appeared to be catching. Fortunately, the Random House lawyers convinced the Museum that it did not have a case.

The Israel Museum has done something similar, however. It now charges $150 to take a picture of the outside of the building! This is perfectly legal since it owns the land from which the picture would be taken.

Of course museums are under severe budgetary constraints. But is this not going a little far? Law is only one aspect of our subject. Many public museums now assert a monopoly over the artefacts in their collections in what may be a perfectly legal way. It used to be that professional photographers were permitted to photograph objects in museum collections. We would often get the same image from several photographers and we would choose the best, just as we still do with site shots. There was healthy competition. But the museums have now adopted a new rule: Only their own photographer is permitted to photograph their objects. In this way they exercise a monopoly over the distribution of photographs of the object and can charge monopoly prices for their photographs. For that reason, we often forego pictures from the British Museum, for example, because we cannot afford its prices. On the one hand, we can sympathize with the museum; it needs the money. On the other hand, it is limiting access to what is essentially public property.

Let me return to *Qimron v. Shanks*. What is its present status? As I mentioned, it is now *sub judice* in the Israel Supreme Court—and it has been there for a long time. My guess is that it will still be a long time before it is decided. It has been briefed and rebriefed and briefed again. I am told that originally it was assigned to a three-judge panel that did not include the Chief Justice. He reassigned the case, however, so that he is now a member of the panel. At what was supposed to be oral argument, the Chief Justice opened by saying this was a 'fascinating' case—and then suggested that the parties compromise. Without consulting their clients, both lawyers said no. The court then took the case under advisement without further argument.

The reason I think it will be a long time before it is decided is this.

Although it is obviously a very important case—and the court knows this—it is not an A-priority matter in terms of the timeliness of a decision: it can wait. And it is not a case in which an opinion can be written in a couple of days. It will take a week or more to write an opinion dealing with all the issues, most of which I have not even mentioned. When do busy judges get a chance to set aside a week or more to deal with such a case? I hesitate to say never, but at least it will be a long time.

There is another matter which should tell us that the court has once again turned its attention to this case. A group of American copyright lawyers has filed a motion to file a brief *amicus curiae* in support of our position. Israel does not have a regular *amicus* practice. I am told that this is only the second case in which such a motion has been filed. Presumably when this motion is decided, we will know that the case has again come to life. Until then, we will just have to wait. [The motion for permission to file the *amicus* brief has since been denied, and the Supreme Court decided the case not long thereafter, affirming the decision of the lower court.]

Although I cannot predict the outcome, I can tell you what I think it should be. I think the court should reverse the holding on *droit moral* because it is statutory in Israel. Therefore it cannot be presumed to be the same in all enlightened countries and the plaintiff failed to prove American law.

On the copyright issue, I would send the case back for a new trial to examine the nature of the reconstructions that Qimron placed in brackets. The lower court should then determine whether Qimron was entitled to a copyright in these reconstructions. That matter is sufficiently complicated that maybe the parties would then compromise and the opinion of the lower court would be expunged.

Part II

PRINCIPLES OF INTELLECTUAL PROPERTY AND COPYRIGHT LAWS

The Application of American Copyright Law to the Dead Sea Scrolls Controversy

Cindy Alberts Carson

1. *The Copyright Suits*

In November 1991 Hershel Shanks, Editor of the *Biblical Archaeology Review* and outspoken critic of the international team's handling of the Scrolls, published a two-volume facsimile edition of the Scrolls.[1] In Shanks's introduction to the facsimile edition he reproduced 120 lines of a 132-line international team reconstruction of a portion of one the Scrolls known as the MMT.[2]

Various members of the international team had worked on the MMT document for more than 30 years. Professor Elisha Qimron of Ben-Gurion University, a philologist with expertise in the Halakha, joined the group working on the MMT in 1980, and put together a composite text of the team's reconstruction and his analysis of the likely content of missing text.[3] Copies of portions of the 300-page composite text of the MMT (including parts of the 132-line reconstruction) had been distributed to other scholars and reproduced without permission in scholarly journals during the late 1980s.[4]

Less than ten weeks after the publication of the facsimile edition, Professor Qimron filed a copyright infringement suit in Israel against

1. R. Eisenman and J. Robinson (eds.), *A Facsimile Edition of the Dead Sea Scrolls* (Washington, DC: Biblical Archaeology Society, 1991).

2. 'Miqṣat Ma'aseh ha-Torah' or 'Some Rulings Pertaining to the Torah'. See *Biblical Archaeology Society v. Qimron*, No. 92-5590; Eastern District of Pennsylvania (10 February 1993; LEXIS, GENFED library), p. 2.

3. Asher Felix Landau, 'The Dead Sea Scrolls and the Recognized Rules of Copyright', *The Jerusalem Post* (April 11 1993).

4. 1992–1994 Copyright Law Decisions (Commerce Clearing House), para. 26,241. The full text is printed in E. Qimron and J. Strugnell, *Discoveries in the Judaean Desert*. X. *Qumran Cave 4:* V. *Miqṣat Ma'aśe Ha-Torah* (Oxford: Clarendon Press, 1994), pp. 44-63.

Hershel Shanks for an injunction and damages.[5] Shanks and the Review brought a declaratory judgment action to decide the copyright infringement issue in the United States District Court for the Eastern District of Pennsylvania in September 1992.[6] Mr Shanks eventually dropped the American suit.[7]

On 30 March 1993 the Jerusalem District Court awarded Professor Qimron the equivalent of US $55,000 in statutory and mental anguish damages in his copyright infringement suit against Shanks.[8] Professor Qimron's request for the equivalent of US $250,000 in damages was reduced by the court when it found that Professor Qimron had failed to show that the unauthorized publication had caused him actual pecuniary loss.[9]

Two months later, Shanks appealed to the Israeli Supreme Court.[10] In August of 1993, Professor Ben-Zion Wacholder of Hebrew Union College and Professor Martin Abegg of Grace Theological Seminary asked the United States District Court for the Eastern District of Pennsylvania for a declaratory judgment that a Scroll project they were working on would not infringe Professor Qimron's copyright.[11] The suit was prompted by a letter which Professors Wacholder and Abegg received from Professor Quimron's attorneys in February 1993, threatening suit if any use was made of Professor Qimron's reconstructed text. Professors Wacholder and Abegg said that they did not intend to reproduce Professor Qimron's work, but rather intended to fill in the missing fragments of the MMT with their own original research.[12]

5. Shanks's book was published in November 1991; Professor Qimron filed suit on 14 January 1992 (*Qimron v. Shanks*, 3 [5753-1993] P.M. 10, District Court of Jerusalem (1993), p. 3).

6. 1992–1994 Copyright Law Decisions (Commerce Clearing House), para. 26,240.

7. 'Dateline', *The Legal Intelligencer* (16 July 1993), p. 5.

8. 'Qimron is Author of MMT Reconstruction, Jerusalem Court Holds', *BAR* May–June 1993), p. 69.

9. Abraham Rabinovich, 'Court Awards Dead Sea Scrolls Translator NIS 100,000', *The Jerusalem Post* (31 March 1993).

10. Abraham Rabinovich, 'Dead Sea Scrolls Publisher Appeals Conviction for Copyright Violation', *The Jerusalem Post* (4 June 1993), p. 16.

11. Jonathan Groner, 'Dispute Over Sacred Scrolls Lands in US Court', *Legal Times* (20 September 1993), p. 2. *Wacholder v. Qimron*, No. 93-4097, Eastern District of Pennsylvania (filed July 29, 1993).

12. Groner, 'Dispute Over Sacred Scrolls', p. 2.

However, they had seen Professor Qimron's work and did not believe that they could purge it from their minds.[13] Further, their work was likely to be similar since it would be driven by the context of the existing fragments.

2. *Choice of Law in Qimron v. Shanks*

The alleged infringement which prompted *Qimron v. Shanks* occurred in the United States. It is generally recognized that the laws of the place of infringement apply no matter where the suit is brought.[14] The Israeli District Court acknowledged that American copyright law should apply, but, under the 'presumption of equal laws' doctrine, reached the conclusion that, in the absence of proof to the contrary, it would be presumed that Israeli copyright law was identical to US copyright law.[15] In fact, it is not. While the US is a signatory to the Berne Convention, American moral rights law, unlike that of Israel, is limited to the protection of the rights of visual artists.[16] More importantly, the Israeli standard for 'originality' under copyright is not the equivalent of the American standard.[17]

3. *US Copyright Law Generally*

Under US law, copyright is granted only in original works of authorship which have been fixed in a tangible medium of expression.[18] A person who is found to be an author for the purposes of copyright is granted certain exclusive rights with regard to the work,[19] and the

13. Groner, 'Dispute Over Sacred Scrolls', p. 2.

14. Melville B. Nimmer and David Nimmer, *Nimmer on Copyright*, IV, s. 17.05 (1997). But see *Bridgeman Art Library v. Corel Corp.* (25 Federal Supplement 2d 421; Southern District of New York; 1998).

15. Jeffrey M. Dine, 'Authors' Moral Rights in Non-European Nations: International Agreements, Economics, Mannu Bhandari, and the Dead Sea Scrolls', *Michigan Journal of International Law* 16 (1995), pp. 545, 570.

16. Title 17, U.S.C., s. 106A (1997).

17. See Lisa M. Weinstein, 'Ancient Works, Modern Dilemmas: The Dead Sea Scrolls Copyright Case', *American University Law Review* 43 (1994), pp. 1637, 1649-51.

18. Title 17, U.S.C., s. 102 (1988).

19. The rights of reproduction, display, performance, distribution, and the right to prepare derivative works. Title 17, U.S.C., s. 106 (1988).

power to prevent others from exercising those rights.[20] Two competing policies underlie the enforcement of the author's copyright. One policy is that of encouraging authors to produce by giving protection to the expression of their ideas for a limited time. The other policy is that of making the underlying ideas or facts available for others to use and build upon. For this reason, an author's expression of an idea or fact is protected from copying, but the underlying idea or fact is not. Because the distinction between the underlying idea or fact and its expression is not always clear, US courts look for some evidence of creativity in determining whether protectable expression can be found. If no protectable expression can be found, or if the copyright term on protectable expression has expired, the material will go into the public domain where it is freely available to anyone. If protectable expression can be found, and the copyright term has not expired, the author may still lose some control over the material under the doctrine of fair use which permits copying for certain purposes, such as scholarship.[21]

4. *Copyright in the Arrangement, Translation and Interpolations*

Clearly, there is no copyright interest in the content of the Scrolls as written by the Scroll authors.[22] If the Scroll authors had been able to avail themselves of a paleo-copyright lawyer two thousand years ago, they would have been able to copyright their expression of what, they would argue, is historical fact. Today, their expression is in the public domain, and the facts on which they based their expression are unprotectable.[23]

20. Title 17, U.S.C., s. 106 (1988).

21. Title 17, U.S.C., s. 107 (1988).

22. The direct descendants of the Scroll authors could have an intellectual property interest in the Scrolls as unpublished manuscripts, but only if their property right in the Scrolls themselves could be shown.

23. 'We have already seen the problems that have arisen in the distribution of the content of the Dead Sea Scrolls even without copyright protection, and presumably few people today advocate affording copyright protection to such discoveries. The short, technical answer is that recognizing copyright in the process of fixation...does not imply that we must afford copyright protection to new discoveries of old literary works, because the discovery does not result in any new fixation. Translations of such discoveries would presumably be protected, of course, just as any other translation, and...a new fixation that made the work more widely available would have limited protection against direct, mechanical copying. The content

There are three elements of the text which may be protectable. The first is the arrangement of the fragments into a coherent, if incomplete, document. The second is the translation of the characters on the fragments, for the purpose both of arranging the fragments and of creating a document which can be read by those who are not Biblical scholars. The third is the interpolation of scholarly reconstructions of missing clauses.

a. *Protectability of the Arrangement of the Fragments*

The arrangement of the Scroll fragments may be copyrightable.[24] In some instances, the compilation of otherwise unprotectable facts[25] has been deemed copyrightable where the means of compilation itself is not obvious and is, at least to some degree, creative.[26] For example, the names of the citizens of a town would not be protectable, nor would the arrangement of the names if simply placed in alphabetical order. However, if the names were categorized in a non-obvious or creative way, such as by the occupation of their owners, the arrangement may be protected.

If the length of time the Scroll scholars have spent in deciphering the Scrolls is any indication, the arrangement of the Scrolls is not obvious in the sense of being easy to determine. Nonetheless, the arrangement may be obvious if the fragments really only make sense if they are arranged in one particular order. The reason for the delay in deciphering experienced by the Scroll scholars may not mean that they are selecting between several possible arrangements each of which makes

of the work, however, would not be protected'. Dennis S. Karjala, 'Copyright and Misappropriation', *Dayton Law Review* 17 (1992), pp. 885, 907 n. 80.

24. The Copyright Act 1976 defines a 'compilation' as a 'work formed by the collection and assembling of pre-existing materials or of data that are selected, coordinated, or arranged in such a way that the resulting work as a whole constitutes an original work of authorship' (Title 17, U.S.C., s. 101 [1988]). Copyright in a compilation 'extends only to the material contributed by the author of such work, as distinguished from the pre-existing material employed in the work, and does not imply any exclusive right to pre-existing material' (Title 17, U.S.C., s. 103 [1988]). For a discussion suggesting that US Courts would not find reconstructions of ancient texts to be copyrightable, see Weinstein, *Ancient Works, Modern Dilemmas*, pp. 1655-70.

25. Facts are not protectable under US copyright law. See Title 17, U.S.C., s. 102(b) (1988).

26. Title 17, U.S.C., s. 102(a) (1988 and Supplement II 1990).

sense; rather the difficulty may simply lie in handling the large volume of Scroll fragments and dealing with missing fragments. For example, if some nefarious person were to run a Gutenberg Bible through a paper shredder, it might take years to piece the various strips together, but the very reason for the delay would be that there is only one correct way for the strips to go together. The delay is caused by the process of finding the one correct way through trial and error.

That the process is difficult, painstaking and complex does not, in and of itself, make the result copyrightable. It would, no doubt, be extremely time-consuming to list alphabetically the name of every American citizen, but the hard work of doing so does not change the fact that the names are unprotectable facts, and that the means of collation is obvious and available to anyone. American and Israeli courts[27] have, since *Feist Publications, Inc. v. Rural Telephone Service Co.*,[28] consistently rejected the 'sweat of the brow' approach to copyright. The Court in *Feist* stated that the 'sweat of the brow' doctrine arose from an ambiguity in the language of the US Copyright Act 1909.[29] The language of the US Copyright Act 1976 is clear, however, and requires at least some minimal amount of intellectual creativity. In compilations, therefore, the 1976 Act virtually requires that the creativity come from the selection or arrangement of the otherwise unprotectable material. Physical or economic effort is not enough to transform unprotectable material into protectable material. The *Feist* Court stated that the 'sweat of the brow' doctrine 'flouted basic copyright principles', the net result of which was the 'handing out of proprietary interests in facts'.[30]

In *Feist*, the Court held that originality is a constitutional requirement of copyright, and that to be original, a work must possess 'at least

27. Israel's intellectual property law follows an Anglo-American model. For example, because the *Qimron* case was one of first impression, the Jerusalem District Court used American case law to support its decision. See *Qimron v. Shanks*, pp. 22-23, trans. pp. 14-15.

28. (1991) 111 Supreme Court 1282.

29. *Feist Publications Inc v. Rural Telephone Service Co.* 111 Supreme Court 1282 (1991), p. 1290.

30. *Feist*, p. 1292. For a strong pre-*Feist* argument for the protectability of labor-intensive factual compilations, see Denicola, 'Copyright in Collections of Facts: A Theory for the Protection of Non-fiction Literary Works', *Columbia Law Review* 81 (1981), p. 516.

some minimal degree of creativity'.[31] Under this definition, bare facts are unprotectable, but the compilation of bare facts may be protectable if it meets the originality requirement.[32] This level of originality, however, need not be very high. The Court only required that the 'selection and arrangement of facts cannot be so mechanical or routine as to require no creativity whatsoever'.[33] Rural Telephone's alphabetical arrangement did not pass even this minimal test: 'There is nothing remotely creative about arranging names alphabetically in a white pages directory… It is not only unoriginal, it is practically inevitable. This time-honored tradition does not possess the minimal creative spark required by the Copyright Act and the Constitution.'[34] Similarly, the arrangement of documentary fragments into their original order is, while tedious, both mechanical and conventional.

When reconstructing the biblical texts, the international team was guided by more modern versions of the same texts. With non-biblical material, members of the team have had to match handwriting and compare the torn edges of fragments, frequently making educated guesses based on content.[35] Fragments may be matched by following the patterns of damage likely to be inflicted by rodents, insects and humidity on a rolled-up scroll. After the scroll has deteriorated into fragments, these patterns remain.[36] Matching based on suppositions about context are mechanical as well in that, while they require specialized knowledge and high level applications of logic, they do not require, and should not demonstrate, any level of originality.

If the arrangement of the fragments is, as has been argued, much like the completion of a jigsaw puzzle, the arrangement should not be protected.[37] If there is only one correct solution to the puzzle, that solution is a fact, and is, therefore, unprotectable. If, on the other hand,

31. *Feist*, p. 1287.

32. *Feist*, p. 1289.

33. *Feist*, p. 1296.

34. *Feist*, p. 1297.

35. Hartmut Stegemann, 'How to Connect Dead Sea Scrolls Fragments', in H. Shanks (ed.), *Understanding the Dead Sea Scrolls* (Washington, DC: Biblical Archaeological Society, 1993), pp. 245-55 (245).

36. Stegemann, 'How to Connect Dead Sea Scroll Fragments', pp. 249-53.

37. The analogy is apparently apt—one of the founding members of the international team called the Scrolls, '[T]he world's greatest jigsaw puzzle'. K. Botsford, 'Scrolls Better Dead Than Read?', *The Independent* (12 October 1994), Weekend p. 29.

the fragments are small enough, irregular enough or unrelated enough, their arrangement may be a matter of conjecture, but, ultimately, there is really only one correct answer.

b. *The Protectability of the Translation*

Translations of public domain works are regarded as new works subject to copyright.[38] The protectability is only of the translation however, and does not extend to the underlying work. The Scrolls are written in ancient Aramaic and Hebrew. Legible Hebrew Scrolls do not require translation to be readable by anyone able to read modern Hebrew.[39] While translations from Aramaic into Hebrew or from Hebrew into English are protectable, that protection is very thin, and does not extend to the underlying work.

c. *The Protectability of the Interpolations*

It is a fact that the Scroll authors made certain statements in the Scrolls, even if the exact content of those statements is, given the condition of the Scrolls, unknowable in any absolute sense. The Scroll interpreters are seeking to reproduce these statements exactly, understanding, at the same time, that this goal may be unattainable. Professor Qimron's years of work on a small section of the Scrolls was ultimately about making his interpretation as accurate as possible under the circumstances. He sought, as have all Scroll interpreters, to restore the authors' statements to their original form. If he was successful, his work should not be protectable,[40] any more so than would be the work of a potter who glued together the pieces of a broken ancient vase, even if there were pieces missing which required the potter to extrapolate from the existing shape or pattern of the vase.[41]

38. Title 17, U.S.C., s. 86 (1982) (defining a translation as a derivative work and extending copyright in a derivative work only to the author's contribution).

39. Many of the Scrolls require transcription due to fading, soil or damage. Stegemann, 'How to Connect Dead Sea Scrolls Fragments', pp. 246-47.

40. 'However, it is unsettled whether or not, for example, the newly reconstructed emendations of the Dead Sea Scrolls are independently copyrightable' (Kenneth L. Port, 'Foreword: Symposium on Intellectual Property Law Theory', *Chicago Kent Law Review* 68 [1993], p. 585).

41. 'The prevalent contemporary understanding identifies authorial subjectivity as the hallmark of original works of authorship: original works reflect the personalities of their authors or, at the very least, embody their creators' subjective choices in the selection or arrangement of material' (Jane C. Ginsburg, 'Creation and

In general, protectability requires creativity. Creativity requires a degree of discretion, which permits the possibility of alternative outcomes. If there is no discretion in the act, if the actor must perform in only one way, with no opportunity for variance based on personality and preference, there is no creativity. If the potter follows the pattern of the vase, restores the shape, matches the color and decoration, and in every way exactly reproduces the original artist's work, then his work is no more copyrightable than that of any other workman.[42]

Apparently, Professor Qimron's work required discretion. The gaps that he filled made up, by his estimation, 40 per cent of the text, and it was not always evident what the missing words would be in any given fragmented passage.[43] Based on his expertise in the Halakha, his knowledge of ancient Aramaic and Hebrew vocabulary and syntax, and his years of working with the original text, Professor Qimron was able to gauge the likely meaning of any given line, and the words that were most likely used in areas where the text fragments were insufficient. That other scholars might differ in this interpretation is evidenced by Professors Wacholder and Abegg's desire to create their own interpretation.[44] This difference, however, is not an effort to make an individual scholar's work distinctive or reflective of his personality, but rather is each scholar's attempt to make his interpretation of the fragments comport with the fact of the original authors' statements.

Commercial Value: Copyright Protection of Works of Information', *Columbia Law Review* 90 [1990], pp. 1865-1938 [1865, 1867]).

42. See, e.g., *Hearn v. Meyer*, 664 Federal Supplement 832; Southern District of New York (1987) (denying copyright protection for identical fine art reproductions of public domain book illustrations).

43. Even with his years of work, Professor Qimron was not able to fill all of the gaps in the MMT. All reconstruction decisions were based on evidence and in some places there was simply not enough evidence of what the missing words might be. The result is not particularly readable, for example:

> Aaron should [... ... ... And]
> [concerning] the hides of cattle [and sheep that they
> ... ... from]
> their [hides] vessels [... ... ... to]
> [bring] them to the sanctuary [... ... ...]

(Qimron and Strugnell, *Discoveries*, p. 49 [reconstructions appear in brackets]).

44. Even John Strugnell and Elisha Qimron disagree on many of the MMT interpretations which they worked on together for ten years (H. Shanks, 'MMT as the Maltese Falcon', *BAR* [Nov.–Dec. 1994], pp. 48, 51).

d. *Do the Creative Elements Confer Protectability on the Remainder of the Text?*

Mr Shanks's attorney asked the Israeli District Court whether an artist or workman restoring the Sistine Chapel should be entitled to copyright protection when his only 'creative' contribution to the great painting was to fill in blank areas where the original paint had flaked off.[45] While the workman is entitled to protection for those areas which represent actual creative effort, if any, his small contribution should not allow him to protect the painting as a whole. Professor Qimron claimed copyright protection, not just for his suppositions where the text of the Scrolls was missing, or for his contribution to the arrangement of the text fragments, but for the text as a whole.[46]

There is some point at which the quantity of the Sistine Chapel workman's effort might entitle him to protect the entire ceiling. If the original painting was gone and the workman sought to recreate it, his entire recreation may be protectable if sufficiently creative. If he recreated 90 per cent of the ceiling, the whole ceiling would be similarly protected. At some point, however, the workman's contribution will become insufficient to support his claim for protection of the entire ceiling, although the exact location of that point is unclear. Professor Qimron claims to have recreated 40 per cent[47] of the section of text in which he claims a copyright.[48]

Some courts have used what has been called a 'totality' approach to, in essence, convey copyrightability by association.[49] According to the

45. Abraham Rabinovich, 'Court Hears Copyright Dispute on Dead Sea Scrolls', *The Jerusalem Post* (26 February 1993).

46. *Biblical Archaeological Society v. Qimron*, 1992–1994 Copyright Law Decisions (Commerce Clearing House), paras. 26,240, 26,241 (Professor Qimron claimed copyright in 'the text of the deciphering').

47. 40 per cent of Professor Qimron's reconstruction was interpolated material (*Qimron v. Shanks*, 3 [5753-1993] P.M. 10, 16, trans. p. 4). It appears that at least 20 per cent of the missing text remains unreconstructed.

48. Abraham Rabinovich, 'Court Hears Copyright Dispute on Dead Sea Scrolls', *The Jerusalem Post* (26 February 1993).

49. '[The totality] approach may be defined as any legal theory that accords noncopyrightable facts some measure of copyright protection when these facts are somehow combined with copyrightable expression into a protected totality'. G.L. Francione, 'Facing the Nation: The Standards for Copyright Infringement and Fair Use of Factual Works', *University of Pennsylvania Law Review* 134 (1986), pp. 519, 522.

leading authority on American copyright law, copyright protection is 'granted for the very reason that it may persuade authors to make their ideas freely accessible to the public so that they may be used for the intellectual advancement of mankind'.[50] For this reason, the limited monopoly granted by copyright applies only to the expression of ideas, not the ideas themselves. The totality doctrine protects otherwise unprotectable ideas merely because of their close association with the expression of the ideas, despite the fact that this conflicts with the goal of copyright law.[51]

One version of the totality approach is the theory of 'wholesale usurpation',[52] according to which courts find infringement of copyright in factual works if the subsequent user appropriates 'the total entity with its unique and protected mosaic, comprising the overall arrangement and selection of facts'.[53] A similar result is reached under the Copyright Act with regard to sound recordings of public domain works.[54] While no protection is given to the underlying fact of the composition, the performance of that composition is protected from direct copying of the actual sounds fixed by the recording.[55]

Wholesale usurpation adopts the philosophical tenets of the Berne Convention concept of *droit moral*, or moral right, specifically, that the author has a natural right to the fruits of his labour which must be protected.[56] The concept of *droit moral* focuses not on incentive and

50. Francione, *Facing the Nation*, p. 538 (citing Melville B. Nimmer and D. Nimmer, *Nimmer on Copyright* [10 vols.; New York: Matthew Bender, 1997] III, s. 13.03[A] [1985]).

51. 'The totality approach in any form fundamentally perverts the goal of copyright law to promote science and the useful arts through the production and dissemination of literary and artistic works… It simply makes no sense to recognize that certain material is not capable of copyright protection because of "the basic purpose of copyright law", but then to allow the admittedly unprotectable material to receive protection' (Francione, *Facing the Nation*, p. 552).

52. Francione, *Facing the Nation*, p. 522 n. 19. See also *Hoehling v. Universal City Studios* (1980) *Federal Reporter* 618 2d 972, 980, Second Circuit; certiorari denied, (1980) 449 US Supreme Court 841.

53. Francione, *Facing the Nation*, p. 522; see, *Harper & Row, Publishers, Inc. v. Nation Enterprises* (1983) *Federal Reporter* 723 2d 195, 203, Second Circuit; reversed on other grounds, (1985) 471 US Supreme Court 539.

54. Title 17, U.S.C., s. 114(b) (1988).

55. Title 17, U.S.C., s. 114(b) (1988).

56. See generally R. Denicola, 'Copyright in Collections of Facts: A Theory for

free access, but rather on the unjust enrichment of the usurper, and for that reason has been given a very limited application in the United States.[57]

In Professor Qimron's suit in the the Jerusalem District Court, Judge Dalia Dorner stated that Professor Qimron had a moral right 'to have his name applied to the work in the accepted manner and to the accepted extent' and to object, *inter alia*, to 'any derogatory action which may be prejudicial to his honor or reputation'.[58] The portion of the work reproduced was the MMT reconstruction, rather than any part of Professor Qimron's admittedly original 300-page commentary. The 120 lines of the reconstruction were reproduced exactly as written, having been taken from a Polish scholarly journal, which had reproduced the translation without permission. Since no change was made in the work, the only possible 'derogatory action' would be either the failure to acknowledge Professor Qimron or the failure to publish the complete 132-line reconstruction. The failure to publish the complete reconstruction did no damage to the integrity of the work since the 120-line segment represented a natural break in the work, recognized by Professor Qimron himself when he circulated the work to his associates.[59] The failure to give attribution to Professor Qimron specifically was not an attempt by Shanks to take credit for the work himself.[60] Instead, attribution was given to the international team as a whole (a degree of vilification regarding the delay was also directed at the team

the Protection of Nonfiction Literary Works', *Columbia Law Review* 81 (1981), pp. 516-42 (516).

57. Title 17, U.S.C., s. 106A.

58. Asher Felix Landau, 'The Dead Sea Scrolls and the Recognized Rules of Copyright', *The Jerusalem Post* (11 April 1993). Judge Dorner was quoting Israeli moral rights law. See *Qimron v. Shanks*, trans. p. 28.

59. Since the Polish journal had also only published the 120-line segment, Shanks had no access to the complete version of the reconstruction in any case. See *Qimron v. Shanks*, trans. pp. 4-5 (describing circulation by the *Qumran Chronicle*).

60. The issues to which Judge Dorner referred are the Berne Convention's protection of an author's artistic integrity and paternity. Specifically, an author has a right to have a work published or exhibited in its complete, unadulterated form, and to have his name associated with the work. See generally Roberta Rosenthal Kwall, 'Copyright and the Moral Right: Is an American Marriage Possible?', *Vanderbilt Law Review* 38 (1985), p. 1 (discussing moral rights inside and outside the United States); Mayer Gabay, 'Israel Adopts Moral Rights Law', *Journal of the Copyright Society* 29 (1982), p. 462 (providing text of the Israeli law).

as a whole). While Professor Qimron's name was not mentioned individually, the MMT reconstruction included work by other members of the team, and Professor Qimron, as a member of the team, was included in any reference to the team as an entity.

The underlying theory of wholesale usurpation is that a subsequent author may not enjoy the fruits of the prior author's labour, by, for example, doing no independent research, and instead 'bodily appropriat[ing]' the research of the prior author.[61] If this approach prohibits the 'use of an author's research then the doctrine is clearly a totality approach, because protection of research or labor is tantamount to protecting the facts found by that research or labor'.[62]

> The valuable distinction in copyright law between facts and the expression of facts cannot be maintained if research is held to be copyrightable. There is no rational basis for distinguishing between facts and the research involved in obtaining facts. To hold that research is copyrightable is no more or no less than to hold that the facts discovered as a result of research are entitled to copyright protection.[63]

An extreme approach would be the view taken by some scholars that facts and the interpretation of facts are no different from any other form of literature. This relativistic approach[64] argues that the selection of events or items to be deemed fact (as opposed to myth, lies, etc.) is subject to the effect of the interpreter's personality, biases, and belief system, and that factual interpretation and selection therefore have the requisite creative or personality component to be authorship.[65] Congressional intent, however, was quite clear: 'Copyright does not preclude others from using the ideas or information revealed by the author's work. It pertains to the literary [work]...in which the author

61. Francione, *Facing the Nation*, p. 582.

62. Francione, *Facing the Nation*, p. 582.

63. Francione, *Facing the Nation*, p. 585.

64. See Jane C. Ginsburg, 'Sabotaging and Reconstructing History: A Comment on the Scope of Copyright Protection in Works of History After Hoehling v. Universal City Studios', *Journal of the Copyright Society* 29 (1982), pp. 649-50. See also J.C. Ginsburg, *Creation and Commercial Value*, p. 1906.

65. '[T]he news element—the information respecting current events contained in the literary production—is not the creation of the writer, but is a report of matters that ordinarily are *publici juris*; it is the history of the day' (*International News Service v. Associated Press* (1918) 248 US Supreme Court 215, 234).

expressed intellectual concepts'.[66] That some selection, organization and interpretation must occur with factual information in undeniable; that it confers upon the fact the status of protectable literature is not.[67]

Courts have been more willing to find wholesale usurpation when the unjust enrichment enjoyed by the copier is clear. For example, in an article about the life of a famous person each quote is a fact; journalistic ethics would not permit the creation of quotes from whole cloth or the alteration of quotes. Therefore, it would seem that the portion of the article containing the quotes is unprotectable. But what if the quotes are particularly significant and were only discovered by the author through contacts or sources particular to him? In this case the copier is taking, with virtually no labor, a fact which only the author, through his labor or knowledge, could have acquired.[68] While most courts reject the 'sweat of the brow' approach to copyright, which would protect otherwise unprotectable items simply because of the labor involved in acquiring them, they are much more willing to find these items to be protectable where the author, due to his efforts, is the only source of the item, and the copier appears to be getting a 'free ride' by copying. However, in these cases there is generally competition between the author and the copier, and the copied item is something which contributes greatly to the marketability of the author's work.

For example, original survey maps have consistently received copyright protection, even though, since they are striving for accuracy, their arrangement of pre-existing data is almost certain to lack the 'spark of creativity' demanded by *Feist*.[69] Courts have given copyright protection, at least against wholesale usurpation, more because they recognize that the social desirability of having accurate maps outweighs free access to the mapmaker's research than because of the

66. House Committee on the Judiciary, Copyright Law Revision, House of Representatives Report No. 1476, 94th Congress, Second Session (1976), p. 56.

67. In *Meyers v. Mail & Express Company*, *Copyright Office Bulletin* 36 (Southern District of New York, 1919), p. 479, Judge Learned Hand said that the selection of facts is not protectable even though 'into that selection may go the highest genius of authorship, for indeed, history depends wholly upon a selection from the undifferentiated mass of recorded facts'.

68. See generally *Harper & Row, Publishers, Inc. v. Nation Enterprises* (1983) *Federal Reporter* 723 2d 195, 203, Second Circuit; reversed on other grounds (1985), 471 US Supreme Court 539.

69. See Karjala, *Copyright and Misappropriation*, p. 895.

quantum of effort invested by the mapmaker in compiling his data. A person who takes the mapmaker's data is getting, at no cost to himself, the value of the mapmaker's labor. The mapmaker, as a consequence, loses the incentive to expend the labor.

In the Dead Sea Scrolls situation, the international team is the only source of the factual component of the Scrolls, but this is so through their own design. The uncollated fragments are clearly unprotectable facts, because the team has, at that point, expended no effort which could be usurped. Scholars have been denied access to the uncollated fragments, however, and have had to rely on the team's work in progress for certain portions of the Scrolls. Unlike a competing reporter who can attempt to get an interview from his own sources, or a would-be cartographer who can use his own resources to map an area mapped by a competitor, scholars have had no alternative method for gaining access to the Scrolls. At the point where collation has taken place, the team may be able to argue that they have expended enough energy to warrant protection (although they should also be able to show competition and damage to their own market), if it were not for the fact that their refusal to reveal the uncollated material is the reason for other scholars having to use the collated material.

Copyright law grants a monopoly, but only for a limited time.[70] With regard to facts which are given protection because of their propinquity to protectable expression, that time limit should be reduced. In *International News Service* (hereafter, *INS*),[71] the US Supreme Court found a 'quasi-property' interest in the Associated Press's report of events (as distinguished from the reportage, which would, of course, be protected by copyright), but only while the news stories were 'fresh'.[72] The international team has controlled access to the Dead Sea Scrolls for almost 45 years. The release of the contents of the fragments, as

70. 'Limited times' [for the existence of copyright] were established precisely for the purpose of allowing material to pass rather quickly into the public domain' (John S. Lawrence, 'Copyright Law, Fair Use, and the Academy', in John S. Lawrence and Bernard Timberg [eds.], *Fair Use and Free Inquiry*, [New York: Ablex, 1980], pp. 3, 9).

71. *INS* was decided under an unfair competition, rather than a copyright, theory; 248 US Supreme Court 215, pp. 234-35.

72. Richard S. Epstein, 'International News Service v. Associated Press: Custom and Law As Sources of Property Rights in News', *Virginia Law Review* 78 (1992), pp. 85-147 (92).

opposed to their collation, interpretation or interpolation, could have occurred at any time in that period. In this case the factual information is still 'fresh', in the sense of not being generally known, only because the international team has refused to reveal it.

One could argue that without the security of copyright protection, Professor Qimron and others would have no incentive to labor for decades over the Scrolls, and that, because it is socially desirable and unlikely to be remunerative, this sort of painstaking, exacting, but uncreative, work is as deserving of protection as any creative, literary work.[73] In reality, however, it is unlikely that scholars engage in research with the hope of vast financial rewards. Those financial rewards that there are come indirectly, as the result of an enhanced scholarly reputation. Other, more meaningful, rewards include the broadening of human knowledge (which goes to the dissemination goal of copyright) and the recognition of one's peers.[74] Certainly, nowhere is the tension between free access to knowledge and the copyright holder's proprietary interest more at odds than in an academic setting.[75]

While it is possible that the failure to protect the non-creative components of research will result in the wholesale theft of hard-won intellectual effort by unscrupulous 'scholars' and the abandonment of continued research by scholars unwilling to support 'free riders', or to continue work without the economic incentive that copyright protection brings, this result is unlikely. Just as in nature, it is unwise for a parasite to kill its host, and, generally, self-interest requires that equilibrium be maintained. One commentator has pointed out that repeat players in an industry have a powerful incentive to respect the customary rules if they wish to stay in the game.[76] It is only when aberrational events occur, such as a long-term monopoly, that these players are likely to take the risks inherent in breaking the rules.[77]

73. Ginsburg, *Creation and Commercial Value*, p. 1908.

74. 'Glory is the reward of science... It was not for gain, that Bacon, Newton, Milton, Locke, instructed and delighted the world...' (Ginsburg, *Creation and Commercial Value*, p. 1908 n. 163) (quoting Lord Camden speaking before Parliament in 1774).

75. But see *Mazer v. Stein* (1954) 347 US Supreme Court 219 ('The economic philosophy behind the clause empowering Congress to grant patents and copyrights in the conviction that encouragement of individual effort by personal gain is the best way to advance public welfare...').

76. Epstein, *Custom and Law*, p. 101.

77. See, e.g., *International News Service v. Associated Press* (1918) 248 US

Even if facts or factual interpretation were protectable, the 'author' must still be able to prove that infringement occurred. Because there are only a very limited number of ways in which a fact can be expressed, it has been argued that a different standard should be used in determining whether factual interpretation has been infringed.[78] In wholesale usurpation cases, that standard seems to be virtual identity.[79] In Shanks's case, 120 lines were copied verbatim. With regard to Professors Wacholder and Abegg, however, there was no intent to copy. Nonetheless, their work was likely to be very similar, if not virtually identical. To avoid infringement, Professors Wacholder and Abegg would have needed to ensure that their wording was at least slightly different from Professor Qimron's. However, if Professor Qimron's work is accurate, Professors Wacholder and Abegg would be forced to be less accurate merely to avoid infringement. Either the fact that the Scroll authors must have said a particular thing in a particular place in the Scrolls is protectable or it is not. If it is, only one person, the first person under all common law notions of property, can have a protectable interest in the interpolations.[80] If the first interpolator is allowed to obtain protection, the fear of rushed and haphazard scholarship voiced by those who object to open access may be realized in a different context.

e. *Fair Use*

There is no question but that Hershel Shanks copied, and that Professors Wacholder and Abegg were likely to copy, Professor Qimron's reconstruction of the MMT, and that, therefore, if any portion of Professor Qimron's work is copyrightable, they will have infringed, at least with regard to that portion. Despite this, the uses to which the Huntington Library, Hershel Shanks and Professors Wacholder and Abegg have put the Scrolls may be acceptable.

Supreme Court 215. 'In retaliation [for INS's pro-German positions], the British and French authorities cut INS personnel off from the front lines and barred them from using the entire European cable system' (Epstein, *Custom and Law*, p. 92). If INS wanted to report from the front, it had little choice but to appropriate AP's stories. See Epstein, *Custom and Law*, pp. 92-93.

78. Francione, *Facing the Nation*, pp. 570-74.

79. *Hoehling v. Universal Studios* (1980) *Federal Reporter* 618 2d 972, 980, Second Circuit; certiorari denied (1980) 449 US Supreme Court 841.

80. See generally Richard S. Epstein, 'Possession as the Root of Title', *Georgia Law Review* 13 (1979), p. 1221.

Up until the publication of the Scroll photographs by the Huntington Library, and the very limited release of a few 'bootlegged' portions of the Scrolls, the international team had complete control over the Scrolls and denied access to all outsiders. This has meant that no other scholars or academics were permitted to contribute their expertise to the deciphering of the Scrolls or to challenge the work of the international team. In the 40 years the Scrolls were sequestered, experts in the field who could have contributed to Scroll knowledge have died or retired without being able to add to the understanding of the Scrolls.

The stated purpose of American copyright law is 'to promote science and the useful arts'.[81] This is effected in two ways: first, a monopoly is given to authors to encourage authorship by allowing them to benefit commercially from their labor; and second, the monopoly is strictly limited by time and by the doctrine of fair use to encourage others to use the author's labor as a stepping stone for their own pursuits or to exploit the fruit of the author's labor when he has abandoned it. Ultimately, the goal is to encourage societal, intellectual and technical development, and the protection of the author is secondary to that goal. This should particularly be the case where the author's monopoly restricts access, not just to his creative effort, but to the facts on which his effort is based. Nothing would be more abhorrent to the underlying policy of copyright, and of all intellectual property law, than to restrict access to material that is, and should be, in the public domain.

The doctrine of fair use makes clear where the drafters' priorities lay. The author's power to control and exploit his work is limited where the copier infringes the copyright in order to increase the public store of knowledge.[82]

Section 107 of the US Copyright Act lists the factors for consideration when determining whether a given use is fair:

1. the purpose and character of the use, including whether such use is of a commercial nature or is for nonprofit educational purposes;
2. the nature of the copyrighted work;

81. US Constitution, Article 1, s. 8, clause 8.

82. '[T]he fair use of a copyrighted work...for such purposes as criticism, comment...scholarship, or research, is not an infringement of copyright.' Title 17, U.S.C., s. 107 (1988, Supplement II 1990).

3. the amount and substantiality of the portion used in relation to the copyrighted work as a whole; and
4. the effect of the use upon the potential market for or value of the copyrighted work.[83]

These considerations apply to unpublished works as well.[84] In addition to the consideration of these factors, courts have found fair use where other compelling factors exist.[85]

The Huntington Library's revelation of their photographs of the Scrolls was non-commercial.[86] The library did not sell its photographs or attempt to use them to raise funds. If anything, the library's revelation might have had a negative fiscal effect if individuals had become hesitant to loan or donate items to the library as a result.[87] The Huntington Library's release of the Scroll photographs does not interfere with the international team's commercial interests. It would be very unusual indeed if the international team had intended to sell photo-

83. Title 17, U.S.C., s. 107.

84. Title 17, U.S.C., s. 107.

85. Essentially, the fair use doctrine is 'an equitable rule of reason' (*Harper & Row, Inc. v. Nation Enterprises* [1985] 471 US Supreme Court 539, 560, quoting House of Representatives Report No. 1476, 94th Congress, 2d Session, p. 65).

86. In the 1960s President Warren G. Harding's love letters to a woman not his wife were donated to the Ohio Historical Society, over the objection of family members. After the letters were returned, it was discovered that the Historical Society had made microfilm copies of them. 'Whether the Society could photocopy the origial letters and provide access to or lend [them] as a means of preserving the originals, is unclear... Such activities seem wholly unlikely to interfere with the basic economic interest secured by the copyright in the letters...' (Robert Cogswell, 'Copyright Law for Unpublished Manuscripts and Archival Collections' [ed. R.M. Mersky; *Law Library Information Report* 14 (1992)] p. 59) (quoting Professor James R. Treece).

87. The Huntington Library received approbation from many other libraries and research centers. See Daniel Wood, 'Library That "Freed" the Scrolls Hears a Jericho-like Blast of Support', *Christian Science Monitor* (8 October 1991), p. 12. Nonetheless, potential donors might have had second thoughts. One of the reasons the Library of Congress gave for its release of Justice Thurgood Marshall's papers shortly after his death, despite objections from his family and colleagues, was the importance of showing future donors that donative intent would be respected. See, e.g., 'The Marshall Files: The Complaints and the Library's Response', *The Washington Post* (27 May 1993), p. A20, (excerpting Justice Marshall's instrument of gift, and including statements by James Billington, Librarian of Congress; Chief Justice William Rehnquist; and former Chief Justice Warren Burger).

graphs of the Scrolls to interested academics. It is customary in academia to make purely factual material available to fellow scholars without any fee beyond the cost of reproduction. This is the approach which the Huntington Library took with its photographs.

Professor Qimron argued that since he intended to publish and sell a book[88] dealing with his analysis of the Scroll fragments he was given to study, Mr Shanks's work would cause him to lose sales.[89] The two-volume work which Mr Shanks compiled on the Scrolls was intended for sale.[90] However, Professor Qimron's work made up only one page of Mr Shanks's two volumes, and appeared in the Foreword rather than in the main body of the work. It is unlikely that anyone purchased Mr Shanks's two-volume set for the opportunity of reading Professor Qimron's one-page 'contribution', or that they would choose not to purchase Professor Qimron's several hundred-page book merely because one page of it was reproduced elsewhere.

Professors Wacholder and Abegg's intent was to use the same material Professor Qimron had used as the basis for their own analysis of the Scrolls, with, in all likelihood, similar results. Ultimately, their interpretation will be published and perhaps sold. While their alleged infringement would be commercial to some degree, it is most likely that their main purpose in publishing would be academic rather than commercial.[91]

Neither Mr. Shanks's nor Professors Wacholder and Abegg's work is what might be termed 'light reading'; it is likely that their work would only be of interest to a very narrow audience of people with a serious interest in biblical scholarship in general or the Scrolls in particular.[92] Such readers are likely to purchase all available relevant material and

88. Professor Qimron's book was published on 30 June 1994.

89. However, Judge Dorner found that Professor Qimron had failed to prove this contention (Abraham Rabinovich, 'Court Awards Dead Sea Scrolls Translator NIS 100,000', *The Jerusalem Post* [31 March 1993]).

90. The price of Shanks's book was US$200. Only 300 copies were sold (Shanks, *Maltese Falcon*, p. 49).

91. Fair use is more likely to be found when the copying is for scholarly purposes. See, e.g., *Williams and Wilkins Co. v. United States* (1973) *Federal Reporter* 487 2d 1345, Court of Claims; affirmed by an equally divided Court (1975) 420 US Supreme Court 376 (*per curiam*).

92. However, there has been a exponential increase in the number of popular books on the Scrolls. Bob Summer, 'The Dead Sea Scrolls', *Publishers Weekly* (10 January 1994) at 27.

to take the view that one scholar's opinion is not a perfect substitute for all other scholars' opinions on the same topic.

Fair use may occur when infringement cannot be avoided without putting unreasonable restraints on intellectual or technological progress. In *Sega Enterprises v. Accolade, Inc.*,[93] Accolade, a maker of computer games compatible with Sega's Genesis system, disassembled a Sega computer game cartridge to determine how to construct the interface for their own games. In the process of disassembly, the Accolade engineers transformed the Sega game's machine-readable object code into a code readable by humans. In doing so, the Accolade engineers copied Sega's copyrighted object code. Their purpose was to understand that part of the object code which would allow their games to run on the Genesis system, not to copy any particular game or the specifics of any particular game. When Accolade constructed their own compatible games using the copied interface object code, they sold them under the Accolade label and made no attempt to pass them off as Sega games. The only portion of the Sega code which Accolade actually copied into their own game programs was the interface code.[94]

While Sega admitted that that portion of the object code which governed the interface was strictly functional or factual and not protected by copyright, they argued that Accolade's copying of the entire code in order to find the interface code was an infringement.[95] The court agreed that Accolade's disassembly was 'wholesale copying'.[96] The court pointed out, however, that since the object code is virtually unreadable by humans, the only means for accessing the unprotected functional aspect of the program was through copying the protected aspect of the program.[97] Sega argued that Accolade admitted that humans could 'read' the object code to some degree without the aid of computer disassembly. This is true in the sense that a human could, very slowly, transcribe the binary object code, but doing so is as much copying as is computer transcription of the binary object code. Whether done by a computer or by hand, the binary code must be transcribed before it can be translated, since no one is capable of memorizing the innumerable bits of binary information and translating it mentally.

93. 1992 977 *Federal Reporter* 2d 1510, Ninth Circuit.
94. 977 *Federal Reporter* 2d 1516.
95. 977 *Federal Reporter* 2d 1525.
96. 977 *Federal Reporter* 2d 1527.
97. 977 *Federal Reporter* 2d 1525-26.

The court found that since Sega's programs contained functional aspects that could not be examined without copying, they were entitled to a lower degree of protection than are other, more traditional, literary works, the factual or functional components of which are readily accessible.[98] The court argued that a finding that disassembly was a per se unfair, use would, in effect, give the copyright owner a *de facto* monopoly over the unprotectable functional aspects of the work.[99]

Even if the international team's collation or interpretation is protected by copyright, other scholars would need to copy the team's copyrighted material in order to make their own analyses of the contents of the Scrolls. The most obvious reason for this is that the international team has physically controlled the fragments and has not allowed others to engage in their own attempts to put the pieces of the 'jigsaw puzzle' together. The only way that other scholars can engage in their own 'from scratch' analysis, has been to 'disassemble' the work that the international team has done. By reducing the team's work to its component parts, the fragments, other scholars can gain access to the unprotectable, factual aspect of the Scrolls. This cannot be done without copying. No scholar, no matter how brilliant, is capable of remembering the contents of thousands of fragments, mentally rearranging them and translating them. Any other result would permit copyright holders to deny access to unprotected factual information by ensuring that the factual information is only available in a copyrighted document.

While it was not discussed in any depth in *INS*, the apparent reason that INS violated news industry custom by taking AP news was that INS had been barred by British and French authorities from using the

98. 977 *Federal Reporter* 2d 1514. The court found fair use in necessity: 'Although the question is fairly debatable, we conclude based on the policies underlying the Copyright Act that disassembly of a copyrighted object code is, as a matter of law, a fair use...if [it] provides the only means of access to those elements fo the code that are not protected by the copyright and the copier has a legitimate reason for seeking such access' (977 *Federal Reporter* 2d 1518).

99. '[T]hat computer programs are distributed for public use in object code form often precludes public access to the ideas and functional concepts contained in those programs, and thus confers on the copyright owner a *de facto* monopoly over those ideas and functional concepts. The result defeats the fundamental purpose of the Copyright Act—to encourage the produciton of original works by protecting the expressive elements of those works while leaving the ideas, facts, and functional concepts in the public domain for others to build on' (977 *Federal Reporter* 2d 1527).

European cable system.[100] With no other access to information about events occurring on the front during the First World War, INS was faced with the choice between financial ruin caused by not reporting the leading story of the day and professional malapprobrium for taking the facts of that story, although (usually) not its expression. One scholar has argued that the property doctrine of necessity should have been applied to the quasi-property in *INS*, permitting INS to use AP's factual information when other access to that information had been blocked by AP's monopoly, as long as INS paid just compensation.[101] This argument for compulsory licensing is even more compelling when, as in the case of the Dead Sea Scrolls, the monopoly is caused by the potential licensor, rather than by outside events.[102]

Even if the arrangements, translations or interpolations of the international team should be protected, the factual basis of their work should be made available to other scholars to ensure that a complete picture of the Scroll contents, as seen by scholars of different disciplines, backgrounds and perspectives, becomes clear. When one group controls access to the facts, the ability of others to add to the store of knowledge is stifled. An analogy can be drawn with patent law. One goal of patent law is the dissemination of information.[103] While the patent holder is given a monopoly on the manufacture, use, and sale of his invention, the public is given free access at a very early stage to the specifications and technology of the invention so that further innovation will be facilitated.

The courts' interpretation of the scope of each patent may also serve to encourage innovation; a narrow reading of the patent's scope permits greater use of the patent's technology, while a broad reading limits use. Interestingly, some scholars believe that the monopoly given to patent holders is not limited or expanded based on balancing the desirability of encouraging innovation with the desirability of allowing

100. See Epstein, 'International News Service v. Associated Press', p. 92.

101. Epstein, 'International News Service v. Associated Press', p. 119.

102. See generally Ginsburg, 'Creation and Commercial Value', p. 1865 (arguing that works of 'low authorship', for example, compilations, should be subject to a compulsory license for derivative use).

103. See, e.g., Title 35, U.S.C. s. 112 (1988) (setting forth disclosure requirements in patent specifications).

others to exploit that innovation.[104] Instead, they argue that patents are protected more strenuously by courts when they believe that the patent holder is in the best position to supervise the exploitation of the patent in a systematic and efficient way.[105] If the patent is for a threshold invention upon which other inventions will build, and the patent holder has the means to build on that invention quickly and efficiently, courts are more likely to consider the patent to be a broad one. If, on the other hand, the invention is complete and the patent holder is not likely to build on it, the patent will be narrowly construed.[106]

While patent law obviously does not apply, the international team's control of the Scrolls and refusal to allow others to participate in the process of collation has been very similar to the monopoly control a patent holder tries to exercise over his invention. Like the patent holder, the international team has tried to control all new uses to which their find is put. If the above 'best user' view is an accurate description of the reasoning behind modern patent decisions, a similar view could be applied to the Scrolls. The Scrolls are a work in progress, much like a threshold invention. The international team, having spent decades with the Scrolls themselves, and having amassed a constituency of biblical scholars of excellent repute, appear to be in the best position to exploit and expand upon Scroll knowledge. Under the 'best user' approach, the international team's scope of protection should be broad, and others can, and should, be prevented from using the Scrolls until the team has done all it can with them. This argument fails, however, if, due to mismanagement, politics, ego or conspiracy, the international team's monopoly is not the quickest or most efficient way to interpret the Scrolls. Even under the 'best user' approach, a resource-rich patent holder for a threshold invention should not be granted broad patent protection if it does not use its resources to expand upon and exploit the invention.[107]

104. See generally Mark F. Grady and Jay I. Alexander, 'Patent Law and Rent Dissipation', *Virginia Law Review* 78 (1992), p. 305.

105. Grady and Alexander, 'Patent Law', p. 331.

106. Grady and Alexander, 'Patent Law', p. 318.

107. '[T]here is a need to spur the creation of [information]...[b]ut once the [information] is effectively developed, the information may well have greater value if it is used by many people simultaneously than if it is used and kept by one person alone (a new mathematical theorem may be a good illustration of this phenomenon). Therefore, granting perpetual property rights in information creates, at the margin,

5. *Conclusion*

Access to the content of historic documents does nothing to diminish the owner's property interest in the documents themselves. If the content consists of public domain or purely factual information, there is no copyright interest to be infringed. Under American law changes in, or additions to, the original content in the form of arrangement, translation or interpolations may not be independently protectable if they do not evidence a sufficient 'creative spark' to meet the requirement of originality. Expression which meets the threshold requirement of originality may do so only marginally and, therefore, be more likely to be subject to the fair use exception of American copyright law. Even if the expression clearly meets the originality requirement, copying for the purposes of scholarship or commentary, particularly where no economic harm results, should be considered fair use.

small additional incentives to gather the information, but it reduces, no doubt to a far greater extent, the beneficial use of the information once it is made available' (Epstein, 'International News Service v. Associated Press', pp. 114-15).

COPYRIGHT LAW AND THE DEAD SEA SCROLLS: A BRITISH PERSPECTIVE

Hector L. MacQueen*

1. *The Issues*

The issues raised by the case of *Qimron v. Shanks*[1] are truly ones of profound importance for the world of scholarship and, indeed, any other world in which the discovery and generation of information has significance. Writing in the *Michigan Journal of International Law*,[2] and drawing on the perspective of US law, Professor Cindy Carson has

* Professor of Private Law and Director, Shepherd & Wedderburn Centre for Research in Intellectual Property and Technology, University of Edinburgh. I am grateful for the comments of the participants in the conference, and also to Jöelle Godard, Willem Grosheide, Jeremy Phillips, Irini Stamatoudi and Wojiech Kowalski. In this article, the following system of abbreviations is used for the principal statute and standard texts on British copyright:

CDPA 1988	Copyright, Designs and Patents Act 1988
Copinger	K. Garnett, J. Rayner James and G. Davies (eds.), *Copinger and Skone James on Copyright* (London: Sweet & Maxwell, 14th edn, 1999).
Laddie, Prescott & Vitoria	H. Laddie, P. Prescott and M. Vitoria, *The Modern Law of Copyright and Designs* (London: Butterworth, 2nd edn 1995).
O.J.	Official Journal of the European Communities

1. 3 [5753-1993] Pesakim shel Bete ha-Mishpat ha-Mehoziyim be Yisrael [Judgments of the District Courts of Israel] [P.M.] 10 (D Jerusalem 1993). The outcome of an appeal to the Israeli Supreme Court was awaited at the time of writing.

2. C.A. Carson, 'Raiders of the Lost Scrolls: the right of scholarly access to the content of historic documents', *Michigan Journal of International Law* 16 (1995), pp. 298-348. I gladly acknowledge my indebtedness to this stimulating piece for what follows. See also her contribution to the present volume.

put forward a powerful case for regarding the work of the international team on the Dead Sea Scrolls as falling outside the scope of copyright protection, essentially on the basis that the task of editing the scrolls lacks that 'spark of creativity' which is necessary before any work may have such protection.[3] The task of transcribing, piecing together and deducing the probable additional content of the fragments that have come down to us is in the end merely a process of reproducing an uncopyrightable fact or set of facts, namely what the original writers of the documents actually wrote. The mere expenditure of editorial skill and labour or, in the American phrase, the 'sweat of the brow', in producing an edition of the Scrolls does not justify copyright protection.

This paper argues that, at any rate viewed from the perspective of British copyright law, an opposite point of view is tenable and appropriate. While British law would share the American aversion to conferring copyright upon facts or information per se, and indeed upon ideas, it will give protection to the form in which information or ideas are expressed. The essence of the argument to counter Professor Carson's position is quite simple, namely that in the British copyright tradition, skill and labour in producing an independent form of expression *is* enough to attract copyright, at any rate if it is skill and labour of the right kind. In the view put forward here, editorial activity of the level required to produce acceptably scholarly editions of such intractable and difficult material as the Dead Sea Scrolls evidently are does indeed involve appropriate skill and labour of the kind meriting the law's reward of copyright for the editor.

A second-level point is that the British tradition is currently subject to change in some degree, and hence to pressure to change its approach altogether, to come into line with the European norm requiring works to be 'the author's own personal or intellectual creation' before they can enjoy copyright. This, it is generally accepted, is a higher standard than skill and labour, although its relation to the American 'spark of creativity' is perhaps more debatable. Although it would seem that this higher Continental standard does take editorial work out of the protection of copyright properly speaking, German law has nonetheless recognised that the editor does have some claim to legally enforceable rights

3. For this requirement of US copyright law, see above all the decision of the Supreme Court denying copyright protection to a telephone directory, *Feist Publications, Inc. v. Rural Telephone Co.* (1991) 111 US Supreme Court 1282.

in his or her work. This position has now won the endorsement of the European Union in a Directive promulgated in 1993.[4]

As Professor Carson herself observes,[5] the requirements of American copyright law are coloured by its background in the US Constitution, which provides that the purpose of copyright laws (and patent laws) is 'to promote the progress of science and useful arts, by securing for limited times to authors and inventors the exclusive right to their respective writings and discoveries'.[6] There is no equivalent to this in either British or, even more so, European copyright laws, which are founded much more on the basis of respect for the personality of the author and its expression in his or her work. Thus, British law has given explicit recognition since 1989 to the author's so-called moral rights to be identified and to object to derogatory treatment of his work.[7] Implicit too in British law is a relatively weak version of another of the moral rights often called on the Continent the right of dissemination or divulgation[8]—that is, the right to decide not to publish one's copyright work but to maintain its privacy and non-availability to anyone else. In Britain, this right follows from the author's exclusive right to issue copies of the work to the public, which in general he cannot be compelled to exercise.[9] We do not, however, go as far as French law, which gives the author a right to withdraw an already published work from circulation, albeit subject to the publisher's claim for compensation.[10]

A final question to be raised is whether the subsistence of copyright inhibits or promotes scholarly access to information.

4. See further below, pp. 111-12.

5. Carson, 'Raiders of the Lost Scrolls', p. 325 (see n. 2 *supra*).

6. US Constitution, Art. 1 s. 8.

7. CDPA 1988, ss. 77-89.

8. See French Intellectual Property Code 1992, Art. L.121-2; German Copyright Act 1965, s. 12(1).

9. CDPA 1988, s. 18. The main qualification to the proposition in the text follows from the decision of the European Court of Justice in *RTE and ITP v. Commission* (the '*Magill*' case) [1995] E.C.R. I-743, holding a refusal to grant copyright licences to be abuse of monopoly power, but in very special circumstances which make the case not a safe basis for generalizations, especially in the context of the Dead Sea Scrolls.

10. French Intellectual Property Code 1992, Art. L.121-4.

2. *Copyright in the Dead Sea Scrolls*

A starting point is that British copyright law would not agree with the US position that there is now no copyright in the unpublished Dead Sea Scrolls themselves.

Up until 1 August 1989,[11] an unpublished manuscript enjoyed copyright until it was published, whereupon the copyright would run for only 50 years more.[12] Thus, so long as a manuscript remained unpublished, whenever first written, it had a perpetual copyright. The British courts seem never to have been called upon to address the question of copyright in genuinely ancient documents which had been written before the establishment of statutory copyright early in the eighteenth century, although by then it was already common for the contents of mediaeval and earlier manuscripts to be made more widely available through published editions. Nothing in successive Acts of Parliament touched upon the question, while the so-called common law copyright in unpublished works, enabling objection to be taken to unlicensed publication, which existed until the Copyright Act 1911 came into force[13] generally involved relatively recent works such as private letters and lectures.[14] A major obstacle to the question arising would of course have been the identification of the owner of the copyright, given the anonymity of the originals and the centuries which had passed since their composition; and so far as I have noted, eighteenth- and nineteenth-century editions of mediaeval works appeared with the permission of whomsoever was the owner of the physical manuscripts, as distinct from that of the other intangible rights which might have existed in them.

The Copyright Designs and Patents Act 1988 provided that existing copyrights in unpublished material would come to an end at midnight on 31 December 2039, that is, 50 years after the 1988 Act came into force.[15] However, in 1993 the European Community issued a Directive to harmonise the term of copyright in its Member States.[16] For literary

11. The date upon which CDPA 1988 came into force.
12. See Copyright Act 1911, s. 17; Copyright Act 1956, s. 2.
13. Common law copyright was abolished by the Copyright Act 1911, s. 31.
14. On common law copyright see *Laddie, Prescott & Vitoria*, paras. 2.2–2.7.
15. CDPA 1988, Sch. 1 para. 12(4).
16. Council Directive 93/98/EEC, [1993] OJ L290/9; implemented in the UK by

works such as the Dead Sea Scrolls, published or unpublished, it was determined that the period of protection should be the lifetime of the author plus 70 years.[17] This immediately raised the tricky problem of the anonymous work where the identity, and hence the lifetime, of the author is not known, with the result that the ordinary period of protection cannot be determined. The Directive's resolution of this conundrum distinguishes two cases for treatment:[18]

1. *work published*: copyright lasts for 70 years from publication (unless the author's identity becomes known during that period, in which case the normal term applies);
2. *work unpublished*: copyright lasts for 70 years from creation and then expires (unless the author's identity becomes known during that period, in which case the normal term applies).

The Directive left unclear what its effect upon existing copyrights was to be. The British implementation, which came into force on 1 January 1996, declared that copyright in an existing work should continue to subsist until the date on which it would have expired under the 1988 provisions if that date was later than the date under which it would expire under the new provisions.[19] It would thus seem that the Dead Sea Scrolls, at least so far as unpublished, will only lose their copyright as anonymous unpublished works on 31 December 2039, since under the new rules their copyright would have expired nearly 2,000 years ago, 70 years after their creation! The new rules will, however, enure to the benefit of the copyright owners should a Scroll have been published at any time since 1 August 1989, since the new seventy-year period will carry the right well beyond the end of the year 2039.[20]

Who owns the copyright? The general principle is that the author is

the Duration of Copyright and Rights in Performances Regulations 1995, amending CDPA 1988.

17. Term Directive, Art. 1(1); in the UK, see now CDPA 1988, s. 12 (as amended).

18. See Term Directive, Art. 1(3) and (6); in the UK, see CDPA 1988, s. 12(3) and (4).

19. Duration of Copyright Regulations 1995, reg. 15(1).

20. Further on the current copyright position for anonymous unpublished material, see G.P. Cornish, *Copyright: Interpreting the Law for Libraries, Archives and Information Services* (London: Library Association, 3rd edn, 1999), pp. 30-32 (questions 75-82).

the first owner of the copyright in a work.[21] But we have no idea of the individual identity of the writer or writers of our fragments, still less of their descendants in the present day, or of any rules of inheritance which might have governed a right not known to exist at the time (or for many centuries afterwards). For practical purposes, therefore, the issue of ownership of copyright in ancient and anonymous manuscripts can be taken to be coterminous with the current ownership of the physical embodiment of the work. The uncertainty at the core of this approach is, however, indicative of the problems to which the lengthy posthumous term of copyright can give rise.

3. *Protectability of Editorial Work*

If we turn from the Scrolls themselves to consider the position of those who edit them, we have at least the comfort of dealing with the rights of identifiable and often living persons; or, if dead, then at least the date of their death and the identity of their descendants can probably be discovered without undue difficulty. But do they have copyright in their work? There is no problem about what may be called the editorial apparatus: introductions, translations, textual notes, glossaries and other similar material will all fall clearly within the scope of general copyright protection.[22] The big question is the position of the version of the original text produced by the editor.

British law would, I think, tend to answer the question in favour of the editor, at least in principle. (Much might depend on the precise facts of any given case.) First, the editor's work is written down and is thus a literary work.[23] Writing for these purposes includes any form of notation or code, whether by hand or otherwise and regardless of the method by which, or medium in or on which, it is recorded.[24] Thus the editor's reproduction of the symbols inscribed on the Scrolls is writing, and the fact that he uses a computer to record his version of what he sees, rather than a pen or other writing instrument, matters not.

The second point is the crucial one. The literary work must be

21. See CDPA 1988, ss. 9 and 11.

22. See, e.g., *Black v. Murray* (1870) 9 M. 341 (works of Sir Walter Scott).

23. CDPA 1988, s. 3(1) (''literary work' means any work, other than a dramatic or musical work, which is written...').

24. CDPA 1988, s. 178.

original to qualify for copyright.[25] Originality as it has been interpreted by the courts is not a high hurdle for would-be claimants of copyright, and in considering it the judges seem often driven by an observation made by Mr Justice Peterson in 1916: 'What is worth copying is worth protecting.'[26] The test may be epitomized as requiring an author to exercise skill and labour in creating his own form of expression, which must be arrived at independently of any previous work. However, a work that is derived from another may still be original if there is sufficient independent input from the author of the second work.[27] However, while 'scholarly editors may disagree about many things...they are in general agreement that their goal is to discover exactly what an author wrote and to determine what form of his work he wished the public to have.'[28] Are they then in a position like that of the persons described as follows in a recent Privy Council case about the Lego brick?

> Take the simplest case of artistic copyright, a painting or a photograph. It takes great skill, judgment and labour to produce a good copy by painting or to produce an enlarged photograph from a positive print, but no one would reasonably contend that the copy painting or enlargement was an 'original' artistic work in which the copier is entitled to claim copyright. Skill, labour or judgment merely in the process of copying cannot confer originality... A well-executed tracing is the result of much labour and skill but remains what it is, a tracing.[29]

As a matter of principle, however, I would argue that at least the editor of an ancient or mediaeval manuscript is not a mere tracer or slavish imitator of another's work. The Lego brick case is important for its observation that the mere expenditure of skill and labour is not enough to create a copyright, for the reasons given above; the skill and

25. CDPA 1988, s. 1(1) ('Copyright is a property right which subsists in... (a) original literary...works').

26. *University of London Press Ltd v. University Tutorial Press Ltd* [1916] 2 Ch. 601 at 610.

27. On originality see *Laddie, Prescott & Vitoria*, paras. 2.56-2.72; *Copinger*, paras. 3.85–3.104.

28. Thomas Tanselle in 1976, as quoted without citation of source by David Hewitt, in 'General Introduction' to Walter Scott, *St Ronan's Well* (ed. Mark Weinstein; The Edinburgh Edition of the Waverley Novels; Edinburgh: Edinburgh University Press, 1995), p. xii.

29. *Interlego AG v. Tyco Industries Inc.* [1989] A.C. 217, *per* Lord Oliver at 262-263.

labour involved must be of a relevant kind. The issue in the case was whether there were any rights in the third-generation Lego brick, which looked just like its predecessor Lego bricks, but was a better, stronger and more durable brick. The skill and labour had thus gone into the non-artistic qualities of the brick's design and was accordingly irrelevant to the artistic result, which was all that copyright could protect.[30]

By contrast, an editor engages in literary skill and labour to produce a literary result. The operation is one of interpretation of a given body

30. See also the recent New York case of *Bridgeman Art Library Ltd v. Corel Corp* 25 Fed. Supp. 421, 1999 (District Judge Lewis A. Kaplan), in which the court applied UK law to the question of whether photographs of public domain works of art were the subject of copyright so that their unauthorised digitisation and inclusion in CD-ROMs was infringement. Judge Kaplan held that, since the photographers aspired to produce as exact as possible a copy of the subject of the photograph, their work lacked originality under UK law and could not be protected. The judge relied on the *Interlego* case and passages in *Copinger and Skone James on Copyright* (ed. E.P. Skone James, J.F. Mummery, J. Rayner James and K.M. Garnett; London: Sweet & Maxwell, 13th edn, 1991); para. 3.34, and *Laddie, Prescott & Vitoria*, para. 3.56. However, it is submitted that he gave insufficient weight to the comment in the last of these sources that originality may 'reside in such specialties [sic] as angle of shot, light and shade, exposure, effects achieved by means of filters, developing techniques etc'. The *Copinger* passage is para. 3.95 in the new 14th edition, published in 1999, and it now includes the following sentence: 'A photographer who takes a picture of a work of art, such as a painting or a sculpture, may be treated as being in the same category, in that he may bring to the process of photographing the work considerable skill as regards the angle from which to take the photograph, the lighting, the use of the right film and filter, and so on'. See also para. 3.104: '...a photograph which is intended to reproduce a work of art, such as a painting or another photograph. Provided that the author can demonstrate that he expended some small degree of time, skill and labour in producing the photograph, (which may be demonstrated by the exercise of judgment as to such matters as the angle from which to take the photograph, the lighting, the correct film speed, what filter to use, etc.) the photograph ought to be entitled to copyright protection, irrespective of its subject matter'. Judge Kaplan quotes the *Interlego* dictum that 'skill, labour or judgment merely in the process of copying cannot confer originality'; but it is submitted that the skill and labour in *Bridgeman* is the skill and labour relevant to the production of a photograph, which is a distinct kind of artistic work. And see *Antiquesportfolio.com plc v. Rodney Fitch & Co. Ltd* ([2001] F.S.R. 345), in which Neuberger J. held, following Copinger, that a photograph of a single static item was an original artistic work, because it could be said that the positioning of the object, the angle at which it was taken, the lighting and the focus were all matters of judgment, albeit in many cases at a very basic level.

of material on which another possessed of the same basic skills and knowledge might well produce a different outcome. In other words, transcribing an ancient document is not a purely mechanical process even where it survives entire, and the end result, no matter what the intention of the editor may have been, cannot be taken as merely an unoriginal reproduction of what the original author wrote.

This proposition is also supported by some directly relevant (although limited) authority. In *Evans v. Tout* [31] in 1909, the plaintiff had produced scholarly editions of ancient Welsh manuscripts, which 'were as nearly as possible an exact transcription from the original, but great labour, skill, and expert knowledge was required to decipher the manuscript, and in many cases the reading was, owing to defects in the original, a matter of conjecture'. The manuscripts had been previously published by others. The case was settled on the basis that Evans's work was protected by copyright. Earlier, in 1903 in *Parry v. Moring and Gollancz*,[32] the editor's copyright in his edition of the letters of Dorothy Osborne was accepted as the basis of an injunction against a competing edition which had admittedly appropriated the first editor's text, albeit with corrections made from the originals. The case is, however, significantly different from *Evans*, in that the first editor had not simply transcribed but had modernized the text. Interestingly, he had also arranged the undated letters in their probable date order. Both cases thus have resonances for the Dead Sea Scrolls controversy.

However, both cases also involved settlements rather than court decisions and as such their authority is extremely limited. But they continue to be cited in standard modern texts,[33] and it seems clear that they are supported by other, more general authority. Most conspicuous in terms of general principle is the 1900 decision of the House of Lords in *Walter v. Lane*,[34] where a newspaper reporter who took a full transcription of a speech orally delivered by Lord Rosebery was held to have a copyright in his work. The case has been doubted on the basis that, being dependent on another work, the reporter's work was not original;[35] but it has been vigorously defended by writers[36] and followed in

31. [1905–10] M.C.C. 213.
32. [1901–1904] M.C.C. 49.
33. *Laddie, Prescott & Vitoria*, paras. 2.63 (n. 1), 2.64 (Illustration 1).
34. [1900] A.C. 539.
35. See *Roberton v. Lewis* [1976] R.P.C. 169 *per* Cross J. at 175.
36. See *Laddie, Prescott & Vitoria*, paras. 2.68-2.71; *Copinger*, para 3.87.

other cases.[37] The view seems to be that the reporter is exercising a skill and labour which is in fact independent of that of the speech-maker or speech-writer, albeit that the result is identical. Similarly, in *Warwick Film Productions Ltd v. Eisinger*[38] in 1967, it was held that copyright subsisted in transcriptions of shorthand notes of the proceedings in the trial of Oscar Wilde.

The case for the editor's copyright is *a fortiori* where the editorial task involves the comparison of more than one manuscript in order to determine what the initial author wrote. In such cases it is extremely rare that the Ur-copy has survived or is available; every surviving manuscript will itself be a copy of some earlier one, and the editor's task will be to interpret the relationships of these manuscripts to each other and to the ultimate original in order to produce a version of what that original may have been. Another case may be where the only surviving manuscript is known to be a copy of some preceding document, and the editor's task includes overcoming the defects arising in the copying process. The whole problem of getting behind a manuscript to reach an unavailable original has been nicely described by the legal historian, T.F.T. Plucknett:

> Some times an obscurely written word in the original has been variously misunderstood by long successions of copyists. More often (and this is essentially so in a long and laborious task) the copyist works mechanically, heedless of the sense of his text—which indeed he may not comprehend... Sometimes a scribe is too ambitious and may introduce 'corrections' into a text which is actually quite accurate—if only he had understood it. More often he is tricked by his eyesight. Thus it is extremely common for the same word (especially in a technical work) to occur twice in close proximity. The scribe will copy a phrase ending with the first occurrence of the word, and at the next glance at his exemplar he will continue copying from the second occurrence of the word, thus omitting the intervening passage. In the sesquipedalian jargon of the textual critics this is familiarly known as homoeotelenton [sic], which is deemed to be a special case of haplography.[39]

Another issue of particular importance in the Dead Sea Scrolls

37. *Sands & McDougall Pty Ltd v. Robinson* (1917) 23 C.L.R. 49 (High Court of Australia); *Express Newspapers plc v. News (UK) Ltd* [1990] 1 W.L.R. 1320 (Browne-Wilkinson VC).

38. [1969] 1 Ch. 508.

39. T.F.T. Plucknett, *Early English Legal Literature* (Cambridge: Cambridge University Press, 1958), p. 54.

controversy is where the manuscript material is fragmented and the question arises of the relationship of the fragments to each other. Professor Carson's doubts as to the protectability of this aspect of the editor's work are again related to the observation that ultimately the relationship of the fragments is a matter of fact which the editor aspires to recreate as accurately as possible.[40] My tentative view would be that any such assembly of the fragments is no more than the editor's attempt to *express* what is undoubtedly a fact, and as such the selection and arrangement of the fragments, being the product of skill and labour, could be a protectable work in itself, just like an anthology of poetry or the combination of algorithms and routines which go to make up the totality of a computer program.

Returning to our main theme, as already observed, the long-standing 'low' British point of entry for copyright protection is now subject to some degree of pressure for change to a higher standard.[41] Two sources of such pressure can be identified. One is the perception in some quarters that the low British standard admits too many undeserving works to the pantheon of copyright works. Quite apart from the observations of the court in the Lego brick case already mentioned, Mr Justice Laddie, in a lecture entitled 'Copyright: Over-Strength, Over-Regulated, Over-Rated?',[42] has talked of 'the pernicious refrain' that what is worth copying is worth protecting, adding that 'we should not be handing out monopolies like confetti while muttering "this won't hurt"'.[43] Another leading English judge has hinted at his dislike of the approach of protection following copying, pointing out that 'it is not the law that copying as such is unlawful'.[44]

40. Carson, 'Raiders of the Lost Scrolls', pp. 324-26 (see n. 2 *supra*).

41. Note, however, that some commentators favour removing the standard altogether: see M. Sherwood-Edwards, 'The Redundancy of Originality', *International Review of Industrial Property and Copyright* 25 (1994), pp. 658-89.

42. Published in *European Intellectual Property Review* 17 (1996), pp. 253-60 and reprinted in H.L. MacQueen and B.G.M. Main (eds.), *Innovation, Incentive and Reward: Intellectual Property Law and Policy* (Hume Papers on Public Policy, 5.3; Edinburgh: Edinburgh University Press for the David Hume Institute, 1997), pp. 1-16.

43. Quotations at *EIPR* 17 (1996), p. 260; *HPPP* 5 (1997), p. 15.

44. *Hodgkinson & Corby v. Wards Mobility Services Ltd* [1995] F.S.R. 169, *per* Jacob J. at 173. The case was about passing off rather than copyright. In full the relevant passages of Jacob J.'s judgment read as follows: 'Some think that copying is unethical; others do not. Often the copyist of today becomes the innovator of

The second source of pressure to raise the standard of originality in Britain is the copyright harmonization process underway in the European Union.[45] It has long been known that the law in other Member States of the Community has deployed a higher standard, usually expressed in a formula embodying phrases like 'personal intellectual creation'. When the European Community has sought harmonization with regard to new subject-matter such as computer software and databases, the phraseology used to describe the works qualifying for protection has generally not been the British 'original' but the Continental 'intellectual creation'.[46] The phrase has now found its way into the British legislation implementing the Database Directive in particular, where emphasis is also placed upon the process of 'selection and arrangement' of material by the author as the manifestation of his 'personal intellectual creation'.[47]

tomorrow. Copying is said by some to be part of the lifeblood of competition, the means of breaking *de facto* market monopolies and keeping down the price of articles not protected by special monopolies such as patents and registered designs. Others say that copyists are parasites on innovators. None of this matters. Certainly it is not the law that copying as such is unlawful: the common law (and I am concerned with the common law) leans against monopolies. [at 173]... I turn to consider the law and begin by identifying what is not the law. There is no tort of copying. There is no tort of taking a man's market or customers. Neither the market nor the customers are the plaintiff's to own. There is no tort of making use of another's goodwill as such. There is no tort of competition. I say this because at times the plaintiffs seemed close to relying on such torts. For instance, Mr Morcom reminded me of the old adage, "Anything worth copying is worth protecting"' [at 174-75].

45. In addition to the Term Directive already discussed, see the Directives on the legal protection of computer programs (91/250/EEC, [1991] O.J. L122/42), rental rights (92/100/EEC, [1992] O.J. L346/61), satellite broadcasting and cable transmission (93/83/EEC, [1993] O.J. L248/15)), and the legal protection of databases (96/9/EC, [1996] O.J. L77/20). At the time of writing a further draft Directive on copyright in the information society (COM(1999) 250 final, [1999] O.J. C180/6) was under consideration. See new Directive 2001/29/EC [2001] O.J. L167/10.

46. Computer Program Directive, Art. 1(3); Database Directive, Art. 3(1). See also German Copyright Act 1965, s. 2(2): 'personal intellectual creations alone shall constitute works within the meaning of this Law'. The French copyright legislation speaks of 'works/creations of the mind'; see, e.g., French Intellectual Property Code 1992, L.111-1, L.112.

47. CDPA 1988, s. 3A(2) (added by Copyright and Rights in Databases Regulations 1997, reg. 6).

Coupled with the observations in the Lego brick case, this may mean that the standard of effort needed to obtain copyright in Britain is being, or has been, raised to Continental standards. But does this mean that the editor's copyright will be lost? Neither French nor German copyright laws would see an unpublished old manuscript as being the subject of copyright protection in itself beyond the standard period of the author's lifetime plus 70 years.[48] Although French law states that the authors of translations, adaptations, transformations or arrangements of works of the mind enjoy copyright,[49] it would appear that the person who edits and publishes some pre-existing unpublished work is not seen as deserving of author's rights of protection.[50] The German Copyright Act does provide, however, that editions of non-copyright texts are protected in a manner akin to copyright 'if they represent the result of scientific analysis and differ in a significant manner from previously known editions of the works or texts'.[51] The editor is the owner of this right.[52] The only major difference from ordinary copyright is that the period of protection is much shorter than the usual lifetime plus 70 years, being now 25 years from publication (the period was ten years until a 1990 amendment to the law).[53] The provision exists because it is thought that otherwise the editor would get no protection from ordinary copyright, but deserves some more limited rights in his work.[54] French and German law also provide what is now a 25-year term of protection for posthumous works which are disclosed after copyright has expired; however, the right belongs to the owners of the work who have it published, not to the editors as such.[55]

The German protection of the scientific edition has now found its way into Community law. Article 5 of the Term Directive says that

48. French Intellectual Property Code 1992, Art. L.123; German Copyright Act 1965, s. 64.

49. French Intellectual Property Code 1992, Art. L.112-3.

50. A. Lucas and H.J. Lucas, *Traité de la Propriété Littéraire et Artistique* (Litec, 1994), pp. 201-202, 651.

51. German Copyright Act 1965, s. 70(1).

52. German Copyright Act, s. 70(2).

53. German Copyright Act, s. 70(3).

54. G. Schricker, *Urheberrecht Kommentar* (Munich: C.H. Beck, 2nd edn, 1999), pp. 1133-38.

55. French Intellectual Property Code 1992, Art. L.123-4; German Copyright Act 1965, s. 71 (amended in 1995 to extend the period of protection from 10 to 25 years).

'Member States may protect critical and scientific publications of works which have come into the public domain', although a maximum period of 30 years from first publication is laid down. Article 4 of the same Directive also follows French and German law, in providing that 'any person who, after the expiry of copyright protection, for the first time lawfully publishes or lawfully communicates to the public a previously unpublished work, shall benefit from a protection equivalent to the economic rights of the author.' Here the protection is to be 25 years from the first publication. The UK has implemented Article 4 in the Copyright and Related Rights Regulations 1996,[56] but does not yet seem to have taken any steps with regard to the permissive Article 5, perhaps because it does not have to do so given the existence of copyright protection in Britain already.

4. *Copyright, Access and Scholarship*

Does the existence of copyright in the original manuscripts and in the edited version thereof inhibit scholarly activity in relation to the Dead Sea Scrolls or any other manuscript material, published or unpublished? Should we be concerned that the traditions of scholarship are in fact inconsistent with the protection of intellectual property? Ought the law to be changed?

A first point would be that the history of the Dead Sea Scrolls suggests that the issue of access to the originals themselves is far more important than any copyright which may exist. If access is restricted to a very small group of individuals, then the only work which others can carry out in relation to them is through the publicly available work of that group. The fact that others want that access evidences the earlier point that the views of scholars on the interpretation of the material may well legitimately differ, and surely supports the argument that, even if the aim of editorial work is to establish what the initial author wrote, what an editor produces is in the end that editor's version, based upon personal skill and knowledge, of that fact, that is, a form of individual expression.

Should there be a general right of access to material such as the Dead Sea Scrolls? I think that, whatever the correct answer to this question may be, it cannot be an unqualified 'Yes'.[57] Qualifications would

56. Reg. 16.

57. The French Intellectual Property Code 1992, Art. L.111-3, provides that the

include the owner's right to privacy (if I am the private owner of valuable historical material, am I really obliged to set up the facilities required to fulfil a public right of access?), and the archivist's need to protect the originals from excessive or inappropriate physical handling and treatment. Many of these concerns can be met, however—and in the case of the Dead Sea Scrolls, seem to have been met—by the production of facsimile versions which are relatively readily available to the scholarly community and other members of the public who wish to examine them. Digitization and the Internet promise further advances on this front.

The existence of copyright in an editor's work does not of itself prevent access to the underlying documents. In British terms, it prevents, first, copying of a 'substantial part' of the editor's work, substantiality being an issue of the quality rather than the quantity of what is taken.[58] If another editor goes into the sources and produces an independent version, then a new copyright comes into existence, and there is no infringement of the earlier copyright, even in the unlikely case of an identical result being reached. Copyright will also prevent the unauthorized issue to the public of either the original or subsequent copies of the editor's work;[59] but again this has no effect on the underlying documents save that, inasmuch as the underlying documents have copyright, this provision may support the right of the holder to deny access to a member of the public.

An editor's work may be used by others, in particular if it is published, although that is not absolutely necessary. Nothing in the present British copyright law prevents use of and commentary upon any other person's copyright work, even when it is unpublished. It is when actual quotation or paraphrasing occurs that copyright issues begin to arise. British law has no 'fair use' doctrine akin to that found in the United States Copyright Act, in which there is a general principle permitting fair use with a non-exclusive listing of some specific examples of what constitutes fair use.[60] In the UK, by contrast, there is a very specific and

owner of the copyright in a work may not compel an owner of the physical original of a work to give access to it unless it is manifest abuse of right not to do so.

58. CDPA 1988, s. 16(3)(a); *Ladbroke (Football) Ltd v. William Hill (Football) Ltd* [1964] 1 W.L.R. 273 (HL), *per* Lord Reid at 276.

59. CDPA 1988, s. 18.

60. Title 17, U.S.C., s. 107 (1976) ('fair use...for purposes such as criticism, comment, news reporting, teaching (including multiple copies for classroom use),

exclusive list of 'permitted' acts, although these are sometimes grouped under the heading 'fair dealing'.[61] These include copying for purposes of private study or research (which certainly does not permit quotation in published work),[62] or for purposes of criticism or review.[63] It is open to question whether the latter gives immunity to someone who copies chunks of another person's work and appends to each chunk some critical comment.[64] Criticism or review requires a 'sufficient acknowledgement', which means 'identifying the work in question *(i.e. being criticised or reviewed)* by its title or other description, and identifying the author *(i.e. the editor)*' in such a way that it is clear that the position and claim of the author of the original work is recognised by the critic/reviewer.[65] There is perhaps here some link with the moral right of the author to be identified as such when his work is published.[66] It has also been suggested that it may be unfair to subject unpublished work to criticism or review where the author never intended to publish it;[67] it might also be unfair to publish comment on a work which had not yet reached the stage at which the author had decided to publish, given the existence of the right not to publish mentioned earlier.

Finally, we might consider what the consequences would be if an editor doing his or her best to produce as accurate a version as possible of what some unknown author actually wrote or intended to write were

scholarship or research, is not an infringement of copyright'). Various factors are listed for consideration in determining whether use is fair, such as nature and purpose of use and of copyright work, and the amount, substantiality, and competitive effect of use.

61. CDPA 1988, ss. 28-76; see in particular ss. 29 (research and private study) and 30 (criticism, review and news reporting).

62. CDPA 1988, s. 29. See *Sillitoe v. McGraw-Hill Book Co. (UK) Ltd* [1983] F.S.R. 545, where a study guide for students included quotations from another copyright work; the fact that this work would be used for the private study and research of third parties (the students) did not justify the copying by the publisher.

63. CDPA 1988, s. 30.

64. See *Hubbard v. Vosper* [1972] 2 Q.B. 84, CA, discussed in *Pro Sieben Media AG v. Carlton UK Television Ltd* [1999] F.S.R. 610, CA.

65. CDPA 1988, s. 178. See further *Sillitoe v. McGraw-Hill Book Co. (UK) Ltd* [1983] FSR 545 and *BBC v. British Sky Broadcasting Ltd* [1991] 3 W.L.R. 174.

66. CDPA 1988, s. 77.

67. *British Oxygen Co. Ltd v. Liquid Air Ltd* [1925] Ch. 383; *Beloff v. Pressdram Ltd* [1973] R.P.C. 765.

to be denied copyright in that work on the grounds that he or she was merely reproducing someone else's earlier work.

First, when it came to negotiating with publishers about the publication of the work, the editor's only bargaining tool would be the physical inaccessibility of his or her work. This would encourage, rather than discourage, the secreting of work; sharing with others in the usual academic way would be wholly inadvisable. Similarly, there is lacking an incentive in subsequent scholarship to improve upon any edition already available by working upon the original sources.

Second, a publisher who knew that the editor's work was in the public domain might well feel disinclined to make the significant investment of its own skill and labour in producing and marketing what is bound to be a work with an extremely limited market, when at any time a competitor could step in with an undercutting rival publication. Publication is also, I would argue, the best way to encourage entry by others into the field of scholarship concerned, by giving that initial access that whets the appetite and the ability to tackle the originals in succeeding generations of researchers. Publication will not occur unless the publisher who lives and dies according to the ability to turn a profit can be given sufficient lead-time in the market place to recoup the initial outlay required to make the work available.

Third, if the editor is told that the more he or she strives for accuracy the less likely he or she is to gain the protection of copyright, an incentive may arise not to seek accuracy, but instead to introduce embellishments and adjustments designed to reflect the editor's creative spirit. Again, the aims of scholarship in the field of editing texts could be subverted. This is not an area where progress is likely to be made through imitation.

I conclude, therefore, that, on balance, copyright in this field serves to promote rather than to damage scholarly interests, and that the really important question raised by the controversy of the Dead Sea Scrolls is that of access to the originals themselves.

CHOICE OF LAW REGARDING COPYRIGHT AND THE DEAD SEA SCROLLS: THE BASIC PRINCIPLES

Paul L.C. Torremans

1. *Introduction*

Copyright is at the centre of a major controversy surrounding the Dead Sea Scrolls. Professors Carson and MacQueen examine the application of American and British copyright law respectively to this controversy in their contributions to this book. My contribution will steer clear of substantive copyright law and focus on the fact that the alleged infringement of the work of Professor Qimron and the International Team concerning the Dead Sea Scrolls has occurred in more than one jurisdiction. This raises the issue of which copyright law applies to the claim.

It is crucial to grasp the point that under the rules of international private law a court may have to apply rules other than those of the country in which the court exercises jurisdiction to the facts before it. Further, quite apart from the question of infringement raised in the *Qimron* case, there is the even more fundamental problem of copyrightability. Do the works at issue attract copyright protection in the first place? Once more the issue of choice of law arises, because not all national laws use the same criteria of originality, the root requirement for copyright protection of literary and artistic works. The answer to the question of whether protection exists at all may differ depending on the applicable national copyright law.

I will deal first with the issue of copyrightability, and then address questions about infringement. The approach I take to the subject is based on the Berne Convention, the basic framework of which applies to all Member States of the Berne Union. Whenever necessary, I use American or United Kingdom copyright law to illustrate the issues.

2. *Copyrightability*

The national treatment obligation in the Berne Convention, i.e. the obligation to treat a foreigner in the same way as a national, may require Member States to grant protection to works produced in other Member States, but the exact modalities of that protection are not specified. Nothing in the text indicates how to address the issue of which law should govern the protection of a work. Nor do the UK Copyright, Designs and Patents Act 1988 or the US Copyright Act 1976 contain any detailed guidance on the issue of which law to apply when conflicts arise.

The issue has not yet been addressed directly by the courts in the UK, but it can be said that the creation of copyright leads to an exclusive right that restricts competition. It would seem to follow that the United Kingdom's public policy dictates that the creation of a copyright exercisable in the UK will be governed by the provisions of the Copyright, Designs and Patents Act 1988. If protection is sought in the UK, the 1988 Act should apply as the law of the protecting country.

In the US, too, this issue was virtually ignored for many years, but recently the courts have had to address it head-on in two cases. One, the *Itar-Tass* case,[1] was concerned with Russian news articles which were copied in the US and incorporated by a Russian, Kurier, in a New York publication. The second, the *Corel* case,[2] was concerned with the alleged copying of photographs in both Britain and the US. In each case issues of choice of law arose. In both, the concern was over which law applied to copyright infringement, but the scope of copyright and copyrightability was also addressed. The *Corel* case is particularly informative in this respect. The *Itar-Tass* case further deals with the issue of the law applicable to the ownership of copyright, but a full

1. *Itar-Tass Russian News Agency; Itar-Tass USA and Fromer & Associates, Inc. (Plaintiffs-Counter-Defendants-Appellees), Argumenty I. Fakty; Moskowskie Novosti Komsomol-Skaya Pravda; Union of Journalists of Russia; Ekho Planety; Megapolis Express; Balagan Israeli Comic Magazine; Moskowsky Komsomolets: AR Publishing Co., Inc. and Yevgen I. Fromer (Plaintiffs-Appellees) v. Russian Kurier, Inc. (Defendant-Counter-Claimant-Appellant) and Oleg Pogrebnoy (Defendant-Appellant)* (1998) 153 F.3d82, 47 USPQ 2D 1810 (2nd Cir.).

2. *Bridgeman Art Library v. Corel* (1998) 36 F Supp 2d 191 and 25 F Supp 2d 421.

discussion of this point would lead too far afield from the issues of present concern.[3]

For current purposes, we should turn first to the issue of copyrightability and the scope of copyright. In *Itar-Tass*, the Second Circuit Appeals Court held that the national treatment rule in the Berne Convention does not provide a full answer to all the choice of law questions that arise in a copyright context: specifically, whether or not a work attracts copyright protection, or what the scope of such copyright protection is. The Court then went on to consider copyright as a form of property to which the standard Second Restatement rule—that the law of the state with the most significant relationship to the property and the parties determines the interests of the parties in the property—fell to be applied.[4] In a copyright context, that judgment seemed to mean the law of the country of origin, i.e., the law of the country where the works had been created and published. The decision led the court to choose Russian law as the applicable law. Thus if the work attracted copyright in Russia, it would receive the protection of copyright in the US, even if US law would not have recognized the work as copyright had it been produced in that country. The court was happy to conclude that the law that determines whether or not a work attracts copyright will also determine the scope of the right that is granted.

In the *Corel* case, the United States District Court for the Southern District of New York[5] first went down a very similar path, but was later forced to reconsider its position. In its second judgment, dated 18 February 1999, the court looked at the provisions concerning copyright in the US Constitution before turning its attention to the Berne Convention Implementation Act (BCIA) 1988, in particular sections 3(a) and 4(c) of that Act.

Section 3(a) states that:

3. For further details see Paul Torremans, 'Jurisdiction and Choice of Law Issues in United states Intellectual Property Cases: From Dodging the Bullet to Biting It', *Intellectual Property Quarterly* (1999), p. 372.

4. *Itar-Tass v. Russian Kurier, Inc.* (1998) 153 F.3d82, 47 USPQ 2D 1810 (2nd Cir.), at 90.

5. The first case was reported as *Bridgeman Art Library Ltd v. Corel Corp.* (1998) 25 F Supp.2d 421 (Southern District of New York). The second judgment in this case was delivered on 18 February 1999.

> The provisions of the Berne Convention—(1) shall be given effect under title 17, as amended by this Act, and any other relevant provision of Federal or State law, including the common law, and (2) shall not be enforceable in any action brought pursuant to the provisions of the Berne Convention itself.

Section 4(c)[6] adds that:

> [n]o right or interest in a work eligible for protection under this title may be claimed by virtue of, or in reliance upon, the provisions of the Berne Convention or the adherence of the United States thereto.

The court inferred from these provisions that Congress cannot have had the intention to see any other law but the US Copyright Act apply to the issue of copyrightability in the US. This interpretation places particular emphasis on the wording of section 4(c) of the BCIA 1988. The application of any foreign law would in this view necessarily occur 'in reliance upon the provisions of the Berne Convention or the adherence of the United States thereto', and is, therefore, excluded in the same way as the solution that would give any direct effect to the provisions of the Berne Convention itself. It would not be appropriate to apply a foreign law as a result of a provision in the Berne Convention if the Convention itself cannot be relied upon directly.

The *Corel* court thus arrived at a very different solution from that of the *Itar-Tass* court. I submit that the outcome in the *Corel* case is better, because it leads indirectly to the application of the law of the protecting country. To be sure, the matter is complicated. English and Scottish private international law do not have an equivalent to the rule that property issues are governed by the law of the state with which the property and the parties have the most significant relationship. The British approach is based more upon the *lex situs* (the law of the place where the property is located). I have pointed out elsewhere that, with regard to immaterial rights like copyright, such an approach, when taken in combination with the limited guidelines provided by the national treatment rule in the Berne Convention, leads to the applicability of the law of the protecting country in determining copyrightability. The *Itar-Tass* court's approach is, in my view, incompatible with the national treatment rule, in that it applies the law of the country of origin, which means that in one country different persons will receive different rights in similar works. The Berne principle of

6. Now codified at Title 17, U.S.C. s. 104(c).

national treatment means that the same private international choice of law rules should apply to all authors. It is my view that national treatment should go further, and that the same substantive rules should also apply to all authors and rightholders within the territory. This view leads, inevitably, to the application of the law of the protecting country. The approach taken by the *Corel* court seems to lead to the right conclusion, even if the reasoning is not properly based on the correct interpretation of the Berne Convention and the application of the rules of private international law, but rather on domestic US law.

The next matter for discussion must be: how do we determine what kinds of issues are ones involving copyrightability for the purposes of private international law? For current purposes, we can restrict our discussion to the question: does the editorial work of Professor Qimron meet the requirements of copyrightability? That is, we should consider whether Qimron's edition of MMT is original in the first stage, before we turn to the scope of copyright protection and the related issue of copyright infringement as the second stage.

a. *The Types of Works That Will Be Protected*

Article 2 of the Berne Convention restricts itself to stating the principle that 'literary and artistic works', which include 'every production in the literary, scientific and artistic domain', will be protected, and Article 2bis allows for certain limitations without requiring Member States to introduce them. The precise definition of the types of works that will be protected, and the decision whether or not to introduce any limitation, is left to the Member States and their domestic legislation.[7] As a result, differences exist among the laws of the Member States, even if not large ones. The law of the protecting country determines whether a work comes within a category of works that will be protected and, if so, in which category. In practice, there is no doubt that all the works involved in the Dead Sea Scrolls case are literary works, with the exception of the photographs, which are artistic works. All of these works can be protected, irrespective of whether US, UK or Israeli copyright law applies. Originality seems to be much more of an issue between these legal systems, however.

7. Compare in this respect Art. 2(1) Berne Convention and ss. 1-5B Copyright, Designs and Patents Act 1988.

b. *Originality*

Works are not granted copyright protection simply because they come within the scope of one of the categories of works that are protected, or within the general definition of literary and artistic works. Copyright protection also requires works to be original. The issue of what law is applicable is particularly relevant here, because national copyright systems have no uniform legal definition of the concept of originality. In other words, depending on which law applies, certain works may be granted copyright protection or may be refused it for lack of originality. The chapters in this book that deal with substantive copyright make it very clear that, whilst British copyright law will probably view all works involved as original, this may not necessarily be the case under US copyright law.

Since originality is a core factor in the decision whether or not a work will attract copyright protection, it seems logical to apply the law of the protecting country. Its criteria for originality will be used, therefore, to determine whether any of the works produced by Professor Qimron attract copyright protection. Thus, Israeli copyright law will apply if the question is whether they will attract copyright protection in Israel, US copyright law if the question is whether they will attract copyright protection in the US, and so on.[8]

3. *Infringement*

a. *The Scope of the Right*

Once copyright has been created, it is important to know what the content of the exclusive right will be. How far will the protection, and the restriction of competition, extend? Logically speaking, the issue is inextricably linked with the decision to grant copyright, because it determines exactly what is being granted. The issue should, therefore, be decided under the same applicable law, that of the protecting country.[9] The law of the place where the right is used has to decide

8. *Bridgeman Art Library Ltd v. Corel Corp.*, United States District Court for the Southern District of New York, judgment of 18 February 1999. The judgment explicitly confirmed and applied this rule.

9. See *Novello & Co. LD v. Hinrichsen Edition LD and Another* [1951] 1 Ch. 595, and see also Art. 34 para. 1 of the Austrian Private International Law Statute that contains the same rule, and Schack UFITA 108 (1988), p. 51.

whether the right exists and what is its content.[10] No specific provision, however, in any national copyright legislation deals directly with this issue.

This point concerning choice of law is important in practice because the Berne Convention does not define the scope of protection in a rigid way. Rather, it sets minimum standards for the Member States to build upon. While it is generally accepted that the copyright holder has the exclusive right to reproduce the work and make public representations of it, certain national legislations add to this right the exclusive right to distribute copies of the work, that is, to make the first sale of each authorized copy.[11]

The issue of the scope of an immaterial right such as copyright is inextricably linked with the concept of infringement. The beneficiary of an immaterial right only receives those rights that can be enforced whenever they are infringed. In light of the fact that the national treatment principle leads to the application of copyright laws on a territorial basis, as far as the scope of protection is concerned, it seems logical to assume that in cases of infringement the law which the protecting country will apply will be the *lex loci delicti* (the law of the place where the delict [tort, or wrong] was committed). An English court has recently dealt with an international copyright infringement case on this basis,[12] and although this was primarily a jurisdiction case, it seems clear that the courts will eventually apply the *lex loci delicti* to the infringement issue also.

The US court in the *Itar-Tass* case dealt with the issue of choice of law in regard to real copyright infringement, and the first *Corel* judgment also considered the point. Both courts considered infringement to be a separate matter from the existence of the copyright, and one for

10. See Michael Walter, 'La liberté contractuelle dans le domaine du droit d'auteur et les conflits de lois', 89 (1976) RIDA 44, at 51 and, for an example, see the judgment of 1 March 1989 of the *Arrondissementsrechtbank* (Dutch court of first instance) in Leewarden, *United Feature Syndicate Inc v. Van der Meulen Sneek BV* [1990] Bijblad Industriële Eigendom 329, the scope of copyright in the Garfield dolls in the Netherlands was determined by Dutch law (law of the protecting country), rather than under US law.

11. E. Ulmer, *Intellectual Property Rights and the Conflict of Laws: A Study Carried Out for the Commission of the European Communities, Directorate-General for the Internal Market and Industrial Affairs* (Deventer: Kluwer, 1978), p. 36.

12. *Pearce v. Ove Arup Partnership Ltd* [1997] 2 W.L.R. 779; [1997] 3 All E.R. 31.

which another choice of law rule existed. They classified copyright infringement as an issue of tort, leading them to apply the *lex loci delicti*. In the *Itar-Tass* case, the copying of the news articles had taken place in the US. The Court of Appeals for the Second Circuit, therefore, having applied Russian law to the copyrightability issue, applied US law to the infringement issue.[13] It must, none the less, be made clear that in the view of the court only those rights that in the first place had come into existence under Russian law could be infringed. US law governed only the issues whether or not certain acts in the US amounted to an infringement and what the consequences of the infringing activity were. Similarly, it was said in the first *Corel* judgment[14] that the alleged copying had mainly taken place in England and that English rather than US law was, therefore, applicable to the infringement issue.

This solution of applying the *lex loci delicti* to the issue of copyright infringement should be regarded as the right one. James Fawcett and I have argued that copyright infringement is tortious in nature and that the normal rules of choice of law in tort should be applied.[15] As the outcome of the *Itar-Tass* case shows, this is the most sensible approach and leads to results that are acceptable and even desirable. The synergy between the *lex loci delicti* and the territoriality principle means that in practice it is the law of the country where protection is sought, that is, the law of the protecting country, which determines the scope of the protection offered by copyright. In copyright cases the *lex loci delicti* corresponds therefore to the law of the protecting country.

Moral rights give rise to a few delicate issues, however, and need to be considered separately. Whether one sees moral rights as an integral part of copyright or as separate rights, the law of the protecting country determines the precise content of the moral rights that are granted.[16] Either they are part of the scope of the copyright that has been granted,

13. Ulmer, *Intellectual Property Rights*, pp. 91-92.

14. *Bridgeman Art Library v. Corel Corp.*, 36 F Supp 2d 191 and 25 F Supp 2d 421.

15. J. Fawcett and P. Torremans, *Intellectual Property and Private International Law* (Oxford: Clarendon Press, 1998), Ch. 11.

16. The term 'rights' in the Berne Convention includes both pecuniary and moral rights, see Jane C. Ginsburg, 'Conflicts of Copyright Ownership Between Authors and Owners of Original Artworks: An Essay in Comparative and International Private Law', *Columbia-VLA Journal of Law and the Arts* 17 (1993), p. 405, also the analysis of the John Huston case below.

or, if they are seen as independent rights, they come into being automatically through the creation of the copyright. For reasons of uniformity, it is logical in these circumstances to accept that they are governed by the same rule. Article 6bis (3) of the Berne Convention, which explicitly states that the law of the protecting country governs the means of redress in relation to moral rights, confirms that the law of the protecting country applies. The specific means of redress for each moral right are linked so strongly to the moral right in question that it would make no sense to separate them from the applicable law.

Moral rights can also be seen as personality rights linked to the person of the author of the work. From a choice of law point of view, they can then be classified as forming part of the personal law of the author. In copyright terms, the law of the country of origin could provide an alternative to that of the country where protection is sought, because the author has close links to the former. But the common law approach to substantive copyright and moral rights, which is based upon commercial exploitation of the work rather than upon author's rights, has never gone down the path of tying moral rights to personality rights. The 'personal law' approach is, therefore, to be rejected.

Jon Holyoak and I have argued that moral rights should be seen as fundamental rights that protect the author against the abuse of his work.[17] From this point of view, the UK's approach to moral rights should form part of its public policy. This approach would have important implications in a situation where a case is litigated in the UK, but where the law to be applied is in general not the Copyright, Designs and Patents Act 1988, but the *lex loci delicti*. Rather than applying this law, however, the court would be obliged to apply the UK's provisions on moral rights, if the standard of moral rights protection in the applicable law were lower than that of the Copyright, Designs and Patents Act 1988. It needs to be stressed that this approach does not replace the choice of law rules and the law of the protecting country altogether. Public policy considerations, and eventually the application of the law of the forum (the court in which the litigation is taking place), can only be considered at a later stage of the court's discussion.[18]

17. J. Holyoak and P. Torremans, *Holyoak and Torremans Intellectual Property Law* (London: Butterworths, 2nd edn, 1998), Ch. 13; see also I. Stamatoudi, 'Moral Rights of Authors in England: The Missing Emphasis on the Role of Creators', *Intellectual Property Quarterly* (1997), p. 478.

18. See Jane C. Ginsburg and P. Sirinelli, 'Authors and Exploitations in Inter-

It is doubtful whether this argument about the public policy character of moral rights could also apply to US copyright law. The absence of strong and explicit moral rights protection under the provisions of the US Copyright Act seems rather to lead to the conclusion that the US does not regard moral rights as an issue that touches upon its public policy.

National rules which can be characterised as 'mandatory' operate in a slightly different way. Such rules are directly applicable[19] and the choice of law process is not followed at all. If the provisions of the forum on moral rights are mandatory, therefore, they are directly applicable, irrespective of the content of the law of the protecting country. The French Cour de Cassation took this approach[20] in the *John Huston* case when holding that colorization of black and white Huston films infringed the director's moral rights.[21] I submit, however, that the nature of moral rights as rights only coming into operation when the copyright work is used abusively does not justify regarding them as mandatory rules. The traditional approach of applying the rule of the protecting country, plus the public policy of the forum in exceptional cases, is far

national Private Law: The French Supreme Court and the Huston Film Colonization Controversy', *Columbia-VLA Journal of Law and the Arts* 15 (1991), pp. 135, 139 (an English translation of the judgment is attached as an appendix).

19. French legal terminology refers to the rules as *règles d'application immédiate*, which characterizes them very well.

20. Different decisions were reached at first instance and upon appeal; see Judgment of 23 November 1988 of the Tribunal de Grande Instance de Paris, [1989] Recueil Dalloz Sirey 342 (Jurisprudence), annotated by Audit, and *Revue Critique de Droit International Privé* (1989), p. 372, annotated by Gautier; Judgment of 6 July 1989 of the Cour d'Appel de Paris, [1990] Recueil Dalloz Sirey 152 (Jurisprudence), annotated by Audit; and *Revue Critique de Droit International Privé* (1989), p. 706, annotated by Gautier; Judgment of 28 May 1991 of the Cour de Cassation, *Revue Critique de Droit International Privé* (1991), p. 752, annotated by Gautier. In this case, French law was both the law of the protecting country and the law of the forum, but that fact does not influence my conclusions.

21. For an in depth analysis of the case, see J.C. Ginsburg and P. Sirinelli, 'Authors and Exploitations'; Jane C. Ginsburg and P. Sirinelli, 'Auteur, création et adaptation en droit international privé', in RIDA 150 (1991); see also Jane C. Ginsburg, 'Colors in Conflicts: Moral Rights and the Foreign Exploitation of U.S. Motion Pictures', *Journal of the Copyright Society of the USA*, 36 (1988–89), p. 81; *idem*, Jane C. Ginsburg, 'Conflicts of Copyright Ownership', p. 395.

more suitable.[22] The same law would then also be applied to all issues that form part of the scope of copyright.

b. *Exceptions to the Rights*

Restrictions placed on the exclusive right of the copyright-owner modify the content of that right. So, if the law of the protecting country governs all issues relating to the content of the exclusive right granted by copyright, the exceptions to the rights granted to the copyright holder, such as fair use, are the next issue to be faced. The precise scope of the rights granted is, indeed, only to be determined after these exceptions have been taken into account. For example, the exceptional right of a user to make a copy for personal use restricts the right-holder's exclusive right to make copies of the work. Further exceptions might exist for reporting current events, research and private study, and so on.[23] The same exceptions obviously also play a role as defences against copyright infringement claims.

When all these considerations are applied to the case of the Dead Sea Scrolls, it becomes clear that the whole question of infringement in relation to any of the works produced by Professor Qimron that attract copyright protection should be answered by Israeli copyright law if the alleged infringement took place in Israel, by US copyright law if it took place in the US, and by British law if it took place in the UK.

c. *Civil Remedies*

The final issue is that of the civil remedies available if the claims of infringement are made out: injunctions, damages, and so on. This also includes the matter of who can sue, for example whether a licensee can sue independently for infringement of copyright, or whether he needs to rely on the copyright owner to take action for him. The remedies available determine the real scope of the right involved and should, therefore, come under the law of the protecting country.[24] Traditional procedural restrictions apply, however, in the situation where the law of the protecting country is not also the law of the forum. For example,

22. See Ginsburg and Sirinelli, 'Auteur, création et adaptation', p. 21.

23. For a full catalogue of these exceptions, e.g. under UK law, see Chapter 3 (sections 28-76), Copyright, Designs and Patents Act 1988.

24. See for an example in case law the judgment of 17 June 1992 of the German Bundesgerichtshof (Supreme Court), [1993] GRUR Int. 257 and see E. Ulmer, *Intellectual Property Rights*, p. 35.

the issue of quantification of damages will be governed by the law of the forum.[25]

4. *Conclusion*

The law of the protecting country governs issues of copyrightability. In other words, whether or not the work of Professor Qimron attracts copyright—especially whether they are original works for the purposes of copyright—is a matter that will be decided by Israeli copyright law as far as copyright protection in Israel is concerned, by US copyright law as far as copyright protection in the US is concerned, and by British copyright law as far as copyright protection in Britain is concerned.

Once the works attract protection, the issue of infringement of copyright can arise. Here the law of the protecting country becomes the *lex loci delicti.* The question whether there has been copyright infringement in Israel should, therefore, be decided under Israeli copyright law and, similarly, the question whether there has been copyright infringement in the US or Britain will be decided under US or British copyright law respectively, wherever the court deciding the matter may be located.

Needless to say, in the light of the differences in substantive copyright law on points such as originality and defences to copyright infringement, to name only the most important ones, the eventual outcome of the case will differ depending on the law to be applied.

25. See P. North and J.J. Fawcett, *Cheshire and North's Private International Law* (Butterworths, 13th edn, 1999), Ch 6, specifically pp. 87-88.

Legal Aspects of the Recent History of the Qumran Scrolls: Access, Ownership Title and Copyright

Wojciech Kowalski

Many factors have contributed to making the finds at Qumran one of the most important archaeological discoveries of the last century.[1] The finds come within a lawyer's range of interest not only for their significance in the history of law,[2] but also, and more importantly, because they pose modern questions of a legal nature. The issues are particularly those about accessibility to the scrolls for scientific research, the ownership of the manuscripts, and the copyright on reconstructed texts. Polemics about these problems often take on a fairly fierce character: this volume appears because the matter of the rights to reconstructed texts ended up in a law court. The facts of the case having been discussed in other contributions to this book, I will focus mainly on the legal issues.

1. *Access to Manuscripts, or the Question of Freedom of Historical Information*

The question of access to the Dead Sea Scrolls is not the only one of its kind. There is a general issue about scholars' right of access to newly-discovered historical sources. Although concentrating on the Qumran

1. The author wishes to thank Professor H. MacQueen, Faculty of Law, University of Edinburgh, Reverend Dr J. Kozyra, Silesian Theological Seminar, and Dr Z.J. Kapera, Jagiellonean University, for their invaluable advice, information and material about the Qumran discoveries.

2. Among the various texts found at Qumran were purely legal documents, for example, contracts of sale. They were translated and published by E. Koffman, *Die Doppelurskunden aus der Wüste Juda. Recht und Praxis der jüdischen Papyri des 1. und 2. Jahrhunderts n. Chr. samt Übertragung des Texte und deutscher Übersetzung* (Leiden: E.J. Brill, 1968).

case, Cindy Alberts Carson provides another example of an historical source that was inaccessible for many years,[3] an Aramaic text from the 5th century BC which was discovered in 1890, and which its discoverer intended to publish as soon as possible. He could not fulfil his objective, however, and his assistant undertook the task of publication. He too was unsuccessful, and the next generation then took up the task. In 1994 Carson found that a scientific 'heir' of its discoverer was still working on the manuscript. Promising to publish within the next four years, he represented the fourth generation of researchers holding sole access to the document.[4]

Analysing negative aspects of limited access to historical sources, including the issue of keeping them in the dark, Carson discusses the duties of the holder of such sources. She stresses that 'proper stewardship requires access and preservation', which, if not carried out, results in a broader problem of access to information. She cites periods of history when control or denial of access to sources constituted a means of political domination. In Carson's opinion, the scholarly world is, as a rule, against such an approach, and she supports the idea of publishing information where the only 'gratification' for doing so is proper attribution.[5] This view deserves full acceptance. Truly, those who for such an extensive period excluded others from access to the Qumran manuscripts and to the photographs of their inscriptions had no reasonable grounds for their action, and it proved harmful for a number of reasons. It also needs to be emphasized that, although the contents of the texts are above all of a religious character—at least they are significant to Christians and Jews—they have not had the effect of overturning religious practice and teaching claimed by their sensation-seeking advocates. Those who kept the material inaccessible not only made research difficult for two generations of scholars, but also left the

3. C.A. Carson, 'Raiders of the Lost Scrolls: The Right of Scholarly Access to the Content of Historic Documents', *Michigan Journal of International Law* 16 (1995), pp. 299-348.

4. This text should now be published. See Carson, 'Raider of the Lost Scrolls', pp. 299-348 (299-322) n. 129.

5. Carson cites undesirable practices in the former USSR and during the McCarthy era in the USA. She concludes, 'when governments have tried to limit access to information, academia has traditionally been a bastion of free access', and 'the only thing given in exchange for the use of this information is attribution', 'Raiders of the Lost Scrolls', pp. 317 and 318.

Catholic Church open to false accusations.[6] If the unpublished texts had been lost as a result of improper conservation of the scrolls or had been destroyed, the greatest loss of all (fortunately not realized) would have been to scholarly enterprise. It is well known that the texts were kept in an inappropriate way for many years. They were, moreover, endangered by hostilities of varying intensity in Palestine.[7]

It is hard to question Carson's conclusion that

> Secretiveness has no place in scholarship. By definition, scholarship should enlighten, not obfuscate. Even in the scientific community, where research results often represent a marketable commodity, scholars recognize the inherent contradiction, and ultimate destructiveness, of secret research.[8]

Aside from the issue of freedom of scholarly access to information, publication, like the physical care of the documents, protects the information. That is, publication eliminates fears about any hypothetical damage to, or destruction of, the original sources. For example, the publication of an enormous quantity of source materials saved for Polish scholarship invaluable historical data threatened with destruction because of the ravages of the First and Second World Wars.

While I concur generally with Carson's views, I nevertheless have a question. If freedom of information, so much defended by her, is about totally free access to it, can there never be any restrictions?[9]

6. For example, the Vatican was accused of making access to the scrolls difficult. Some authors based their publications on this accusation, the most successful probably being that of M. Baigent and R. Leigh, *The Dead Sea Scrolls Deception* (London: Corgi Books, 1991). See the comments by J.M. Fitzmyer, *Responses to 101 Questions on the Dead Sea Scrolls* (New York: Paulist Press, 1992); also O. Betz and R. Riesner, *Jesus, Qumran und der Vatican: Klarstellungen* (Freiburg: Herder Verlag, 3rd edn, 1993).

7. It is clear that in the early years after their discovery the Scrolls were not properly treated and stored. The situation was much worse during the 1956 war when they were moved to Amman and stored in the damp basement of the Ottoman Bank. As a result a certain number of the more fragile fragments was definitely lost. See J.A. Fitzmyer as quoted by H. Shanks, 'An Inside—Outside—Look at the Scrolls', *BAR* 19 (March/April 1993), pp. 71-72.

8. Carson, 'Raiders of the Lost Scrolls', p. 347.

9. At this point the distinction between information as such and the material object (*corpus mechanicum*) from which it is derived must be underlined. It is possible to imagine a limitation on access to an object, either to the information or to the object alone, for example, when it constitutes a very important historical

When it comes to information in the widest sense of the word, we should sometimes take into account certain limitations. In principle, the problem goes beyond the confines of the subject under discussion, but for the sake of completeness it should be pointed out that the freedom in question is never open-ended, and that a great deal of information is lawfully kept inaccessible. It is enough to cite protected information such as state, bank or medical records, and other personal data. The phenomenon is so well understood and common that objections are never raised; indeed, sometimes, the question arises if such protected information should not be considered a property right.[10] This conclusion is generally regarded as going too far. We are dealing, not so much with property, but with a set of protective instruments that sometimes functions like a right of property.[11]

Depending on the sort of information, there might sometimes be restrictions. In principle, this statement does not apply to scholarship, although even here one can speak about extraordinary information that should be kept in strict confidence, for instance, information relevant to a country's defence. Should such restrictions affect historical information, however, particularly information obtained by the methods characteristic of archaeology? At first glance, it seems evident that any secrecy or limitation of access is out of the question, except, of course, temporary confidentiality related to contemporary history, such as is often the case when it comes to certain archives. Nonetheless, for sources that concern distant history, two possible limitations should be recognized: the character of the ownership title, and the circumstances in which the information was obtained.

The first limitation applies when the historical source is private property. No matter how difficult it is for scholars to accept, they should recognize the primacy of the right of property, which in a given

document that is accessible only through a microfiche or a photograph. It is difficult, however, to imagine access to an object without access to its information, unless the operation serves an entirely different purpose, e.g. the conservation of the object.

10. See, e.g., N. Palmer and P. Kohler, 'Information as Property', in N.E. Palmer and E. McKendrick (eds.), *Interests in Goods* (London: Lloyds of London, 1993), pp. 187-206.

11. As Palmer and Kohler conclude: 'The point to be made is that the property label is a conclusion not a premise. If some aspects of the law's treatment of confidential information display a proprietary parallel, that does not mean that confidential information is property per se but that in that regard it displays a proprietary characteristic' (see Palmer and Kohler, 'Information as Property', p. 205).

case may be strengthened by the added protection of moral rights. It is consequently difficult to discard Hector MacQueen's argument, 'If I am the private owner of valuable historical material, am I really obliged to set up facilities required to fulfil a public right to access?'[12] It should be understood that his opinion is grounded in UK law, but it is also the rule within many legal systems. That is why legal measures aimed at forcing disclosure of information hidden in private archives, or at giving public access to other kinds of cultural property, are seemingly unimaginable. Yet, as a matter of record, there is an example of such a right, enjoyed by the Polish conservation authorities, who can compel 'the study of objects of presumed historical, scientific or artistic value'.[13] As commentators point out, however, it is a right limited to 'what is necessary to provide effective care for the examined objects'.[14] At least, that is what follows from the text of the act, which declares that the examination of the said objects is carried out 'in order to determine their condition or to prepare documentation'. The regulation is not aimed at the forced disclosure of any information contained within a specific cultural piece of property. It is not easy, however, to conceive how such an examination or documentation would turn out if the holders did not reveal some information data. Highly specialized researchers would succeed in obtaining it.

Another example of an instrument in Polish law with a similar effect is 'the seizure of a monument of a peculiarly historical, scientific or artistic value by the State Treasury'.[15] There are also doubts about the interpretation of this instrument. The regulation constitutes grounds for taking over such a moveable monument 'to make it available for the general public'. Despite the fact that the expression of the act is clear and offers no basis for an expanded interpretation—a judgment confirmed by the authors of the commentary on it[16]—as in the previous

12. L.H. MacQueen, 'Copyright Law and the Dead Sea Scrolls: A British Perspective', in this volume. The author expresses his thanks to Professor MacQueen for making it possible to read his paper before its publication.

13. Art. 18 of the Law of 15 February 1962 on the protection of cultural property, and on museums, *Journal of Laws* (1962), No. 10, entry 48.

14. S. Łazarowicz and W. Sieroszewski, *Przepisy prawne dotyczące ochrony dóbr kultury oraz muzeów* (*Legal Regulations Concerning the Protection of Cultural Property, and on Museums*) (Warsaw, 1970), p. 33.

15. Art. 33 of the law of 15 February 1962 on the protection of cultural museums, *Journal of Laws* (1962), No. 10, entry 48.

16. As they maintained, Art. 33 allows the seizure of a movable object only for

case it is unclear how the monument could be made available to the public without the disclosure of its information. The restriction of the seizure exclusively to the objectives defined by the commentators could also be supported by the rule denying access to archival materials that constitute an important source of historical information.

Regardless of these ambiguities in the regulations, their actual significance is lessened by the fact that they originated at a time when the right to property was not taken seriously into consideration, and when social purposes, at least nominally, took absolute priority. As far as I am aware, 'the forced examination' of cultural property was conducted under them, but rarely and only in exceptional circumstances. Motivated by political purposes rather than by protection, it occurred only in relation to church institutions. It also appears that seizures did not take place at all. The situation changed dramatically after 1989, when the right to property in Poland was fully restored.[17] Consequently, a long awaited and much heralded Cultural Property Protection Act, as set out in its final draft of 11 January 1999, does not anticipate seizure and other similarly operating instruments designed to obtain disclosure of information. Any limitations to the rights of the proprietors of monuments are to be dictated solely by the protection of the national cultural heritage.

The second limitation upon access to historical information can be linked to the method by which scholars acquire it. I am referring particularly to sources of an archaeological character that come to light as the result of excavation work. The norm of availability and publication applies because the finds are usually very rare and more often than not consitute unique sources of information. At the same time I wish to stress that, in the case of archaeological artefacts, we are usually dealing with the value of the object on account of the information that it provides, not with the value as such, or its potential value.[18] After we

'expository objectives', which means 'to place it on exhibition in a museum or other venue open to public viewing, providing that such opening is on clearly indicated days and hours. Łazarowicz and Sieroszewski, *Przepisy prawne dotyczące*, p. 42.

17. See, in particular, Articles 21 and 64 of the new Constitution of Poland, as well as the Law of 28 July 1990 on the amendment of the Civil Code, *Journal of Laws* (1991), No. 55, entry 321.

18. 'Archaeologists do not seek objects as such, but scientific information', *Principles for Partnership in Cross-Cultural Human Sciences Research with a*

have obtained the information, the object becomes irrelevant for scholarship.[19] Owing solely to its value as a document, the archaeological object becomes completely devoid of material value, with the result that the issue of a property right has no importance.[20] Despite the devaluation of the object itself, the public nonetheless seeks an assurance that archaeological information will be made generally available, a consequence being that it cannot become private property. In expressing their opinion about an archaeologically related subject, A. Beith and O.J. Olivier, consultants to the Parliamentary Assembly of the Council of Europe, emphasized, 'The archaeological heritage is first and foremost a common heritage, providing evidence for a better understanding of our common past. It cannot be the property of any private individual.'[21] Recognizing this proposition, the law of many countries considers archaeological finds to be state property.[22] O'Keefe and Prott go so far as to claim that the state is entitled to any

Particular View to Archaeology (Rüschlikon Principles; Rüschlikon, Zürich, Switzerland, 30 September 1994), 'Chapter A. At the Service of the Archaeological Heritage. Principle 1', *International Journal of Cultural Property* 7.1 (1998), pp. 223-30.

19. 'In many cases, once the information has been obtained the objects are no longer of scholarly interest' (L.V. Prott and P.J. O'Keefe, *Law and the Cultural Heritage: Discovery and Excavation* I [Abingdon: Professional Books, 1984], p. 194).

20. As F. Hole and R.F. Heizer underline: 'Archaeological data consists of mud, clay, stone, bone, and fibrous objects, and so they will remain unless they are given a cultural interpretation', *Prehistoric Archaeology: A Brief Introduction* (New York: Holt, Rinehart & Winston, 1977), p. 250. Of course, archaeological objects made of gold or silver, as well as of precious stones have sometimes a very great commercial value, but we have to remember that they represent only a tiny fraction of all finds.

21. This comment was made in the context of a discussion about the use of metal detectors, but more general questions were also addressed See A. Beith and O.J. Olivier, 'Explanatory Memorandum. Council of Europe. Parliamentary Assembly. Doc. 4741-E. Metal Detectors and Archaeology' (*Report of the Committee on Culture and Education*; Strasbourg, 1981), p. 6.

22. Among such countries are the following: Bulgaria, China, Greece, Mexico, New Zealand, Turkey, Poland and Italy; see also Prott and O'Keefe, *Law and the Cultural Heritage*, p. 191, and the regulations quoted in *The Protection of Movable Cultural Property. Compendium of Legislative Texts*, vol. I i II (Paris, 1984). In the majority of cases these laws also declare that all objects as yet undiscovered are the property of the State, government or nation.

information obtained from archaeological research.[23] It then follows that the information acquired must be freely available to all.[24]

If we familiarize ourselves with the procedures that apply to the excavation of sites, we will be surprised to learn that, despite such clear-cut support for the freedom of archaeological information, it is not entirely without restriction. Moreover, coming as it does from a tradition that grew up in their own circles, archaeologists themselves willingly implement the restriction albeit, in principle, temporarily. Over time, it has become an international standard and is legitimized in the relevant international documents. For example, the UNESCO General Conference in 1956 passed its UNESCO Recommendation on International Principles Applicable to Archaeological Excavations.[25] It is a relatively early document, formally sanctioning an existing custom. One of the regulations is the right of an archaeologist to publish his or her research. The right comes under his 'scientific rights', as defined by the Title of Principle 24 of the Recommendation, or even under the notion of 'scientific property', as it is called in the Polish translation, prepared under the auspices of the Polish Ministry of Culture and Art.[26]

23. Prott and O'Keefe, *Law and the Cultural Heritage*, p. 195, also underline that there is no legislation vesting such information in the State.

24. The duty to publish all information gathered from archaeological excavations is declared to be one of the most important; see, e.g., Art. 7 of the European Convention on the Protection of the Archaeological Heritage (revised), *European Treaty Series* 143 (Valetta, 16 January 1992). For more on this Article, see *Council of Europe. Protection of Archaeological Heritage. Explanatory Report on the Revised Convention Opened for Signature* on 16 January 1992 (Strasbourg, 1992), pp. 13-14, also: P.J. O'Keefe, 'The European Convention on the Protection of Archaeological Heritage', *Antiquity* 67 (1993), pp. 406-13 (410). One of the ways in which the duty can be realized is making public access to the excavated material and places possible. For papers discussing the issue, see *Archaeological Sites in Europe: Conservation, Maintenance and Enhancement* (Conimbra, Portugal, 18–20 October 1990); *Council of Europe. Architectural Heritage Series*, No. 22 (Strasbourg, 1992), pp. 35-80.

25. *Recommendation on International Principles Applicable to Archaeological Excavations* (5 December 1956). *Conventions and Recommendations of UNESCO Concerning the Protection of the Cultural Heritage* (Paris, 1985), p. 101.

26. *Conventions and Recommendations*, p. 111; W. Sieroszewski, 'Własność naukowa: prawa i obowiązki prowadzącego wykopy' (Scientific property, rights and obligations of the excavator), in *Ochrona dóbr kultury w ustawodawstwie UNESCO* (*Protection of Cultural Property in UNESCO's Documents*) (Warsaw: OD2, 1978), pp. 103-107.

The 'property' consists of the rights and obligations of the person conducting an excavation, and includes a general guarantee that the State in which the excavation is licensed will respect his rights.[27] As for the first recommendation, it cites the already mentioned right to publish the results of an excavation, which must, however, be exercised within 'a reasonable period of time', i.e. not longer than two years in the case of a preliminary report. Corresponding to this right is the obligation of the appropriate authorities to give an assurance that any finds and related documentation will not be given over for examination to other people for a period of five years after discovery, unless the finder himself provides written consent for it. Within this period of time the authorities are also obliged to prevent any photographing or other reproduction of unpublished archaeological materials.[28]

In essence, this right is repeatedly confirmed in other documents, most often in the form of a general confirmation of 'existing rights to publication'. It is juxtaposed with the obligation that, to obtain proper permission to take advantage of unpublished materials,[29] 'a researcher may have primary access to original materials and documents for a limited and reasonable time'.[30] Sometimes the right is confirmed in a

27. 'The conceding State should guarantee to the excavator scientific rights in his finds for a reasonable period' (Principle 24, point 'a' of the Recommendation).

28. 'The conceding State should require the excavator to publish the results of his work within the period stipulated in the deed, or, failing such stipulation, within a reasonable period. This period should not exceed two years for the preliminary report. For a period of five years following the discovery, the competent archaeological authorities should undertake not to release the complete collection of finds, nor the relative scientific documentation, for detailed study, without the written authority of the excavator. Subject to the same conditions, these authorities should also prevent photographic or other reproduction of archaeological material still unpublished' (Principle 24, point 'b' of the Recommendation. See Prott and O'Keefe, *Law and the Cultural Heritage*, pp. 296-305 for comments on this priority right and connected issues).

29. 'Before studying and/or publishing any unpublished material, archaeologists should secure proper permission, normally in writing, from the appropriate project director or the appointed representative of the sponsoring institution and/or the antiquities authorities in the country of origin.' Archaeological Institute of America, 'Code of Ethics (29 December 1990), Chapter III. Responsibilities to Colleagues. Principle 6', *International Journal of Cultural Property* 7.1 (1998), p. 193.

30. *Society for American Archaeology. Principles of Archaeological Ethics*. According to this document a priority right can be used under the condition that, 'If there is a compelling reason, and no legal restrictions or strong countervailing

more detailed way, when the rules formulated in the Recommendation are repeated with an added guideline stating that, for instance, the entire report should be concluded within eight years from the date of completion of the preliminary report.[31]

Finally, it is worth mentioning that the priority right might sometimes contain a right to give out information about an excavation to the press and other media. This right has long been of crucial significance, the 1920s being a turning point with the publicity surrounding the excavation work that led to the discovery of the tomb of the pharaoh Tutankhamun.[32] The Recommendation does not provide for any rules on the subject, but legislation in certain countries pays the problem some attention.[33]

A brief survey of the UNESCO Recommendation and other documents indisputably indicates that a temporary limitation on freedom of information for a fixed period is commonly recognized and accepted. The purpose of the restriction is the protection of some rights of the archaeologist, but the restriction is, in fact, inconsistent with freedom of information and is antithetical to the strongly emphasized obligation to give out information, an obligation that appears in the same documents. That is why the priority right operates within clearly specified time limits. Some of the documents distinctly underline that exceeding the publication time should result in interested scholars having free access to all the finds of the procrastinating archaeologist.[34]

interests, a researcher may have primary access.' *Principle 5. International Journal of Cultural Property* 7.1 (1998), p. 233.

31. *Rüschlikon Principles*, Chapter D; *Information, Documentation, Publication. Principle* 15. *International Journal of Cultural Property* 7.1 (1998), p. 229.

32. Being a sponsor of excavations, Lord Carnaervon signed a contract with the publisher of *The Times* giving it an exclusive right to publish information on the excavations for a £5000 lump sum plus 75 per cent of the profit gained from publishing the information. Tutankhamun's tomb was discovered in 1922, and by the middle of the next year the peer's income had reached £11,600. See T. Hoving, *The Untold Story* (New York: Simon & Schuster, 1978), p. 154.

33. Certain countries require official permission for the publication of information, and sometimes it is forbidden to make use of photographs for commercial purposes, Prott and O'Keefe, *Law and the Cultural Heritage*, pp. 282-83.

34. 'Failing timely publication, their material and findings are at the free disposal of the competent scientific community', *Rüschlikon Principles*, Chapter D; *Information, Documentation, Publication. Principle 15* (*in fine*). *International Journal of Cultural Property* 7 (1998), p. 229; also the *Principles of Archaeological*

Pursuing this issue a little further, one could certainly demonstrate that the limitation in question does not have the full force of law, because both the Recommendation and the other documents mentioned are merely guidelines, or standards, valid only within the professional corporations adopting them. Nonetheless, as I have already stated, these documents are a formal embodiment of established custom. The fact that the norms are not expressed in the form of generally binding legal acts is congruent with a current tendency: the regulation of certain issues is left in the domain of such guidelines, or is a matter of private ethics, or codes of behaviour within professional circles. Such standards are perceived to be more desirable than those that a legislature might impose.[35]

In light of the above consideration, I would affirm that, in regard to the main subject of this article, the team appointed by Fr R. de Vaux could exclusively take advantage of the scrolls for a certain limited period of time. The period, however, should not have exceeded 'the period indispensable for sound scientific evaluation'.[36] The scrolls discovered at Qumran undoubtedly belong to the category of archaeological materials subject to the regulations stated in the documents I have been discussing. The issues of rights of access and publication apply to the team members. The period of time could last several years—say two to five, or even eight—if we take into account the complexity of the task entrusted to them. The fascination with the discovery and its importance however, led the team, constantly to extend the assignment and, as has been stated before, the task could not be done because of the way in which it was set up and because of the time factor. The project was not completed even after 45 years of exclusive access, and the situation gave rise to widespread criticism of the group instead of an appreciation for their real achievements. Without doubt, we have witnessed an abuse of the priority right granted to an

Ethics, adopted by the *Society for American Archaeology*, state (Principle 5) that the priority right is valid only 'for a limited and reasonable time, after which these materials and documents must be made available to others.' See n. 30 *supra*, p. 232.

35. For more information on the issue see K. Greenawalt, 'Thinking in Terms of Law and Morality', *International Journal of Cultural Property* 7 (1998), pp. 7-20; P.J. O'Keefe, *Codes of Ethics: Form and Function in Cultural Heritage Management*, pp. 32-51.

36. *Rüschlikon Principles*. Chapter D. *Principle 15*. *International Journal of Cultural Property* 7 (1998), p. 229.

archaeologist as a reward for his discovery. The perfectly justified reward is accepted, but the licence is nonetheless a strictly limited one. Almost five decades of restricted access seems unacceptable in light of established international standards. It is understandable that, although such enterprises usually involve an enormous, even noble, personal commitment on the part of the researcher, with the passage of time there is the perception that the object of study is the scholar's personal career. Such a phenomenon happens to be dangerous for scholarship, and the very object of the study, in an extreme case, becomes the exclusive possession of several generations of scholars, as Carson shows.

The documents I quote above warn about this quite common phenomenon and state that 'archaeological work and findings, particularly documentary records and primary field data, are of public interest, not commodities to be exploited for personal enjoyment and profit, and not private property'.[37] In the case of the Qumran scrolls such a tendency was more than discernible.[38]

To conclude the discussion about access to historical information: it should be remembered that even a limited freedom in this field does not cover the scholars' intellectual property, that is, the property which has come into being as a result of their creative work on the discovered sources.[39] Clearly, their creative work is something completely different from the archaeological materials and any other discovered sources. In the field of archaeology, such work could be any interpretation of the discovered objects and is usually inseparable from the

37. See n. 36 *supra*, p. 229. *The Consultants of the Council of Europe* are also alert to the problem: 'One is speaking here of the evidence that can be gleaned from an archaeological context rather than of the objects themselves. The distinction between ownership of archaeological evidence and ownership of an individual object, is, I believe, basic: it rules out any justification for treasure hunting in that this activity destroys or appropriates the archaeological context; it applies also to the archaeologist who should not keep for his personal use the results of an excavation' (Beith and Oliver, *Explanatory Memorandum*, p. 6).

38. This observation was also stressed by Carson who quoted certain remarks made by some persons who had exclusive access to the scrolls. See Carson, 'Raiders of the Lost Scrolls', p. 347, note p. 245 and p. 321.

39. 'With scientific research, however, some secretiveness is understandable in that scientific research represents invention and creation, results which are personal to the researcher and a reflection of his creative genius', Carson, 'Raiders of the Lost Scrolls', p. 34.

documentation and reports of the discovery. Archaeological proceedings emphasize the difference under scrutiny.[40] I will undertake a detailed analysis of the issue in the following sections of this article.

2. *Who is the Owner of the Scrolls?*

In the background to the question about access—a question so often subject to hasty and fraught considerations—we come upon the legal issue as to who is the actual owner of the scrolls. The most considered opinion on the matter comes from Carson, who believes that the Scrolls are the property of Israel. Focusing on how a given Scroll comes into someone's possession, she derives Israel's title to the Scrolls from the fact that they were found in an area belonging to the country that was either bought by the Government or taken over as a spoil of war.[41] Carson stresses, however, that in this context one can contemplate possible rights of 'additional owners', whose title would be based upon a concept of 'cultural business' that produces links between some entity and the Scrolls. In particular, one would take into account an entity's religious, ethnic, geographical, linguistic, or political ties to the material. The criteria that Carson proposes, however, do not, despite her analysis of the history of the finds, bring her any closer to a definitive answer to the question of ownership. Consequently, none of the ties she cites constitutes a reliable indication by which to define an entity's right to specific cultural property.[42] All that is left is the claim that the Scrolls are the common property of mankind. This option does not provide a reply to the question about which of the countries should play the role of the Scrolls' protector. Her approach obviously favours countries that have economic or political power, that is, the countries

40. 'Scholars seeking access to unpublished information should not expect to receive interpretive information if that is also unpublished and in progress', *Code of Ethics. Archaeological Institute of America*. Chapter III Responsibilities to Colleagues. Principle 5. *International Journal of Cultural Property* 7 (1998), p. 193.

41. 'Some Scrolls were found in Israeli-controlled areas, others were ultimately sold to the Government of Israel, and some came to Israel as spoils of war', Carson, 'Raiders of the Lost Scrolls', p. 309.

42. 'Geographic, political, ethnic, or linguistic boundaries are not necessarily the best indicator of who should have the right to cultural property, however', Carson, 'Raiders of the Lost Scrolls', p. 313.

which can take the liberty of purchasing or 'conquering' cultural property.[43]

If one tries to take a position on the issue, it is necessary to make clear that the relationship between cultural property and a specific nation or state is difficult to define. This difficulty, in turn, means that in regard to the many arguments raised by the issue, it is also difficult to come to a decisive legal conclusion, particularly so far as the property right is concerned. Various proposals have been put forward. Some opt for far-reaching legal effects, or for rating cultural property as a world or national heritage; or, ignoring this line of approach, some propose that the property come under some special, *sui generis*, legal regime.[44] The first proposal assumes miscellaneous methods of subordinating cultural property to a general category, namely, the common heritage of mankind. For instance, cultural property that for some nations is its most important and representative could form a collection, which could then be made available for exhibition in museums all over the world.[45] None of the museums would acquire any rights to the displayed objects beyond those of borrowers. This concept leads to the recognition that there can be an 'international cultural heritage'. It would be a new type of property and would belong to the international community. Technically, UNESCO, for example, could administer it.[46] Although the idea of mankind's common heritage has found practical

43. 'When the Scrolls belong to all of humanity rather than to one government, it also becomes more difficult to determine which government should act as their steward... Obviously, this approach favors politically or economically powerful nations that are in a position to acquire cultural property through commerce or conquest', Carson, 'Raiders of the Lost Scrolls', p. 314.

44. See also further proposals suggested for the US, P. Gerstenblith, 'Identity and Cultural Property: The Protection of Cultural Property in the United States', *Boston University Law Review* 75 (1995), p. 671. The author suggests that in the USA 'cultural policies be reorientated so as to provide uniformity of treatment for all cultural property within this nation with the primary purpose of returning control over cultural property to the cultural group that produced the property' (p. 671).

45. S.A. Williams, *The International and National Protection of Movable Cultural Property: A Comparative Study* (Dobbs Ferry: Oceana, 1978), p. 202.

46. The adoption of such a version of the concept of the 'common heritage of mankind' could 'justify the establishment of a concrete *international* cultural heritage, a new sort of property, owned by the international community as such, administered by an international agency (e.g. UNESCO) and made available to all persons for them to enjoy', Williams, *International and National Protection*, pp. 201-202.

application in the law of the sea,[47] and to some extent is put into practice,[48] it is still far from being recognized within the category of property rights. The concept of giving priority to a national cultural heritage presupposes that every effort will be focused on the protection of the integrity of the cultural property,[49] the main criterion which makes its identification possible being the territorial links of its components.[50] It is assumed that the law of each country provides standards which entitle it to keep cultural property within its boundaries; a correlate being a claim for return of property removed without a proper permit. Such protection is primarily concentrated on export control. The property issue is not as important as the guarantee that the specific objects remain in the territory of a given country.[51] As to the nature of

47. See *United Nations. The Law of the Sea* (New York, 1983).

48. See *Convention Concerning the Protection of the World Cultural and Natural Heritage, 16 November 1972, International Legal Materials* (1972), XI, pp. 1358-66. For underwater cultural heritage as the common heritage of mankind, see, in particular, A. Strati, 'Deep Seabed Cultural Property and the Common Heritage of Mankind', *International and Comparative Law Quarterly* 40 (1991), pp. 859-94; also A. Strati, *The Protection of the Underwater Cultural Heritage: An Emerging Objective of the Contemporary Law of the Sea* (The Hague: Martinus Nijhoff, 1995), pp. 11-12.

49. This concept was already discussed before World War Two; see, e.g., Ch. De Visscher, 'La protection internationale des objets d'art et des monuments historiques', *Revue de Droit International et de Législation Comparée* 16.1 (1935), pp. 32-74 and 16.2 (1935), pp. 246-88.

50. This issue is widely discussed by L. L. Engstler, *Die territoriale Bindung von Kulturgütern im Rahmen des Völkerrechts* (Cologne: C. Heymann, 1964). The author assumes that the principle of the integrity of the national artistic and historic heritage (Integrität des nationalen Kunst und historischen Erbes) is accomplished by the principles of inalienability (Unantastbarkeit) and non-transferability (Unantziehbarkeit) of works of art and archaeological objects representative of a given country's cultural heritage. Cultural heritage defined in this way is also subject to reconstitution (Rekonstitution) after cession of a territory or dissolution of multinational states. See, in particular, Engstler's summary, pp. 279-81.

51. See, in particular, Art. 5 of the *Unidroit Convention on Stolen and Illegally Exported Cultural Objects*, which is discussed in this context by L.V. Prott, *Commentary on the Unidroit Convention on Stolen or Illegally Exported Cultural Objects* (Leicester: Institute of Art and Law, 1997), pp. 52-62. This principle is also adopted in the EU Law concerning the control of the export of cultural property, see Council Regulation (EEC) No. 3911/92 of 9 December 1992 on the Export of Cultural Goods, *Official Journal of the European Communities* No. L 395/1, 31. 12. 92, and Council Directive 93/7/EEC of 15 March 1993 on the Return of Cultural

the law protecting cultural heritage, more and more authors tend to regard it as a new category of property that is subject to the specific law of cultural property.[52] They see a limited possibility for the application of the law of property as traditionally comprehended,[53] because the element that entitles the holder to destroy the property does not apply where mankind is obliged to protect its cultural heritage for succeeding generations.[54]

The above discussion highlights the complexity of the task of regulating ownership of cultural property. Regardless of how debatable the concepts may be, one cannot lose sight of the fact that some elements of them already constitute international standards, and, therefore, are of invaluable assistance in the search for the answer to the issue at hand. Let us bear them in mind while looking at the problem of who owns the Scrolls.

The issue demonstrates the difficulties described above. The Scrolls were found on territory having a legal status that in its early and recent history was extremely complex. The current Israeli and Palestinian negotiations show no end to the history and no sign of reasonable stability. The complexity shows up when it comes to the status of law in regard to cultural property and archaeological finds. The problem is aggravated by the lack of complete information relevant to the issue. When the Scrolls were discovered, the area was British mandatory territory, and an Antiquities Ordinance applied that had been in

Objects Unlawfully Removed from the Territory of a Member State, *Official Journal of the European Communities* No. L 74/74, 27. 3. 93.

52. See, e.g., R. Crewdson, 'Cultural Property: A Fourth Estate?', *Law Society's Gazette* 81 (1984), pp. 126-29, and also S. Rodota, 'The Art Trade. Report of the Committee on Culture and Education and Related Documents', *Council of Europe. Parliamentary Assembly*, Doc. 5834-E (Strasbourg: Council of Europe, 1988), p. 8.

53. See, e.g., L.V. Prott and P.J. O'Keefe, '"Cultural Heritage" or "Cultural Property?"', *International Journal of Cultural Property* 1 (1992), pp. 307-20. W. Kowalski also examined this problem in his presentation at the Conference, 'Cultural Tensions: The Case of Museums', University of Edinburgh, 12–13 September 1997, see the Conference's report, Tim Schadla-Hall, *Art, Antiquity and Law* 3 (1998), pp. 101-102.

54. 'The present generations have the responsibility to identify, protect and safeguard the tangible and intangible cultural heritage and to transmit this common heritage to future generations', Art. 7, *Declaration on the Responsibilities of the Present Generations Towards Future Generations. UNESCO. Records of the General Conference*, 29th Session, 1997, *Resolutions* (Paris, 1998), I, p. 69.

existence since 1929 (there were also executive acts in 1930 and 1933).[55] Those who write about the finds at Qumran do not provide us with the exact content of those regulations. All that we know entitles us to assume that archaeological finds, and hence the Scrolls, had to be reported to the Department of Antiquities, and that it was forbidden to export the finds abroad.[56] Carson gives a more pointed interpretation. She states, 'Under the laws of the British mandate in Palestine, private ownership of the Scrolls would have been prohibited'.[57] Having only this limited information, it is rather difficult to determine the legal status of the Scrolls after they were found. It is hard to define the legal effects of the transactions that then took place. They could be invalid from the very beginning, which would bring into doubt the legality of subsequent sales. In every case, however, the Scrolls eventually ended up in public collections, usually located in Israel, that is, in the area of their discovery. Are they lawfully there now despite this uncertain background? Lack of information makes it impossible to judge the case on national law grounds, but we can at least evaluate it in the light of the standards of international law.

It seems that in this context decisive importance attaches to the storage of the Scrolls in the country where they were found, despite discovery taking place before the formation of the State of Israel. Should a territory become part of another country, two factors come into play: the general principle of defining the components of a national cultural heritage, and the rules regulating the status of cultural

55. Prott and O'Keefe, *Law and the Cultural Heritage*, p. 49. New regulations were issued by Israel only in 1978.

56. According to E. Wilson, when the Syrian Metropolitan showed the Scrolls to Dr Trever for the first time, he 'explained to him that the antiquity laws of Palestine required that all such discoveries should immediately be reported'. The Metropolitan assured Dr Trever and other scholars in the American School of Oriental Research, 'that in future he would scrupulously co-operate with the Department of Antiquities and the School'. In another part of his book, Wilson writes that 'an outcry had been raised by the Department of Antiquities of Jordan, whose director is the British Harding, that the Metropolitan Samuel had had no right to take the Scrolls out of the country, and that Americans had no right to publish them and had connived with the Metropolitan in committing an illegal act. It was intimated that steps would be taken if he ever came back to Jerusalem'. E. Wilson, *The Dead Sea Scrolls: 1947–49* (Glasgow: Collins, 1985), pp. 18 and 113 respectively.

57. Carson, 'Raiders of the Lost Scrolls'. p. 302.

property. In regard to the former, we ought to invoke the UNESCO Convention on the Means of Prohibiting and Preventing the Illicit Import, Export and Transfer of Ownership of Cultural Property.[58] Article 4 of this Convention states that the national cultural heritage of each country embraces the finds discovered on its territory.[59] Prott and O'Keefe add that this regulation also means that this concept of heritage includes the objects created by extinct cultures, or cultures not or no longer residing in the territory in question.[60] Bearing in mind the Convention text, we can assert that when contentious issues arise in connection with archaeological discoveries, and hence the Scrolls, the decisive factor for national status should be the territorial link. Similarly, the same link is definitive also for the issue of what constitutes cultural property. The question is: what happens to cultural property when the territory where it has been found changes status? The rules enabling an evaluation of the situation I present elsewhere,[61] but I will cite my conclusions here.

The treaties and methods used by countries in at least the past century and a half teach us that, both in the matter of ceding territory and in that of the break-up of multinational states, the dominant element in deciding the status of movable cultural property is the principle of the territorial link. The criterion of a given country's closeness to *patrimoine intellectuel* comes second.[62] I must underline that the

58. *Conventions on the Means of Prohibiting and Preventing the Illicit Import, Export and Transfer of Ownership of Cultural Property* (Paris, 14 November 1970), *International Legal Materials*, 10 (1971), p. 289.

59. Art. 4. '...property which belongs to the following categories forms a part of the cultural heritage of each State... (b) cultural property found within the national territory.'

60. 'The national cultural heritage also includes cultural property found within the national territory (this would cover, e.g., archaeological remains of neighbouring or extinct cultural groups found within a territory now belonging to a different cultural group)', see Prott and O'Keefe, *Law and the Cultural Heritage*, p. 737.

61. W. Kowalski, 'Repatriacja dóbr kultury w sytuacji cesji terytorialnej i rozpadu państw wielonarodowych' (Repatriation of Cultural Property after Cession of Territory or Dissolution of Multinational States), Polska Fundacja Spraw Międzynarodowych. Studia i Materiały, Vol. 16 (Warsaw, 1998). This article also appeared in Russian in *Restytucyja kulturnych kasztounascjej* (Minsk: Nacjanalny; Nawukowa-aswetny Cemtrumja Franciska Skaryny, 1997), pp. 21-52 An English edition is in preparation.

62. The term *patrimoine intellectuel*, which refers to cultural heritage, was for

standard applies only to situations where, because of the lack of confirmed information, it is impossible to define the place of origin of specific objects; in other words, when the determination of the territorial link is practically impossible. In general, then, we can state that the cultural property connected with, and usually present in, the seized territory, belongs to the current sovereign power.[63] It is the contemporary internationally recognized custom which, besides treaty practice, is also supported by the solution accepted in the Vienna Convention on the Succession of States in Respect of State Property, Archives and Debts 1983.[64] If we put aside the issue of archives, the Convention is not directly applied to cultural property. Rather, it states that moveable cultural property is granted to the succession country in accordance with the principle of territorial link.[65]

If we do not wish to elaborate on the question of the ownership of the Scrolls beyond the issue as it presents itself now, it is enough to say

the first time used in this context in Art. 177 of the Peace Treaty with Hungary of 1920. See *Traité de paix entre les Puissances Alliées et Associées, et la Hongrie, signé au Trianon le 4 juin 1920. Societé des nations. Recueil des Traités* (1920), No. 10. For more details on this issue, see Kowalski, 'Repatriacja', pp. 30-31.

63. Consequently, such a state can also claim those elements of its heritage that were removed from its territory before another state seized it. The most appropriate term to be used in this context is 'repatriation', which should be kept separate from other terms such as 'return', or 'restitution' as well as from 'repatriation' when used to describe another situation. See W. Kowalski, *Liquidation of the Effects of World War II in the Area of Culture* (Warsaw: Institute of Culture, 1994), p. 13; Engstler, *Die territoriale Bindung*, pp. 279-82, W. Kowalski, *Art Treasures and War. A Study on the Restitution of Looted Cultural Property, Pursuant to Public International Law* (London: Institute of Art and Law, 1998), pp. 1-2. Compare also L.V. Prott's distinction between claims for repatriation of cultural property advanced by the original inhabitants of a territory, which are subject to national laws, and internationally advanced restitution claims, which are subject to international public law. See his 'Restitution of Cultural Property', *University of British Columbia Law Review* 29 (1995), Special Issue, p. 45. On such 'internal repatriation', see further, 'Symposium: The Native American Graves Protection and Repatriation Act of 1990 and State Repatriation related Legislation', *Arizona State Law Journal* 24 (1992), pp. 229-40.

64. *Vienna Convention on Succession of States in Respect of State Property, Archives and Debts, U.N. Doc. A/Conf. 117/14* (7 April 1983).

65. See Art. 14 (2b), Art. 15 (1d), Art. 17 (1b) and Art. 18 (1c). For more details on the Convention, see Kowalski, 'Repatriacja', p. 34.

that in assessing their situation the general guideline should also be that of the territorial link to the place where the object was found. Nothing seems to stand in the way of claimimg that the Scrolls have been taken over together with the territory, in agreement with the above principle of Succession[66]—all the more true because this principle of the territorial link is easy to establish with archaeological material. We do not need to consider other criteria, which, in the case of biblical texts, are truly difficult to apply, as Carson has demonstrated.

I put forward my suggestion despite the fact that I am fully aware of the extreme complexity of the political situation in the area where the scrolls have been found, and that the circumstances are not easy to judge by standards of international law. That is why I expect counter-arguments, backed by different assessments of the facts connected with the turbulent modern history of the area. My aim is to present a general perspective that, using internationally accepted standards, can aid us in assessing the present position of the Scrolls. It is worth mentioning that this perspective is useful and topical because, despite the complicated political circumstances, the principle of the territorial link has been accepted in practice in the area in question. It is also pertinent to note that Israel has obliged itself to return to Egypt all the archaeological finds excavated at Sinai in keeping with the resolutions of the 1979 Camp David Accord. Carson hints that in this particular case the legal basis was probably different.[67] However, both the basis and the rules mentioned above achieve the same goal in the same manner—they serve to protect a country's heritage on account of the principle of the territorial link.

In sum, the question about the ownership of the Scrolls can be answered as follows. Although it is problematical to say from the point of view of private law who the indisputable owner is, the fact that the Scrolls are currently stored in Israel is in full harmony with the international standards of the protection of cultural property.

66. We cannot, however, talk about 'succession' in the context of the spoils of war, as Carson suggests, 'Raiders of the Lost Scrolls', p. 309, because it is generally accepted that removing cultural property as spoils of war is forbidden, at least, since 1815. See Kowalski, *Art Treasures and War*.

67. Carson, 'Raiders of the Lost Scrolls', p. 312.

3. *Copyright on Scientific Study, Reconstruction and Editions of Texts*

The most disputed issue about the Scrolls has arisen in connection with copyright laws concerning the reconstruction of texts that survive only in a fragmentary state. It was the publication of such a reconstructed text that led to the lawsuit in Jerusalem in 1992. At present, among all the questions that have been subjected to analysis, the one about the rights relating to reconstruction is the 'hottest' one. The reconstruction of a text is necessarily preceded by activities that contribute to its scientific study. Let us look closely at the work conducted on the Scrolls in the stages prior to their publication.

According to the information available, some of the Scrolls were in surprisingly good condition when discovered, despite having lain in caves for over 2000 years. This statement does not apply to all the Scrolls, but only to those that were found in jars, exactly as they had been left. These were fully legible and ready for immediate sale. When they were finally handed over to scholars, the latter could not at first believe that they were authentic. But the majority of the documents were found in dust and their overall condition, usually in very small pieces, was appalling. This bad state of preservation could be attributed to the time when, with Roman troops approaching, they were hastily hidden. The condition of the texts was later greatly affected by the fact that they were dug out by non-professionals who, acting hurriedly, sought to be ahead of the archaeologists. To illustrate: in the fourth cave, that is, the famous 'library', some 40,000 fragments of over a hundred biblical, and more than 300 non-biblical manuscripts, were found during seven days of excavation in 1952.[68] These are the remnants that have been exclusively studied by the research team for over half a century. One of these remnants was the text marked 4QMMT, the subject of the current lawsuit. Because of the complex nature of the reconstruction of its fragments, I shall pay special attention to them.

The first operation that took place after the texts had entered the Palestinian Archaeological Museum was undoubtedly the attempt to fit

68. J.C. Trever, *The Dead Sea Scrolls. A Personal Account* (Grand Rapids, MI: Eerdmans, 1977). See also, e.g., J.-D. Barthélemy, 'Le long sommeil des textes de Qumrân', *Bulletin de la Société Suisse d'Etudes Juives. Supplément de Judaica* 2–3 (1994), p. 7.

together as many fragments as possible. The character of the work is well described by E. Wilson:

> The tens of thousands of fragments—there has been no attempt to count them—have been put away in boxes. The utmost pains, of course, have been taken to keep separate the contents of the different caves and the pieces found in groups together. These range in size from morsels as large as your hand, which may include a whole column, to crumbs with a single letter. Some believe that it will take fifty years to sort them all out and decipher them, but the energetic de Vaux is more hopeful and thinks they may get through it in ten. The fragments selected for study are set out on long tables in a large white-walled room. They are mostly of leather but few are papyrus. In colour, they range from the darkest brown to an almost paper-like paleness, so they give the impression of autumn leaves that have lain in the forest all winter. The ones that are being studied have been flattened under plates of glass; but before they can be thus smoothed out, they have to be rendered less brittle by being put into a 'humidifier', a bell-glass containing moist sponges. When they are taken out of this, they are cleaned with a camel's hairbrush, dipped in alcohol or castor oil. Sometimes the ink comes off along with the marly clay of the caves. Sometimes they flake at the touch of the brush and have to be backed with tape. Sometimes they have turned quite black, in which case they are photographed with infra-red rays and examined through a magnifying glass. The first problem is to bring together—through a study of the various hands of the scribes and the substances on which they have been written—the pieces that belong together. The scholars work on this in a small inner room, equipped with concordances, dictionaries and all the relevant texts. The concordance may place a fragment as coming from a Biblical book or known non-canonical work, and others may be found to fit it.[69]

When this job was finished, a strictly scientific study could be undertaken. This operation consisted in reading through and translating manuscripts and, then, if it was at all possible, to reconstruct missing texts whose fragments were not found among the collected pieces of scrolls. The first two operations, i.e. reading and translating, should create a text consistent with the original and comprehensible to an expert. In the case of texts left over from ancient cultures, such a task is not effortless even if we deal with biblical texts and know them from other manuscripts. The Qumran texts are mainly copies that might not

69. Wilson, *Dead Sea Scrolls*, pp. 108-109.

have been entirely comprehensible to the scribes themselves. The method of copying would have made matters worse. As J.T. Milik explains:

> A book can be copied in two possible ways, from dictation or from a written exemplar before the scribe's eyes. Probably both methods were used at Qumran, as certain modes of spelling are more easily explained as errors of hearing or of pronunciation, others as slips of the eye. Perhaps, as was normal in Greek copying houses, several scribes were engaged in making copies, while one man read a scroll. Either by degrees, or more probably after completing the work, the scribe himself, or sometimes a corrector, checked the copy against its archetype. Additions or erroneous spellings were rarely erased; normally, dots were put above and below the wrong letters, and the corrections or additions were inserted above the line. In the case of a long addition, it overflows the line and runs vertically down the margin.[70]

The job, performed in the heat of the Judaean desert, was long-lasting and wearisome. Assuredly, despite corrections, many mistakes or small alterations of the copied text remained. Moreover, it is not always possible to read unambiguously such created texts because their difficulties go back to the Bible itself. In debatable instances, a careful translator has to adorn the footnotes with 'the possible interpretation of the text and the justification of the adopted form of its understanding'.[71]

A text could only undergo reconstruction if there was a sufficient amount of fragments available to make the operation possible, or if the sense of the text was known thanks to other copies that helped with its reliable completion. Obviously, there is no guarantee that a text reconstructed in this way will be totally consistent with the irretrievable original. The famous dispute over the reconstruction of the text known as 4Q285 furnishes a good example of the problem. Without going into too many details, which are extensively discussed by several authors, it is enough to point out how the controversial line 4 of the cited text is generally understood as '...and the prince of the congregation put [or:

70. J.T. Milik, *Ten Years of Discovery* (ET; Oxford: Blackwells, 1976), pp. 22-23.

71. S. Mędala in the introduction to W. Tyloch, *Rękopisy z Qumran nad Morzem Martwym (Manuscripts from Qumran at the Dead Sea)* (Warsaw: Kiw, 1997), p. 6.

will put] him to death'; but R.H. Eisenman and Wise render this as: 'and they put to death the leader of the community'.[72]

The final action after the reconstruction of a text is to deliver it to a copy-editor who prepares it for printing. The copy-editor's work, however, is of a quite different and autonomous character, a publication process, not one that is connected with the scientific study of the text in question.

After the completion of the various stages of preparing a Qumran text for printing, the issue of copyright arises in regard to each stage of the preparation. It is unquestionably the case that those who carry out the preliminary task of joining together separate fragments are not entitled to such a right. If we bear in mind that Scrolls several metres long had to be reconstructed from a large number of elements,[73] we can agree that it was definitely a very onerous and complicated task that often required talent.

However, despite the great effort that goes into this job, the task does not meet the requirement of 'creativity of an individual character', which is necessary for recognizing a work as the subject of copyright in the European Continental tradition. The aim is not to create something new and original, but to reconstruct something already created, in this particular case the Scrolls with the inscribed texts. The criterion of creativity is in line with the definition of a work that is subject to protection in accordance with Polish law,[74] and is not very different from a similar requirement as defined in the legislation of other countries. American law, which rejected the 'sweat of the brow' doctrine in favour of clearly specified 'at least some minimal degree of creativity', now belongs here.[75] Despite the fact that combining pieces of the

72. See G. Vermes, T.H. Lim and R.P. Gordon, 'The Oxford Forum for Qumran Research: Seminar on the Rule of War (4Q285)', *JJS* 43 (1992), pp. 85-92.

73. 'The size of the scrolls varied greatly. The extremes ranged from 8 metres by 60 centimetres (1Q Isa) to tiny scrolls not higher than 8 centimetres (several examples of the latter come from Cave IV, but their fragmentary state rarely permits us to know their length') (Milik, *Ten Years of Discovery*, p. 23).

74. 'The subject matter of copyright is any expression of creative activity having individual character and manifested in any form, regardless of the value, intended purpose and manner of expression thereof (work)' (Art. 1 of the Law of 4 February 1994, on *Copyright and Neighboring Rights. Industrial Property and Copyright*, March 1995, Poland. Text 1-01, p. 1).

75. Carson, 'Raiders of the Lost Scrolls', p. 325.

Scrolls into integral units was without doubt a 'giant jigsaw puzzle',[76] Polish law would not afford protection to the results. But, as will be argued more fully below, the author of the work will have the protection afforded by the moral right of attribution.

The transcription of an ancient piece of work, which is usually written in a very difficult hand, assuredly requires great knowledge of such script and considerable effort in working with it; yet the exercise is still nothing other than 'copying' a text by means of other letters, most often from the manuscript into typescript or, more popular nowadays, on to a computer.[77] Rights might arise only if a transcription was of a text in a language no longer spoken and was into the same language in its modern form (e.g. Hebrew and Greek). The result of this kind of work is very similar to translation, although the whole operation is performed within the limits of the same language. It is definitely creative because the person doing the work has the opportunity to select modern words that, in their opinion, express the best approximation to what the author wrote many centuries ago. The knowledge itself is not enough to ensure the best choice; a talent that is necessary to keep the text within its genre must assist it. The contemporary version of such a work will be subject to legal protection because, 'Derivative works made from the work of another, in particular translations, transformations and adaptations, shall be protected by copyright without prejudice to the rights in the original work.'[78] As far as one can tell, however, this protection does not apply to the Qumran texts written in ancient Hebrew because they are comprehensible to people who have a good command of modern Hebrew.[79] The problem comes into being when the texts are written in Aramaic or ancient Greek, languages that have gone out of spoken use, or when all the texts are to be made available to readers from other language backgrounds. In the latter case, of course, we are dealing with a typical translation the protection of which as a derivative work is beyond doubt.

76. Fitzmyer, *Responses to 101 Questions*, p. 7.

77. *The Oxford English Dictionary* (Oxford: Clarendon Press, 1989), p. 392, defines the term 'transcribe' as 'To make a copy of (something) in writing: to copy out from an original; to write (a copy)', or 'To write out in other characters, to transliterate; to write out (a shorthand account) in ordinary long-hand'.

78. Art. 2 of the 1994 Polish Law.

79. As underlined by Carson, 'Raiders of the Lost Scrolls', p. 326.

The problem of evaluating the reconstruction of missing fragments of texts looks quite different. As far as legal categories are concerned, the issue does not differ very much from that of reconstructing a partly damaged painting, sculpture, or even a building. The legal status, therefore, of the reconstruction of Qumran texts is not very different from the operation of putting together pieces of the Scrolls so that they make up a whole text or larger fragment. As I have argued elsewhere,[80] the activity of a person restoring a painting consists in the reconstruction of a picture on the basis of the information available to him. If the result of reconstruction is a text that had not been preserved, or of fragments that become a text that fully corresponds to the original, what we are dealing with is a subsequent arrangement of the original work. Such reconstruction or restoration lacks the features of originality and individuality that are necessary for the text to be recognized as an original work of the person carrying out the reconstruction or restoration, and is, therefore, not protected by copyright. This assessment also applies to a copy that is a precise reconstruction of all the elements of an originally copied work.[81] Reconstruction differs from copying in that, conducting often very extensive research, the worker reconstructs a non-existent object, whereas a copyist works with the original. In both cases, arduous work and extensive knowledge are required, yet there is no scope for creativity. Let me repeat: in both cases the result must be a reconstructed piece and, although the work is a great advance in knowledge, from the point of view of copyright the process which produced it disqualifies it as an original work. Quite paradoxically, then, just as the author of an original work can be provided with legal protection, so the author of an unsuccessful reconstruction, whose proposed reconstruction is not correct and who, therefore, despite himself produced something new, inconsistent with the original, can obtain legal protection.

When it comes to the reconstruction of Qumran texts, therefore, we

80. W. Kowalski, 'Conservation of Works of Art under Polish Copyright Law', *Art, Antiquity and Law* 4 (1999), p. 126. See also J. Barta and R. Markiewicz, 'Urheberrechtliche Fragen der Restaurierung von Baudenkmälern', *GRUR* 11 (1986), pp. 705-16.

81. *The Oxford English Dictionary*, p. 915, defines 'copy' as 'A trancript or reproduction of an original. A writing transcribed from, and reproducing the contents of, another; a transcript', or 'Something made or formed, or regarded as made or formed, in imitation of something else; a reproduction, image, or imitation'.

cannot speak of the creation of new copyrightable work. The reconstructed texts are not originals as the result of creativity, but represent scholarly conclusions having their basis in the original text of the manuscript. The possibility that a given text can be reconstructed is determined by knowledge about its content, which, in turn, has been learned from other biblical texts on the same subject matter. Creativity is not involved. This interpretation is also supported by the fact that the task can be performed with the help of a computer. B.Z. Wacholder and M.G. Abegg have reconstructed the Hebrew and Aramaic texts from the fourth cave by means of a computer programme based on a concordance of biblical texts.[82] In order to reconstruct at least some texts that are known from other sources, it is not creativity that is required but an adequately programmed computer. That is why copyright protection of such textual reconstruction is out of the question. In line with what has already been mentioned, copyright protection is possible only in the case of an assertion that there is a discrepancy between the suggested reconstruction and the original. Because fragments of the Scrolls are missing, we do not know the original text. In the case of biblical texts, however, it is quite possible to determine how much a reconstruction conforms to the original because, as I have already said, the texts of the Scrolls are often transcripts of works known from other sources.

The above evaluation of reconstruction relates also to the contentious issue of copyright to the reconstruction of the missing parts of the texts known as 4QMMT. These have been published without the consent of the author of the reconstruction, E. Qimron. In light of the above analysis, the reconstructed fragments of this text do not constitute a work from a copyright viewpoint and thus cannot be protected by copyright. Such an evaluation of the reconstruction of 4QMMT comes not only from general assumptions about legal protection of a reconstruction but, in this particular case, also from Qimron's explanation about the character of his work when carrying out the reconstruction.[83] We have to agree that his effort did not consist in joining together the manuscript pieces in a machine-like manner. Although it is

82. B.Z. Wacholder and M.G. Abegg, *A Preliminary Edition of the Unpublished Dead Sea Scrolls: The Hebrew and Aramaic Texts from Cave Four* (4 vols.; Washington, DC: Biblical Archaeological Society, 1991), I.

83. Hershel Shanks, 'Qimron Defends His Lawsuit—"No Threat to Intellectual Freedom"', *BAR* (March/April 1993), pp. 68-71.

easy to notice that all six fragments at stake make up the same Scroll, to put them together involved extensive studies of Jewish law. Only on the basis of such studies, accompanied by long and arduous work, was reconstruction possible. As Qimron himself emphasized:

> Only on the basis of this research were we able to propose a reasonable reconstruction of the text. Sometimes it took us days of work simply to establish the most plausible placement of a single fragment, or even the most likely reading of a single word.

Further on in the same article, he made the point in this way:

> Establishing the text of MMT was in fact a scientific undertaking that demanded an intimate knowledge of the relevant ancient literature; it demanded paleographic, linguistic and other skills; and above all it demanded creative imagination and authorship.[84]

Qimron himself evaluates his work within the category of a scientific achievement, and it should be definitely regarded as such. For, certainly, only very few scholars in the world are capable of performing the task properly. Furthermore, it entails consultation with specialists representing other domains.[85] However, it is still reconstruction, that is, restoring texts to their previous form, and not a new and unique literary creation. Scientific study undoubtedly requires creative imagination, as stated by Qimron; however, its results are not a new work but a scientific conclusion based on what has already been created, itself the outcome of knowledge and imagination. Consequently, we need to add that Qimron will be entitled to the copyright only of those MMT reconstructed fragments that appear to be inconsistent with the original. In fact, Qimron himself agreed that such a probability should be seriously taken into account when he wrote:

> We hope that our version of MMT will be widely accepted, but we are far from claiming to have produced the only possible version of the text. Many points will inevitably, and legitimately, be the subject of controversy.

Spelling the matter out further, he finally stated:

84. See Shanks, 'Qimron Defends', p. 69.

85. 'There is only a very small number of scholars in the whole world who are capable of doing such original work properly. We consulted various experts concerning problems of reading, placing the fragments and restorations,' Shanks, 'Qimron Defends', p. 69.

> I can say it with assurance that if 100 thoroughly qualified editors were to edit MMT fragments, each one independently of the other 99, the result would be exactly 100 different versions of the text.[86]

These words, in fact, deny the correctness of the reconstruction, so that maybe reconstruction is not the point at all; but rather, as a matter of fact, the version of MMT proposed by Qimron should be protected by copyright.

As suggested above, however, the legal protection of moral rights would apply to the fact of the authorship of the reconstruction, at least within the confines of Polish law. This would be based upon the moral right of attribution. On the publication of the text of the reconstruction, the name of the author should be clearly mentioned. It is possible lawfully to publish two identically reconstructed works that are the results of the independent work of two restorers. As S. Grzybowski wrote with regard to invention, each of the restorers is entitled to the authorship of 'this', that is his own work, and not 'another', that is some other identical reconstruction by someone else.[87] Such reasoning would allow the publication of the texts reconstructed by Wacholder and Abegg, even if these were the same as the texts reconstructed by Qimron. Wacholder and Abegg's legal position is, however, weakened by the fact that they have seen Qimron's reconstruction and for them it is difficult 'to blot out the memory of that work'.[88]

In closing, I also wish to take a position on the issue of the possible rights related to an 'edition', that is the preparation of the texts for publication. As I said before, this task is of a distinct character and may be perceived as a work from the point of view of copyright. This is why all the editorial elements of the publication, such as introduction, comments, and division of content, will be protected. Those elements are of a creative character, reinforced by the fact that they do not directly interfere in the work to which they refer, but help to present the work to readers in a better way.[89] That explains why they do not include, for

86. See Shanks, 'Qimron Defends', p. 69.

87. S. Grzybowski *et al.*, *Zagadnienia prawa wynalazczego (Problems of the Law of Inventions)* (Warsaw: PWN, 1969), p. 68.

88. They tried in 1993 to get a declaratory judgment that their Scroll project would not infringe Qimron's copyright, Carson, 'Raiders of the Lost Scrolls', p. 308.

89. *The Oxford English Dictionary*, pp. 71-72, underlines that the word 'edit' means the work on the material created by somebody else other than the editor. It

example, reconstructions of the texts. It is possible, however, to perceive editorial work that is wider in scope—which seems to be quite common because of discussion about 'the edition' of Qumran texts—when authors have in mind all the tasks connected with the publication of the texts. In such a situation, the legal assessment of the editorial work will depend on the circumstances of a given case, that is, on the character of the activities that were undertaken in relation to the publication of a given text.

4. *Conclusions*

The problem of access to historical information is part of a broader issue of access to information as such which, depending on the character of the information, may be subject to far-reaching restrictions. Such restrictions are justified in the case of historical information that comes from archaeological materials. An international custom accepted in this area allows exclusive rights to the examination of the finds by the discoverers, but the term of this privilege or 'scientific rights' (or even property) is strictly defined. In the case of the preliminary study of the excavation results the period amounts to two years, and the time devoted to a complete study cannot exceed five to eight years. The biblical and other Scrolls found at Qumran surely belong to the category of archaeological finds and, so far as access to them is concerned, should not be treated any differently. They could be subject to exclusive study for some time but to extend that period to over 40 years is beyond comprehension and, therefore, constitutes an abuse of 'intellectual freedom'.

Because of the lack of sufficient information, it is impossible to determine the legal title to the Scrolls. Title is virtually unrealizable in the legal and private sphere, but we can say that the fact that the Scrolls are kept in Israel, that is, in the place where they have been found, is

says, 'To publish, give to the world (a literary work by an earlier author, previously existing in manuscript)', or 'To prepare, set in order for publication (literary material which is wholly or in part the work of others'. Consequently, the word 'editor' means 'One who prepares the literary work of another person, or number of persons for publication, by selecting, revising, and arranging the material'. It is also worth noting that the word 'editorialize' means: 'To write editorials; to make editorial comment; to introduce editorial comments or an editorial slant into a factual account, etc.'

consistent with international standards. This opinion is especially supported by the principle of the territorial link, which in the case of a territory's change of nationality determines the status of a cultural heritage and also provides the basis for including archaeological finds in the cultural heritage of a given country.

The reconstruction of Qumran texts that consists in restoring the fragments of non-existent manuscripts is not subject to copyright. Even though this task requires a great deal of knowledge and substantial effort, it is not the result of a creative act as understood by the law. Rather the task constitutes a scientific achievement to the extent that it determines the original version of the reconstructed text. The lack of copyright protection does not preclude the existence of a moral right of attribution, protecting the fact of the authorship of the reconstruction.

ASSAYING QIMRON'S ORIGINALITY

David Nimmer*

Copyright protection exists for original works of expression. What original expression did Elisha Qimron compose that warranted Judge Dorner's holding that he deserved copyright protection under the laws of the United States?[1] Insofar as his decipherment[2] of MMT succeeded, then plainly the expressive content was imbued into the composition by the Teacher of Righteousness (TR) rather than by Qimron. But the matter wants more examination. This brief excursion investigates that aspect of the multi-fold fascinations to arise out of *Qimron v. Shanks*.[3]

1. *Evaluating the Quantum of Originality*

What did Qimron do to reconstruct MMT? His contributions formed the basis for winning his copyright claim. Thus, to appreciate the core of his case against Shanks, careful attention must be paid to the originality that purportedly undergirds Qimron's acts of authorship.

* David Nimmer, Visiting Professor, UCLA School of Law; Of Counsel, Irell & Manella, Los Angeles, California; Distinguished Scholar, Berkeley Center of Law and Technology.

1. Although the Supreme Court's affirmance veered off into internal Israeli law, the focus here is on general principles, as elucidated by the copyright laws of the United States—the primary subject of Qimron's Complaint. See *Elisha Qimron v. Hershel Shanks and three others* (1993) 69 (iii) Pesakim shel Bete ha-mishpat ha Mehoziyim 10 (District Court of Jerusalem) (hereafter: 'Trial Opin.') at 21, §19 ('everyone agrees that the law of the place of infringement applies to the lawsuit, i.e. the laws of the US').

2. Throughout, its opinion, the Supreme Court refers to *ha-text ha-mephu'anach*, i.e. the 'Deciphered Text'. *Shanks et al. v. Qimron, CA* 2790/93, 2811/93, par. 1 *et seq*. (hereafter: 'App. Opin'.).

3. This chapter derives from a book-length treatment that the author as published concerning authorship and originality, David Nimmer, *Copyright In the Dead Sea Scrolls*, *Houston Law Review* 38 (2001), pp. 1-217.

a. *The Opinions*

In seeking to determine whether Qimron's work contains the requisite originality to qualify for copyright protection under US law, Judge Dorner acknowledges at the outset that if a particular work is a mere duplication of another work, the 'duplicator' is not entitled to copyright protection, no matter how much effort has been put into that work.[4] But Qimron is not a duplicator, she reasons, inasmuch as the original Scroll for MMT has never been fully recovered; the dozens of fragments found relate to more than one scroll; the majority of the fragments did not physically match; and almost half a scroll was still missing even after assembling the fragments.[5] Qimron needed to engage in research in philology and in *halakha* in order to fill in the missing parts, an effort on which he expended 11 years.[6]

These circumstances amply demonstrate that the task of restoration was complex. But Judge Dorner herself realizes that the amount of work put into copying an original work of art is irrelevant when it comes to the originality required to establish copyright protection.[7] Therefore, the sweat that Qimron produced to solve the jigsaw puzzle cannot serve as the basis for copyright protection.[8]

Paradoxically, Qimron's philological expertise and painstaking labor over the decades, if anything, diminish the scope of any copyright protection that he can urge. Consider that one inspired to compose a stream of consciousness ode based on glimpsing the scrolls undeniably obtains copyright protection for her work product.[9] The further that Qimron stands from the poet—the closer his painstaking research and

4. Trial Opin. at 23, end of §21.

5. Trial Opin. at 24, §22.

6. Trial Opin. at 15, §3.

7. Trial Opin. at 23, §22.

8. Judge Dorner specifically rejects protection for fitting together any pieces that physically 'matched'. Rather, her goal is to protect placing of pieces that were not physically connected and filling in lacunae. Trial Opin. at 24, §22 ('composition of the composite text on the basis of halakhic and linguistic research of the author').

9. See, e.g., *Burgess v. Chase-Riboud* (1991) 765 F. Supp. 233 (E.D. Pa.) (recognizing copyright protection for novel based on true historical figure of Thomas Jefferson's slave/concubine). Pristine ignorance of *halakha*, history, and every other scholarly discipline, and spending as little time as possible on the project stand our hypothetical poet at the far end of the spectrum from Qimron. Yet it is she who has engaged in the type of subjective act of authorship that finds protection under the copyright rubric.

analysis bring him to reconstructing TR's words—the less is his protection. At the limiting case in which he is exactly right, he manifestly can claim zero originality.[10] Accordingly, Judge Dorner's ruminations, rooted in an inchoate sense that hard and valuable labor deserves reward, incline in exactly the wrong direction from the copyright standpoint.

Indeed, her conclusion actually matches an earlier view of copyright law, exemplified by *Toksvig v. Bruce Publishing Co.*[11]

That case declared that a biography of Hans Christian Andersen, in which the author personally unearthed various facts and engaged in her own research in the original Danish sources, deserved protection against copying. *Toksvig* posed the question as 'not whether [the defendant] could have obtained the same information by going to the same sources, but rather did she go to the same sources and do her own independent research?'[12]

That requirement of 'independent research' has now been discarded by a unanimous Supreme Court:[13]

> It may seem unfair that much of the fruit of the compiler's labor may be used by others without compensation. As Justice Brennan has correctly observed, however, this is not 'some unforeseen byproduct of a statutory scheme'. It is, rather, 'the essence of copyright', and a constitutional requirement. The primary objective of copyright is not to reward the labor of authors, but '[t]o promote the Progress of Science and useful Arts'. To this end, copyright assures authors the right to their original expression, but encourages others to build freely upon the ideas and information conveyed by a work. This principle, known as the idea/expression or fact/expression dichotomy, applies to all works of authorship. As applied to a factual compilation, assuming the absence of original written expression, only the compiler's selection and arrangement may be protected; the raw facts may be copied at will. This result is

10. In my longer treatment of the case, cited in n. 2 above, I explore the paradox that Qimron's claim to copyright can cover only his errors in reconstruction, as opposed to his successes.

11. (1950) 181 Federal Reporter, Second Series 664 (7th Circuit).

12. *Ibid.* at 667.

13. Adverting to *Toksvig*'s subject-matter regarding the fables of Hans Christian Andersen, a certain treatise offers that '*Feist* has sung the swan song for *Toksvig*, a case that has been long derided in any event as a judicial ugly duckling' (Melville B. Nimmer & David Nimmer, *Nimmer on Copyright* §2.11[E] [2000]). The courts have subsequently joined that treatise in disavowing *Toksvig*. See *Nash v. CBS, Inc.* (1990) 899 Federal Reporter, Second Series 1537, 1542 (7th Circuit).

> neither unfair nor unfortunate. It is the means by which copyright advances the progress of science and art.[14]

But let us look more deeply into the particular circumstances that Judge Dorner adduced as a basis for finding Qimron to have engaged in authorship. Her opinion details two examples:

1. Strugnell believed that the sentences in some parts of the scroll are nine lines long, and therefore the fragments should be assembled lengthwise. By contrast, Qimron's research led him to conclude that the relevant sentence is 18 lines long, and therefore the fragments should be assembled widthwise. That conclusion changed dramatically the content of the recovered scroll.[15]
2. Another part of the scroll was constructed of six tiny fragments in a way that Qimron testified to be speculative. The whole meaning of the paragraph depended on the question whether a missing letter in the text of the word *'orot* was the Hebrew letter *aleph* as Strugnell supposed, so that the reconstructed word would mean 'lights', or whether the missing letter was the letter *ayin*, to reconstruct a Hebrew word that means '[animal] hides'.[16] Following research of the contemporary *halakha* regarding the purity of leather, Qimron concluded that the text should be assembled so that the word at stake would mean 'hides'.[17] The content of the text is far different from the meaning it would have held had the missing word been completed as 'lights'.

When the Supreme Court affirmed, it likewise relied solely on those two examples.[18]

14. *Feist Publications, Inc. v. Rural Tel. Serv. Co.* (1991) 499 United States Report 340, 349-50.

15. Trial Opin. at 24, §22.

16. Herein, the first plural will be translated 'lights', the second as 'hides'. Although the pronunciation is identical, the word with an *aleph* will be transliterated as *'orot*, the one with an *ayin* as *'orot* to signal the difference (but note that quotations remain unaltered, even though some fail to draw the distinction).

17. For a rough analogy to Qimron's task here, compare the emendation of Thomas Nashe's line from 'brightness fell from the air' to 'brightness fell from her hair'. See George Steiner, 'The Uncommon Reader', *No Passion Spent* 1, 7 (New Haven & London: Yale University Press, 1996).

18. App. Opin. par. 14.

Although likewise eschewing reliance on the 'sweat of the brow' doctrine,[19] the opinion's terminology is telling—it refers throughout to Qimron's reconstruction of MMT as the 'Deciphered Text'.[20] That language only highlights the objective nature of the task facing Qimron, and his absence of subjective expression.[21]

In any event, how do the two contributions cited by the courts lie within the realm of copyright? One who takes a work of non-representational art that has traditionally been exhibited lengthwise, and convincingly demonstrates that it is to be rehung widthwise, has not engaged in any copyrightable act of authorship.[22] It is hard to credit the first contribution differently. Moving to the second, it is impossible to maintain that a single letter[23] can a copyrightable composition make.[24]

But these considerations are not conclusive. Perhaps the trial judge simply cited insufficient examples of the evidence adduced to her, and

19. Introducing Judge Dorner's famous two examples, the appellate opinion comments as follows:

> Qimron's work was not, therefore, technical work, 'mechanical', like simple manual labor the results of which are known in advance. His 'inspiration', the 'added soul' that he gave to the Scroll fragments, that transfigured the fragments into a living text, were not only confined to the investment of human resources, like 'sweat', in the sense of 'the sweat of a man's brow'. These were the fruits of a process in which Qimron used his knowledge, expertise and imagination, exercised judgment and chose between different alternatives.

Ibid., par. 14. Earlier, the Court referenced ''inspiration' in the sense of *yitron haruach* [literally, 'advantage of the spirit'] according to one of the interpretations of the words in Malachi 2:15'. *Ibid.*, par. 10.

20. See n. 1.

21. These issues underlie much of *Copyright In the Dead Sea Scrolls*. See n. 3 App. Opin.

22. See *Lee v. A.R.T. Co.* (1997) 125 Federal Reporter, Third Series 580, 581 (7th Circuit).

23. Moreover, even the letter that Qimron changed in the text was not the product of his original authorship. The suggested letter was authored by TR, and recovered by Qimron.

24. Even a single word would not suffice, and a single line is dubious. Judge Frank suggested that copyright protection should be accorded only to extraordinarily fanciful lines, such as 'Euclid alone has looked on Beauty bare'. *Heim v. Universal Pictures Corp., Inc.* (1946) 154 Federal Reporter, Second Series 480 n. 8 (Second Circuit).

the appellate court had nothing further in the record on which to rely.[25] It is therefore necessary to look more broadly before drawing any conclusions as to Qimron's originality.

b. *Qimron's Own Explanation*

For this purpose, developments since trial afford an excellent vehicle to judge the nature of Qimron's contributions. Nine scholarly essays fill the book *Reading 4QMMT*. One of the contributions is by Qimron himself.[26] The philologist-plaintiff there details 'three passages that demonstrate the nature of the text and the way in which it was reconstructed'.[27] Given that the book is aimed at specialists rather than a general audience—and given that Qimron ends his own contribution by noting how he 'anxiously await[s] the critical judgment of my esteemed colleagues'[28]—this work furnishes the perfect vehicle to gauge the originality of Qimron's contributions.[29]

Qimron begins by claiming that his reconstruction of MMT 'probably constitutes 40 per cent of the composite text'.[30] (Strugnell, by contrast, estimates that 'we have about two-thirds, or it depends, between two-thirds and three-quarters of the whole theoretically existent text'.)[31] On several occasions, Qimron claims that reconstruction 'is no more than an educated guess on the basis of the scholar's knowledge and intuition'.[32] These claims, if credited, would seem to demonstrate

25. The latter proposition is dubious. For *DJD*, X was published in 1994, a half-dozen years before the Supreme Court ruled. Justice Türkel acknowledged that this post-trial book 'can shed light on the picture of matters before the Court'. App. Opin. par. 7.

26. See E. Qimron, 'The Nature of the Reconstructed Composite Text of 4QMMT', in J. Kampen and M.J. Bernstein (eds.), *Reading 4QMMT: New Perspectives on Qumran Law and History* (Atlanta: Scholars Press, 1996), pp. 9, 10-11.

27. See Qimron, 'Nature', p. 10.

28. See Qimron, 'Nature', p. 13.

29. Moreover, it can scarcely be contended that Qimron's views were edited against his interest. The editors single out Qimron for their special thanks. Kampen and Bernstein, *Reading 4QMMT*, xi.

30. See Qimron, 'Nature', p. 9

31. Transcript of Recorded Testimony of John Strugnell, taken at Boston, MA, 21 January 1993, made by order of Jerusalem District Court, 110-11 (hereafter: 'Strugnell Testimony'), at 190.

32. See Qimron, 'Nature', p. 9. By contrast, Sussmann, while conceding that there are 'quite a few lacunae', opines that 'the work itself—its aim, significance and the remnants of most of its paragraphs are quite clear' (*DJD*, X, p. 185).

original contributions. Yet it is interesting to juxtapose Qimron's own examples of reconstruction against that standard. Qimron offers three particulars.

As to the first, Qimron explains what he did with a fragment that read simply, 'it from one day to the following one'. He noticed the similarity of this fragment to materials found on another scroll.[33] Qimron suspected that these sources were explicating a biblical controversy arising out of Leviticus 7.15. That commandment contains the imperative of the verb 'to leave'. Qimron further notes as follows:

> Fortunately, I succeeded in finding the word *she-manichim* ('that they leave') on a tiny fragment containing parts of several letters that belong to lines 9 and 11. *These letters establish the placement of this fragment as certain.*[34]

Taking Qimron at his word, this example does not deserve copyright protection. Far from being subjective, an educated guess, a locution for which many variant expressions are possible, the placement is certain. There would appear to be nothing copyrightable here in that objective discovery.[35]

The second example comes from a different fragment of MMT. Qimron modestly notes, 'It was Menachem Kister who first suggested the present placement of this fragment'.[36] Though Strugnell and others disagreed with Kister, Qimron further notes that 'Bezalel Porten believes that papyrology in fact supports Kister's placement of this fragment'.[37] If credited, these circumstances could support a claim by Kister to copyright protection.[38] But they do not support Qimron's claim.

The final example that Qimron adduces is the very one that Judge Dorner adduced in her ruling. It comes from the most extensively

33. See Qimron, 'Nature', p. 10, referencing 11QT 20:12-13.

34. See Qimron, 'Nature', p. 10 (emphasis added; transliteration substituted in place of Hebrew characters).

35. See Title 17, United States Code §102(b) (no copyright for any discovery).

36. See Qimron, 'Nature', p. 12. Elsewhere, Qimron concedes that Kister suggested the order adopted for the entire composite text of MMT. *DJD*, X at p. 201.

37. See Qimron, 'Nature', p. 13.

38. Of course, a separate inquiry would need to unfold to determine whether Kister had an original idea; whether he clothed it in concrete terms; whether he set it down in a tangible medium of expression; and whether the balance of prerequisites for copyright protection are also present.

reconstructed area of the text.[39] Proceeding based on the homophone of the words 'hides' and 'lights',[40] Strugnell had suggested the reading 'lights'.[41] Qimron posited the alternative reading of 'hides'.[42] His methodology is worth quoting:

> I discovered that parts of the words *'orot* and *'or* ('hide' in the singular) are also found on several tiny fragments. I assume that this word must be the basis of some controversial law. The placement, then, of these tiny fragments in the composite text in the restoration of the missing portions was based on the controversial laws found in the Temple Scroll concerning the hides of ritually pure animals... The fact that the fragments which contain the word *'orot* were derived from two separate manuscripts of 4QMMT provides further confirmation for this suggested arrangement. Since this reconstruction is based on the Temple Scroll, it contributes very little which is new to our understanding of this actual law from Qumran.[43]

That passage could support diverse propositions—that Qimron is punctilious, that he is broad in his knowledge, that he is painstaking in his reconstruction, that he is loath to oversell the significance of the matter entrusted to his care. Yet it would seem equally to refute the claim that Qimron injected into this aspect of his reconstruction of MMT any subjective original expression of the sort that must underlie copyright protection.

But let us dig more deeply before drawing any final conclusions as to Qimron's inclusion of subjective elements in his reconstruction. To do so requires examination of the process of Hebrew manuscript reconstruction.

2. *Manuscript Reconstruction*

a. *In General*

Strugnell set forth the essence of the general exercise here:

> Q. For us laymen, could you describe for us the process of transcribing a fragment?

39. See Qimron, 'Nature', p. 11.
40. See Qimron, 'Nature'.
41. Strugnell was later a convert to Qimron's view. See Strugnell Testimony, p. 159.
42. See Qimron, 'Nature', p. 11.
43. See Qimron, 'Nature', pp. 11-12.

> A. Yes, well, the process is trying to give as rough a facsimile as you can on a piece of paper to a piece of leather, not copying the exact style of the script, the copy giving you a copy of what is said there, following the same shape exactly so you can then see what we need, two words to fit in that space and then things like this. * * * And the reconstruction must fit the material data. In other words, if the gap is that large, you must put in that number of words.
> Q. What are joins?
> A. Joins are when…what I talked about as the work of the jigsaw puzzle—When you fit together two fragments and you see the traces where the lameds [*lamed* is the Hebrew letter corresponding to Greek *lamda* and our 'L'] from the bottom one fit with the tops of lameds and so on. As I say, these are less, from my impression overall in the work at Qumran is that there are less, they're not so frequent as the long distance joins, but they're important, obviously.
> Q. In order to give us the proper terminology, what's the overall process called? I know it's of the transcription and the reconstruction and the joins. Is there a term for the overall process?
> A. I suppose it would be reconstruction. Transcription is part of it, but what I want is a reconstruction of the whole.
> Q. What's the object of the reconstruction process?
> A. Well, to recover a book that otherwise is hopelessly lost.
> Q. Well, how do you know if a reconstruction is a good reconstruction or a bad reconstruction, how does one objectively determine the success or the quality of the reconstruction?
> A. That's what you employ critics for. I could read you pages of A.E. Housman on the subject. Good scholars immediately recognize it, and bad scholars don't understand what's happening.[44]

Moreover, turning to MMT itself, Strugnell further elaborates on Qimron's task:

> Q. Imagine ten scholars and each scholar producing a different version even of a line or of a word. Is the version—is each of the ten versions a correct version?
> A. No, in general they're all dubious, some more dubious than the other.
> Q. How many correct versions—
> A. Oh, there's only one, I mean, the correct version is the one of the original composer of MMT, which we can't always get at, but in where we have manuscripts, we can get near to it. * * * It's the same problem as with classical, texts of classical antiquity, and the restoring of the original text of Aeschylus or Homer is a very tricky business, but still the consensus of scholars is that that is a correct reading, that is a correct

44. Strugnell Testimony pp. 95-97 (edited).

> emendation and the like. * * * That is what Qimron is trying to get at in his reconstructed text. He doesn't do it completely because there are large holes left in that text, but where we have any evidence, we can assess whether his reading or someone else's is likely to be either the original reading or near [it].[45]

Reconstructing text is always a delicate operation. Attempts to reconstruct Hebrew poses even more delicate considerations. 'The consonantal foundation of all Hebrew writing—numerous words grow out of a radical of three consonants—is crucial. It allows, indeed makes unavoidable, a polysemic plurality on richness of possible readings probably unmatched by any other written tongue. The same consonantal cluster can, with different vocalizations, be interpreted in wholly different senses'.[46] (As such, Hebrew stands in contrast to truly alphabetic scripts, such as Greek.)[47]

Already by the compilation of the Mishnah in the second century, the rabbis took advantage of Hebrew's 'polysemic plurality...of possible readings' to make homilectical points. An example comes in Exodus 32.16: 'And the tablets were the work of God and the writing was the writing of God engraved upon the tablets.' In tractate *Pirkei Avot* of the Mishnah, Rabbi Joshua Ben Levi explicates that verse: 'Do not read *charut* ('engraved') but rather *cheyrut* ('freedom'). For you are not free unless you engage in study of Torah'.[48]

When Qimron read an *ayin* rather than an *aleph*, what was he doing?

45. Strugnell Testimony at pp. 219-21 (edited).

46. 'A Preface to the Hebrew Bible', *No Passion Spent*, pp. 40, 57. See J. Faur, *Golden Doves With Silver Dots: Semiotics and Textuality in Rabbinic Tradition* (Bloomington: Indiana University Press, 1986), p. 121 ('It is hardly possible to conceive a more 'unreadable' text than one made exclusively of consonants!'). In an earlier age, mastery of Hebrew's polysemic plurality was viewed as a ticket to necromancy. E.L. Eisenstein, *The Printing Press as an Agent of Change* (Cambridge: Cambridge University Press, 1979), p. 277. The advent of the printing press promised access to the hidden secrets, encoded into the Hebrew text; piecemeal publication of works appeared part of a cosmic unfolding, as 'fragments [were] drawn from some vast Ur-book of Knowledge' (p. 279).

47. E.A. Havelock, *The Muse Learns To Write: Reflections On Orality And Literacy from Antiquity to the Present* (New Haven: Yale University Press, 1986), pp. 9, 91. Havelock throws out the intriguing suggestion that the difference stemmed from an ancient 'arms race' in a locale where Greek and Semitic languages co-existed, such as Cyprus or Crete (p. 85).

48. *Ethics of the Fathers* 6.2.

Was he trying to achieve alliteration, or to recall to the reader's mind an apropos biblical verse? Although those strategies would be valid from the quill of any author of a literary text,[49] they should form no part of Qimron's vocation—except in a derivative sense to be discussed in a moment. In other words, for Qimron to turn a phrase nicely to achieve a pleasing aesthetic effect would be for him to leave the realm of history, for which his visa was stamped,[50] and to enter the realm of literature, in which he is an illegal alien.[51]

Yet in a derivative sense, as just mentioned, Qimron could have chosen those tactics. This realm is limited to recapture of what TR desired. In other words, to the extent that Qimron's studies led him to conclude that TR habitually followed two words beginning with *ayin* with a third, then he could have posited the corresponding reading of *'orot* as 'hides' rather than 'lights', to the extent that it occurred following two other words initiated by an *ayin*. Likewise, to the extent that Qimron had learned that TR invariably quoted to the 54th chapter of Isaiah, then he could have brought that knowledge to bear in inserting a citation to that chapter into his reconstruction of MMT.[52]

But to the extent that Qimron inserted either of those hypothetical features into his reconstruction of MMT, it is vital to realize that Qimron was not acting as the author of a literary text. Instead, he was

49. One commentator invokes the 'creative contract...to synthesize information obtained from many sources into a fluid, coherent whole'. L. Stearns, 'Copy Wrong: Plagiarism, Process, Property, and the Law', *California Law Review* 80 (1992), pp. 513-53 (513, 546). Cf. R. Alter, *The Pleasures of Reading in an Ideological Age* (New York: Simon & Schuster, 1989), p. 33 ('strategic selection of vocabulary, shifts in level of diction, juggling of syntax, repetition, metaphorical substitution').

50. The Israel Antiquities Authority conveyed exclusive rights over MMT first to Strugnell, and later to Strugnell and Qimron. The *quid pro quo* for that arrangement was that the two scholars were to prepare a definitive text—not that they would be inspired to aesthetic creations by virtue of their proximity to the scrolls.

51. See C. Brooks, *The Well Wrought Urn* (New York: Reynal & Hitchcock, 1947), pp. 5-6.

52. Gauged by the number of manuscripts recovered, Isaiah was the most popular prophet at Qumran. See H. Shanks, *The Mystery and Meaning of the Dead Sea Scrolls* (New York: Random House, 1998), p. 161. In addition, Qumran yielded some of the most complete manuscripts for that particular book of the bible. Notwithstanding minor textual variants, nothing substantive emerges from the scrolls affecting meaning. See G. Vermes, *The Dead Sea Scrolls: Qumran in Perspective* (London: SCM Press, 1994), pp. 180-81.

acting akin to a psychiatrist who could unravel his patient's thought processes.[53] He no more deserves copyright protection for his insight into the psyche of another than does a shrink for reaching a successful diagnosis.[54] Indeed, to the extent that he succeeded, he simply recaptured words that TR had written millennia ago.[55]

b. *'Read Rather Thus'*

Consider an ancient precursor to the task of textual rectification. This example is probably the most celebrated occurrence[56] of a famous Hebrew locution, *al tikrei...elah*, 'Do not read [thus] but rather [so]!'

The first tractate of the Talmud ends with the following pericope: 'Said Rabbi Elazar in the name of Rabbi Chanina: Sages increase the peace of the world, as it is written "and all your children are learned of God and great is the peace of your children".' Do not read (*al tikrei)* "your children" but (*elah*) rather "your builders" '.[57]

To unpack Rabbi Chanina's insight requires a bit of Hebrew background. The verse cited is Isaiah 54.13. The word in that verse for 'your children' is *banayich*. By revocalizing it, that word becomes *bonayich*, which means 'your builders'. The question arises why the subject verse repeats the word 'children' instead of omitting it the second time and using a substitute ('and great is *their* peace'). Rabbi Chanina concludes that this repetition signifies an alternate reading for the repeated word, thereby deriving from the verse itself the lesson that our *children* are those who *build* our legacy after we are gone.

There are two ways to take Rabbi Chanina's enterprise: inventive or informative.

1. *Inventive*. Perhaps Rabbi Chanina woke up one morning with the juices flowing and wanted to share his original insight

53. Of two proposed reconstructions from an ancient manuscript, 'One of them always makes the better sense if you can get into the writer's mind, without prejudices'. T. Stoppard, *The Invention of Love* (London: Faber, 1997), p. 68.

54. For an elaboration of this point, see *Copyright In the Dead Sea Scrolls*, §III(D).

55. An individual can claim no copyright for the expression composed by another, absent an employment relationship or transfer, both of which are absent in the TR/Qimron relationship.

56. The passage about to be quoted forms part of the weekly Sabbath liturgy. See *Artscroll Prayer Book* (Brooklyn: Mesorah, 1988), p. 328.

57. *Babylonian Talmud Tractate Brachot*, p. 64a.

with posterity.[58] In that event, he was an author, in the copyright sense, of the insight that has come down to us in his name.

2. *Informative*. On the other hand, perhaps Rabbi Chanina wished to transmit a tradition he had heard from his master (and perchance he from his, in a great chain),[59] whereby the holy tongue of Hebrew[60] has encoded within it certain correspondences, the unraveling of which is essential to appreciating the full meaning of the text in Isaiah. Under this view, there is no copyright to Rabbi Chanina's insight. To the contrary, attached to it comes something that might be called 'copy obligation'.[61]

Normative Judaism posits that the sage was not then assuming the modern role of author or critic,[62] to show how clever he was.[63] Even setting aside what some might dismiss as mere folklore,[64] there is

58. The word 'inventive' is not used to conjure up the patent standard of novelty. It might be that others before Rabbi Chanina had already alighted on the same insight. It is enough for copyright that he came up with the insight from his own head, rather than copying it.

59. See Isaiah Horowitz, *Shnei Luchot Ha-Brit* (1649), quoted in 2 *Ha-Enzyclopedia Ha-Talmudit* (1947), 1, n. 7 ('it is passed down, from one person to another').

60. As recently as 1640, an inquisitor, refining the *Index of Prohibited Books*, considered 'vulgar' all tongues save Hebrew and a few select others. D. Julia, 'Reading and the Counter-Reformation', in G. Cavallo and R. Chartier (eds.), *A History of Reading in the West* (Polity Press, 1999), pp. 238, 244 (viz., Greek, Latin, Chaldean, Ethiopic, Persian, and Arabic).

61. D. Nimmer, 'Adams and Bits: Of Jewish Kings and Copyrights', *Southern California Law Review* 71.2 (1998), pp. 219-45 (219, 230-31).

62. He was not trying to change the Masoretic text. See *Artscroll Prayer Book*, n. 56 *supra*, at p. 329; Jacob Tzvi of Mecklenburg, *Ha-Ktav Veha-Qabbalah*, commenting on Exodus 12.17.

63. Epitomizing one view, Abraham Ibn Daud comments, 'Never did the sages…of the Mishnah teach anything, however trivial, of their own invention'. M. Halbertal, *People of the Book: Canon, Meaning and Authority* (Cambridge, MA: Harvard University Press, 1997), p. 55.

64. Strugnell lost his position with the Israel Antiquities Authority when he gave an interview to Ha'aretz, in which he pronounced:

> I think Judaism is a racist religion. Something very primitive. What bothers me about Judaism is the very existence of Jews as a group, as

concrete evidence to bolster that claim. The text itself quotes the insight to 'Rabbi Elazar in the name of Rabbi Chanina'. That internal evidence gives rise to an inference that we are dealing here with a chain of tradition,[65] rather than a lighting bolt.[66]

From the external standpoint, my original research (such as it is)[67] reveals an even more fascinating phenomenon. The Dead Sea Scrolls themselves, for the first time in history, allow us to go behind the *textus receptus* of the Bible handed down by the Masoretes almost a thousand years ago, to investigate whether Rabbi Chanina may indeed have been privy to a different recension of the holy text. The result is startling: the version of Isaiah 54.13 contained in the Dead Sea Scroll of St Marks Monastery[68] reads: 'And all your children are learned of God and great is the peace of your *builders*.'[69]

It would seem, therefore, that Rabbi Chanina was being informative—he is telling us about a variant text that he read. It should go without saying that one whose contribution is only to inform the world that he has read a textual variant cannot achieve any copyright pro-

> members of the Jewish religion... When I look at details in the Halakha, including sex, I think—that's amusing. It's not religion. These people act according to what I call folklore.

See W. Tuohy, 'Dead Sea Scrolls Editor Dismissed', *LA Times*, 3 January 1991.

65. Admittedly, the reference furnishes only one explicit link of that chain. But query why even mention the provenance from Rabbi Chanina to Rabbi Elazar if not to evoke that chain?

66. Some commentators view *midrash* as an exercise in 'creative philology', by which the ancient rabbis imposed their own meanings onto the biblical text. See I. Gruenwald, 'Midrash and the "Midrashic Condition": Preliminary Considerations', in M. Fishbane (ed.), *The Midrashic Imagination: Jewish Exegesis, Thought and History* (Albany: State University of New York Press, 1993), p. 9. But to accuse Qimron of 'creative philology' in that sense borders on the defamatory: '[T]he historian selects his facts, but to suggest that he had manipulated them to produce a more symmetrical structure would be grounds for libel.' See N. Frye, *Anatomy of Criticism: Four Essays* (Princeton: Princeton University Press, 1957), p. 75.

67. This 'research' consisted solely of pulling volumes down from my living room shelf.

68. *Biblia Hebraica Stuttgarttensia* (= *BHS*; Stuttgart: Deutsche Bibelstifung 1967–78) at XLVII (1QIsa[a]).

69. *BHS*, p. 761, n. 13a. Actually, the reading there is *bonayichi*, with an extraneous *yod* at the end of the word, as compared to how Rabbi Chanina is quoted in the Talmud.

tection in the process. As a result, Rabbi Chanina's insight stands outside copyright as being informative, not inventive.

At a higher level, my own 'original' work[70] in this field is but another example of a 'read rather thus'. In other words, the mere fact that I have unearthed a variant text does not confer a copyright on me to prevent future commentators from copying this insight, even in the context of Rabbi Chanina as quoted in the Talmud, juxtaposed against the Dead Sea Scrolls.

3. *Qimron's Reading*

We return now to the famous *aleph* that Qimron transposed to an *ayin*. What role does 'read rather thus' play here? First, it must be forthrightly acknowledged that Qimron was not overtly engaging in the same type of activity as occupied the rabbis who bequeathed *al tikrei* to posterity.[71] For Qimron was trying to reconstruct a previous writing, rather than attempting to make the type of homiletical point which largely concerns the sages of yore. But given that at least one aspect of *al tikrei*, as described above, inheres in preserving a tradition of textual variation, the tasks are not altogether dissimilar.[72]

Second, a preliminary question arises whether Qimron's reading was banal. As Strugnell commented, 'the transcriptions differ according to the difficulty of the manuscript. The reconstruction differs according to what part of the manuscript the wretched worm has eaten away. Sometimes it's very easy to postulate a missing reading, sometimes it's very

70. It reflects *original* research to the extent that I developed it on my own, rather than copying it from Frank Cross, James VanderKam, or any other scholar in the field. However, this is not to remotely imply that this particular insight is *novel*. In other words, among the 6000 items published in Dead Sea Scroll studies that I have not read, see *Mystery and Meaning*, p. 199, my guess is that the point is made, perhaps even often.

71. Qimron, insofar as I am aware, neither claims that 'hides' is a variant of 'lights' nor that the text that he is reconstructing means to preserve two simultaneous readings.

72. Dr Lim, although partially resisting my typology, concedes that *al tikrei* represents 'an exegetical/scribal method already found in double readings among the Qumran scrolls...indicative of the 'polysemic' or 'polyvalent' nature of the biblical texts [that some] would regard...as a technique of variant preservation'. E-mail from Timothy H. Lim to David Nimmer dated 22 September 2000.

difficult.'[73] Imagine that one comes upon a moth-eaten text that reads, 'Oh, say can you see, By * * * early light, What so * * * last gleaming' (the asterisks representing two large lacunae). If the first one had room for ten letters (including punctuation and spaces) and the second for 35 letters, then it would evince essentially no creativity to fill in the two with 'the dawn's' and 'proudly we hailed by the twilight's', respectively.[74] How do Qimron's efforts stack up against that hypothetical? We can assume for current purposes that at least some of his reconstructions were not so pedestrian.[75] Therefore, Qimron can be presumed to have vaulted the hurdle of banality.

With those preliminaries out of the way, it is time to turn to substance. Strugnell read *orot* as 'lights', but Qimron's substitution of a single letter transposed it into 'hides'. It is instructive to compare that transformation against a celebrated predecessor. Genesis 3.21 records that, after the expulsion of Adam and Eve from the Garden of Eden, 'the Lord God clothed [them] with garments of leather'. Of course, the final word of that verse, *or*, is spelled with an *ayin*. But a *midrash* from over 1500 years[76] ago recounts that in the Torah[77] of Rabbi Meir, the word *or* in Genesis 3.21 was spelled with an *aleph,* meaning that God clothed them with 'garments of light'.[78]

73. Strugnell Testimony, pp. 103-104. Later, he expressed himself more forcefully on the subject, 'It's a work which a halfwit could reconstruct', p. 176.

74. For the uninitiated, the hypothesized words form the lyrics to the U.S. national anthem. In parallel fashion: 'When you have something about Adonai El Moshe ['God to Moses'], that's what makes me think to put a *vayedaver* ['and he spoke'] there isn't that difficult'. Strugnell Testimony p. 104 (translations added).

75. In extended testimony, Strugnell opined that for manuscript reconstruction in general, and for MMT in particular, 'it is relatively easy to decipher, let's say ninety, eighty per cent, ninety per cent of a text of a given scroll, but the last ten per cent may take up a lot of work.' Nonetheless, as to the last ten per cent, 'it could have still taken a lot of time and a lot of work to make the necessary improvements, and these improvements could be very significant scientifically for the understanding of the scroll.' See Strugnell Testimony at pp. 155-56. That passage supports the notion that Qimron expended vast sweat of the brow. ('Yes, that's his reading.')

76. R. Alter, *The Art of Biblical Narrative* (London: Allen & Unwin, 1981), p. 11.

77. *Torato shel R. Meir* could refer to a Torah scroll. But the Mirkin Hebrew edition of *Bereshit Rabbah* suggests the interpretation that it refers simply to a collection of R. Meir's thoughts and interpretations of various verses.

78. 'And the Lord God made for Adam and his wife garments of skin (*'or*), and

Although great symbolism obviously attends Rabbi Meir's textual variant—indeed the very name 'Meir' derives from *'or*, and means 'one who enlightens'—that is not the focus here. Instead, what the *midrash* just quoted tells us is that, many centuries before Qimron, the 'light/ leather' homonym was established as a recognized form of textual variation. For Qimron to take Strugnell's 'hides' and to decipher it as 'lights', in short, is a form of reading, not inspiration.[79]

But, more basically, what Qimron did amounts to one species of 'read rather thus'.[80] We have previously noted that Rabbi Chanina cannot claim copyright protection by virtue of revealing the fact that he has seen a different version with a textual variant. Of course, Qimron likewise cannot claim copyright protection over the variants that he has seen by virtue of his unique access to the Qumran stash.

Qimron would attempt to differentiate his situation from that of Rabbi Chanina by pointing out that he did not actually see the text that he is positing. Instead, he applied his scholastic talents to posit a potential reconstruction, based on analogous matters that he discerned in the Temple Scroll, a wholly different document found in Qumran. On that basis, he concludes that he does indeed deserve copyright protection.

But that logic is flawed. Qimron himself admits that *'orot* (with an *ayin*) is 'found on several tiny fragments'[81] of MMT. Qimron, therefore

clothed them.' In R. Meir's Torah it was found written, 'garments of light' (*'or*). This refers to Adam's garments, which were like a torch [shedding radiance], broad at the bottom and narrow at the top.' *Bereshit Rabbah* 20.12 (Soncino edition English translation).

79. Qimron's co-author would seem to support this interpretation. For Strugnell himself volunteered that it is a 'reading' that is at issue here:

> Q. Let's assume that ten scholars were given the same manuscript and would have approximately the same knowledge in the necessary fields and each of them would sit separately in a different room. Is it possible that they would come up with the identical work?
> A. (Pause). They would come with the identical reading, yes, I think quite possible, you know, and there are only two letters that are difficult as far as I remember them.
> Strugnell Testimony, pp. 163-64.

80. *Bereshit Midrash Rabbah* does not present the lights/hide wordplay with that formula. But the claim here is that, functionally, it amounts to the same thing for copyright purposes.

81. See quotation n. 43.

actually did see the variant text upon which he posits copyright protection.[82] The additional feature that he brought to the table was to associate those isolated fragments with the same word appearing elsewhere. That correspondence allowed him to draw the inference that the same material belonged in the place under examination.

An inference is merely a way of 'seeing' something at a higher level. A witness who testifies to seeing something is recounting a fact.[83] A witness who infers something is also testifying to a fact,[84] albeit she subjects herself to cross-examination not only about her vision but also about her reasoning process.[85] A scholar who observes something cannot obtain copyright protection over his observations. A scholar who infers something is in the same category—he simply opens his conclusions to reinterpretation based not merely on the strength of his powers of observations, but of his inference as well.

In sum, it would seem that Qimron's entire copyright claim is premised on the faulty foundation that the textual variants that he indirectly observed entitles him to copyright protection. That conclusion cannot stand.

82. As to *'orot*, Qimron at one point claims, 'Only the top part of the letters has survived.' See Qimron, 'Nature', pp. 11-12. The Hebrew spelling of that word is *ayin-vav-resh-vav-tav*. One would therefore expect to see the top portions of five letters. Yet, as Dr Lim points out, 'the last vav and tav are clearly and wholly preserved and part of resh also. There is no sign of any tops of an ayin or [the first] vav. In other words the first two letters have been reconstructed from the readings of *other* fragments, despite the way that it has been described by Qimron.' E-mail from Timothy H. Lim (cf. n. 72, emphasis original).

83. 'I saw a man in a white coat walk past me.'

84. 'I saw a doctor walk past me.'

85. 'Why do you conclude that the man was a doctor?' 'Because we were at Ichilov Hospital at the time; my colleagues, Nurses Buzaglo and Smith, were addressing him as "Dr Rofeh"; he was ministering to a patient on a gurney; he was giving instructions to Nurses Buzaglo and Smith, about the necessary dosage to give that patient' and so on.

Part III

History of the Study of the Qumran Scrolls

THE ORIGINAL TEAM OF EDITORS

John Strugnell

As my contribution to your discussions, let me first give you in bare outlines the history of the first 35 years of the work of the group of editors who with me edited (and are still editing) the Qumran texts, noticing especially the changes in our project's legal status; this history illustrates nicely some of the problems being considered today. Next I will discuss, more briefly, questions of the degree of protection that the publication of our work enjoyed through copyright or through established scholarly usage, and whether *before publication* a similar protection should be afforded to our long drawn out editorial work and to our 'intellectual property'.

1. *The History of the Project*

Our editorial group had been brought together by the owners of a collection of fragmentary manuscripts, being invited by those owners to study and publish these fragments. Initially, the fragments had all been legally acquired through purchase or through excavation by Jordanian institutions, mainly by the Hashemite Government, represented by Gerald Lankester Harding, then the Director of its Department of Antiquities, and by the Palestine Archaeological Museum, which was at that time an international institution administered by a board of Trustees consisting of Harding (for the Government) and of representatives of the various nations with archaeological schools working in Jerusalem: one of these Trustees, Roland de Vaux, of the French School, had also been actively involved with Harding in the initial excavations and purchasing of the manuscripts. The Museum and the Department of Antiquities, since they did not have on their staffs experts in the study of such fragmentary manuscripts, from 1952 onward invited a group of scholars ('international and interdenominational', as we used to say regularly in those days) to publish these fragments; that group was to work independently but under the general administrative direction of Harding and de Vaux. These two also sought abroad further financing for the work of editing, for purchasing the remaining unpurchased fragments, and for subsidizing the expenses of the various editors over the long periods they would have to stay in Jerusalem.

These scholars were nominated to Harding and de Vaux by, and were subsidized by, the academic authorities of the countries represented among the Museum's trustees, e.g. the American Schools of Oriental Research, the British Academy and the French National Centre for Scientific Research; Mr John D. Rockefeller, Jr, the founder of the Museum, also contributed substantial funds to pay for the Museum's own share in the work (and for my salary as Epigraphist of the Museum). From the beginning onwards, the editorial team distributed its tasks somewhat informally and by 'gentlemen's agreements'; though there may have been some written documents at the start, I never saw them and nothing was specified about the duration of the undertaking or the number of scholars to be involved in it.

As more and more fragments came on the market, the Jordanian Government, realizing it was reaching the end of its financial resources, offered to make an exception to its own Antiquities Law, and proposed in 1954 that institutions in other countries also would be allowed to purchase a share of these fragments; they would, however, have to leave them in Jerusalem until the Jerusalem team had finished the work of editing them and the other fragments—at that point a proportionate number of the reconstructed manuscripts would be distributed and exported to each purchasing institution. As I observed, no target date for the completion of this work was then set or could yet be specified—we did not even know how many fragments were still 'out there', waiting to be bought. The initial Rockefeller funds had been given to support only some of the work of studying, and that for only six years, but as time went on and as our funds ran lower we recognized that work for several more years beyond then would be needed. By 1960, I estimated that had more funds been available then the whole project could have been finished within ten more years or so of intensive work.

The legal status of the manuscripts changed slowly from what it had been at the beginning. First, because of the growing nationalism in Jordan, in 1956 the Government refused to allow any more manuscripts (especially those of Cave 11) to be bought by foreign institutions on the former terms. Henceforth we would have to find universities or libraries who would be willing to purchase fragments not for themselves but for those Jordanian institutions who might legally own them (usually this meant the Government's Museum or the Palestine Museum); to sweeten such unattractive terms we could propose to such universities that they would have at least the right of nominating to the Jerusalem editorial team their own scholars to edit what their funds had bought. Shortly thereafter, the Hashimite Government nationalized and bought back all the fragments which the foreign institutions had previously bought; in those cases of which I have knowledge, a fair repayment was made to them, though sometimes purchasers of smaller lots simply returned their fragments as an outright gift to the Government. A third change in status occurred in 1966 when the Museum was itself nationalized, Scrolls and all. None of these three changes of status, however, affected the authority with which the editorial project continued working—as always, ultimately it depended on the Jordanian Government. Our team however maintained its self-governing status—it was still us and our Chief Editor who continued to invite new scholars into the editorial group; the Government held to its initial agreements and restricted others' access to the fragments until our editors had published them (a matter about which I will speak later) and the now nationalized Museum under its new direction continued to extend its services to us as before.

The nationalization of the Museum had, however, a major consequence; when, in the 1967 war, the Museum and the Old City were occupied by the Israeli army, it was not just occupied but soon after 'annexed' to the state of Israel. The Museum, no longer 'international', and its contents consequently became part of the Israeli government's property—at least in Israel's view, though not in that of most other countries, for what that is worth. At that time our chief editor, de Vaux, was guided by an officer of UNESCO who was trying to supervise the observation of the relevant UNESCO conventions, those of the Hague (with attached Regulations), of 14 May 1954, and perhaps those of New Delhi, of 5 December 1956, on the protection of cultural property in the event of armed conflict (both conventions already ratified by Israel). At that time, we were advised by that officer that those conventions seemed (somewhat broadly interpreted, perhaps) to protect our manuscripts from being absorbed into the archaeological possessions of Israel, and seemed also to guarantee the continuing rights of academic projects that had been established by the preceding authorities, e.g. such as those of our team of editors. (It must be confessed, as I look back over 30 years, that these conventions are now more often breached than observed; and in any case did they regulate the case of annexation, or only that of occupation?)

Looking back, it was probably not these conventions which preserved the autonomy and independence of our project as much as did the *protektsiya* of Yigael Yadin, our influential counterpart among Israeli experts on the Scrolls; it was essentially those attitudes concerning archaeology and academic rights that he shared with de Vaux and us that provided our real *protektsiya* and guaranteed the survival of our project. Between de Vaux, Yadin, and the Government's Director of Antiquities then, Avraham Biran, the pattern and outlines of the continuation of our work were agreed on (i.e. principally on the keeping of the Palestine Museum's manuscript collections in it, and physically separate from the Israeli collections, on the guarantee of our group's autonomy and on the maintenance of our exclusive rights to continue and to finish our project). When I came back to Jerusalem in 1968 to restart after the 1967 war the work on the fragments themselves, it was only further practical details (e.g. photography and other material and financial needs of the work on the project) that still had to be agreed on. Once again, as in the case of the changes of our status under the Jordanians, I find no written record of these agreements; I had them orally from de Vaux as he briefed me for my further but lowlier negotiations with the Israelis, especially with Mr. Broshi of the Shrine of the Book. Once again, 'gentlemen's agreements' were customary, and seem to have sufficed.

At the time of de Vaux's unexpected death in 1971, we had no precedents as to how to replace our Chief Editor. I remember well a day spent with Cross at Harvard as we made transatlantic phone calls to all of our colleagues, one after another, and discussed the situation; we all agreed that we should take the initiative, rely on our former autonomy, and ourselves nominate a new director. We wanted a chief editor who would be from our group, preferably a resident of Jerusalem, a man well seen by the Israelis as well as the Jordanians—and Pierre Benoit of the École Biblique alone fitted the bill. For this occasion Benoit's letters have survived, where he describes his negotiations with both the Israelis and the Jordanians. He sought ratification or confirmation from both authorities of our appointment of him as

'Editor-in-Chief'—even though practically, of course, only one of the parties had any real and physical control of the manuscripts. He insisted especially that it should be stated formally that his and the team's work should continue to be done autonomously and under the same agreed conditions 'as before'.

When, after Benoit had resigned on grounds of sickness, I was appointed by the other editors to be Benoit's replacement as Editor-in-Chief, there were protracted negotiations between 1984 and 1986, again with the Jordanians but especially with the Israelis, and the same formulae of ratification were accepted by the authorities, i.e., that the team's work should go on 'as before', that the team should continue autonomously to choose its members and appoint its Chief Editor (that appointment to be ratified, as before, by the authorities); little thus was changed from our early post-annexation agreements of 1967–68.

However, this generally agreeable collaboration began to turn more tense and more adversarial. Since Scroll questions were beyond the area of specialization of the Director of Antiquities, at my suggestion he set up an advisory committee of scholars, skilled both in publishing projects and in Qumran questions, so as to reassure him whether the work was proceeding sensibly and at a reasonable pace. Unfortunately, those scholars, originally conceived of as *advisors* to the Director, sought for themselves a wider scope, i.e. to become instead *supervisors* of the editorial team, and then to claim for themselves (and their students) the right to edit manuscripts—even though those manuscripts were already being edited by other editors from our team, and though editing such manuscripts was in many cases demonstrably beyond the abilities of the self-called supervisors; next they claimed (without precedent and certainly *ultra vires*) the right to control which new editors we could invite into our editorial group, a matter hitherto exclusively reserved to the editors and the Editor-in-Chief.

Many other conflicts were to follow, some ludicrous, others more grave. Ever more such pressures were being brought to bear, and even if the Antiquities Authority had not taken advantage of a long hospital stay of mine to dethrone me (and that, once more, was against our group's rules), I would probably have had myself to take the initiative and to resign because of the many infractions of the autonomous status that had hitherto been promised our group. Or do you detect the taste of sour grapes?

'Gentlemen's agreements', such as we had made beforehand and during the time when Yadin's influence prevailed, bind only loosely and that especially when you are dealing with Leviathan-like Governments for whom laws and agreements are but words and all too easy to overturn. Though our rights to edit the manuscripts had hitherto been guaranteed by all who could grant them (the excavators, the purchasers, the owners, the Palestine Archaeological Museum and the Jordanian governments)—rights presumably confirmed by the UNESCO conventions and accepted both by academic custom and by our post-annexation agreements with the 'new' owners, as negotiated with Yadin and the Israeli Department—all this could be cancelled as politics or popular pressures demanded.

Since I was not present at my own dethronement, I cannot report with any certainty which of these possible reasons it was which in fact led to that. Instead, it is Professor Tov's turn now to carry on the project and its story to the present—may he have had better luck with it than I did!

2. *Copyright and Other Protections for Our Work*

Next, you may ask, how did I and my colleagues (like many other scholars who have been involved in similar projects of reconstructing and commenting on ancient manuscripts or fragments) see the function of copyright in protecting our work four decades a-borning, and also in protecting our publisher's work; what other defences did we have?

First, what protection was there for our work *after publication?* Since the mid-1950s, almost all of the editions that were published by our group carried a formal statement that they had been copyrighted; this was true of all the books published for us in the 'Discoveries in the Judean Desert (DJD)' Series and copyrighted by the Clarendon Press in the United Kingdom (whose laws are presumably regulative for that Press): it was likewise true of the volumes we published with the Scholars Press, the American Schools of Oriental Research, etc. (in the more recent volumes of DJD 'moral rights' are also claimed for the authors). The same was also the practice with other editions of Qumran Scrolls which lay outside of the scope of our group's responsibility, e.g. those published and copyrighted by the Israel Exploration Society or by Brill. (In some cases a few of our books were instead copyrighted by their authors; this usually happened in order to protect a forthcoming larger edition of a preliminary edition; once, in the case of Elisha Qimron and

MMT, he did this because he was driven to use unusual formulae to defend his work from those who printed and sold it with impunity for their own profit before it had even been first published by Qimron himself.)

It is worth noticing also that with most other ancient works in Greek that have been newly discovered, whether they are completely preserved or only fragmentarily, the practice of other publishers and commentators is similar to ours in the DJD Series. In the major collections of well-preserved classical texts, e.g. the Oxford Classical Library, the Teubner Library, the Loeb Classical Library, the Collection Budé, etc., well-known ancient works, whether literary (e.g. Homer, Plautus) or documentary ones, are usually copyrighted by the publisher; that is also the custom both with editions of papyri of new works almost completely preserved but hitherto unknown (like the plays of Menander), and also with reconstructions of works only fragmentarily preserved on papyrus (e.g. the fragments of Sappho). In the case of a claim of copyright for editions of such (larger or smaller) works, copyright surely expresses no claim on behalf of the heirs of Menander (or of the Teacher of Righteousness), but one on behalf of the economic interests of the publisher or the editor. Such a claim could probably be made by the surviving bodily heirs of a once-copyrighted author of the nineteenth century, if another lost piece by him were recently rediscovered. But between the two extremes, between a lost Menander and a lost Charles Dickens, where do we draw the line?

What protection then does the law offer, by copyright or other devices, and for whom? As I look with my layman's eye at our group's experience with copyrights, it becomes clear that *after publishing* the act of copyrighting protects mainly the *publisher* and his considerable financial investment in the book (e.g. so that it should not be plagiarized and sales diminished). *To the scholar* the protection afforded him from similar plagiarizing *after* the publication of his book would be less important; thus for us the question of protecting our financial interest never arose—we editors never got any royalties—while if any other scholars should improve on our work, surely our interest was not in restricting others from reprinting our work, but in encouraging them to improve on it.

As for our rights guaranteeing the editors exclusive access to the fragments until we had published them—a guarantee often criticized—these rights originated with the initial owners and their successors,

Jordan and Israel; such rights were offered by them as an incentive they used in recruiting the scholarly manpower they wanted—they had no other lure to use to secure the services of mainly unpaid editors other than guaranteeing their rights to bring to a suitable end the work in which they were to invest so much time and effort. There were other reasons too for this restricted access. The manuscripts were only gradually being reconstructed, and early on were far from ready for publication. Again, in 1954–60, when our team was regularly in Jerusalem, other scholars who came to visit our work were mainly interested in the published Cave I and Cave IV manuscripts. Later on, in the period from 1960 to 1985, our editors were only infrequently present in Jerusalem, and as a practical matter there was usually no one around who would have been able to identify any manuscript and show it to others even if its editor had thought this appropriate.

As we look back over the passing years these restrictions seem heavy-handed, but the slow[1] and apparently secretive style of us editors had causes other than any desire of ours to sit Grendel-like on our hoard. The principal cause of delay was the penniless state of the project from 1960 to 1985 (but there were other causes too) while, as for 'restricted access', one should not exaggerate its totality or its novelty; a glance at other projects will show that our practice was not at all unparalleled.

Again, as a matter of fact, in 1954–67, as soon as we had published fragments they were put on exhibition at the Museum, and photographs of them could be purchased there. Furthermore, my colleagues were usually very generous, some by their character more so than others, in making available preliminary transcripts to serious scholars and in discussing these with them; 'restricted access' was hardly iron-clad.

But if such generosity is abused, how can the scholar protect himself? By rigorous restriction of access, or by avoiding in an exaggerated way any discussions with fellow scholars? By neither, I hope, but what other attitude can he adopt other than extreme prudence, or can the law give him any better protection? In general, it is within the

1. In the case of most manuscripts, and not just the Qumran ones, scholars are not so much interested in delaying publication (for what motive?) as in protecting their work from plagiarising or premature publication; but, however noble were our motives for delaying publication of our work, that delay itself may well explain why thieves were tempted to steal it—even if that does not justify the crime itself.

owners' right to enforce the arrangements they had made to ensure orderly publication of their unpublished matter, and they usually do so satisfactorily. Is it to the law, or is it not rather to the acceptable standards of behaviour among scholars, that we should instead look for an answer to Qimron's problem, and to similar questions posed more recently about intellectual rights over still unpublished work? I say 'acceptable standards' of behaviour among scholars; but the experience of our group has shown that this criterion is surely in need of much redefinition in these decadent days.

Before publication, then, the protection of an author's notes and thought from theft must be principally his own responsibility; the stages in his work of identification and reconstruction of the manuscripts were however in our case also recorded by the series of photographs made by the Museum's photographer, who from the beginning regularly stamped on the back of his prints 'Copyright of the Palestine Archaeological Museum'. The force of this claim to copyright was still recognized in our Israeli period by those organizations (e.g. the two Californian centres, and the Oxford Centre) which had been allowed by us to make copies of the Museum's negatives so that they might create 'safe archives', to prevent loss of the manuscripts by fire or the like. Alas, they were no longer observed by the Huntington Library after it inherited the Bechtel Archive, all unaware of the conditions, expressly accepted by Mrs Bechtel herself, under which we had helped her make her copies. Above all, they were not observed by the Eisenman–Robinson–Shanks gang, who published all of the Museum's photos they could procure—how, from whom, and with what right procured I do not know (but, ultimately, they derived from those negatives in the Museum). The authorities had hitherto guaranteed that any access to all the unpublished photographs that recorded our work should, like the fragments themselves, be reserved for us until publication, since they were the unpublished records of our work (preliminary and in progress), the continuing identification and reconstruction of the manuscripts being perhaps our most important intellectual achievement. (Note further that, with half of our manuscripts, a 'work' was an intellectual construct of its editor; it did not exist until the editor had identified the fragments by their handwriting, grouped them, and made the hypotheses and reconstructions that showed the nature of each work. For instance, only slowly did MMT, with many an identification of its fragments, with many a hypothesis and with notable intellectual efforts, grow into the work you now can read and on which we solicited other scholars' private comments to enrich the commentary in our first edition.)

After publication, then, the question of the effects of copyright mainly concerns our publishers;[2] the scholar is more concerned with the protection of their *unpublished* material and work from interference by others—and the scholar is principally responsible for supervising that; not all who volunteer confidential help are trustworthy.

There might, however, be another type of protection, if the meaning of 'fair use' in the case of ancient works could be defined. One might ask of a publisher who copyrights ancient works how much textual change would make a new printing of a play of Menander into a really new edition, one independent of the copyrighted first edition? Is it 'fair use' if a scholar just reprints an earlier edition, merely changing its punctuation, script or spelling? Surely an extensive and original commentary is a new work of scholarship, but where to draw the line between that and a reprint only superficially changed? But as for the scholars who *up to the time of publication* have fought tigerishly to protect their notes and photographs, should they not *thereafter* encourage others to a free and abundant *use* of their book and to improve upon their own early work? Is not that for scholars, in some way, the meaning of 'fair use'? Our publishers may well see things differently, but remember that long ago the functional equivalent of 'publish' was *publici juris facere* ('to make something to belong to the domain of public right').

3. *Of Hares and Tortoises*

The rights of our project having been thus explicitly guaranteed, can they or should they be taken away because of some alarm or other, because, for example, unconvincing accusations were made that we

2. It is only on the rights of the scholarly editor (or editors) after the first publication where I differ from Qimron. Where he has published a text and his commentary on it, does it not then, with all copyright and *droit moral*, become open to fair use and learned discussion of it by other scholars as they work on it accurately, properly, and with all credit duly given? Scholarly discussion does not require any further restraints. That, it would seem, is the practice of editors in other scholarly fields; but protection for a first edition is still essential. Once again the question is one of the definition of 'fair use'.

were unable, too slow, or too few to publish all of the manuscripts allotted to us—was not our project widely but wildly proclaimed the greatest academic scandal of the century?

Calmly reducing these complaints to a measurable size, it will be seen that our performance was in fact as speedy and as foresightfully planned as that of any comparable academic project. As for the *size* of our group, at the start of our work our numbers were not limited by the desire to have a closed circle of congenial *illuminati* but by the financial resources then available to us for inviting and supporting our co-editors, while in later years, as soon as the initial editors and the editor-in-chief had identified suitable new collaborators and secured new sources of finance, the editorial corps in fact grew very rapidly—and this process of enlargement has continued further under my successor as he has brought even more associate editors and funds into the group. As for the gargantuan bulk of the allotments of manuscripts for which each editor was responsible in the earliest days, this resulted necessarily from the nature of our work then, which was one of introducing order into a hodgepodge of fragments of what turned out at the end to be some 800 fragmentary manuscripts, and introducing that order primarily by means of separating out from the fragments those belonging to each manuscript contained there; this work required a smallish group of workers, where each editor would be well aware of the progress of each other's work, and above all would concentrate on each fragment's handwriting as it was identified and compared with those of other similar fragments or manuscripts.

As for our *speed* in publication, during the first 17 years of our work on the fragments (up to de Vaux's death in 1971), our group of scholars, starting with eight members and doubling to 17 (perhaps not so small a group after all), published 303 fragmentary Qumran manuscripts in four volumes of DJD; in the further years up to the end of my chief-editorship in 1990, the team was enlarged greatly by our incorporation of 30 more colleagues, these being not just 'men of Harvard', not just Americans, not indeed just men, but, *mirabile dictu*, women as well. Some seven further volumes (174 fragmentary manuscripts) were published in the 14 years of Benoit's chief-editorship, and seven more (containing 37 largish fragmentary manuscripts) during my own; the pace was quickening! Thus, in the 35 years up to 1990 we had published about one volume in every two years (and about 515 manuscripts of the total of 810 that had to be edited); furthermore many more editions of fragmentary ones were 'in the pipeline', ready or half-ready for the printer.[3]

As you can see, the average pace of the publication of our fragments compares very favourably with that of the collections of fragmentary Greek papyri from Egypt, collections in many ways comparable to ours—indeed their pace was often slower. If we limit ourselves to the larger Greco–Egyptian collections, the size of the allotments for which our various editors were responsible, the number of editors in our team, and the speed with which we published will all be found to be near the norms prevailing in Greek papyrology. Measuring again by volumes published per year (to do so by fragmentary manuscripts, by square centimetres, or by the length of commentary needed might perhaps be slightly more accurate, but would probably make little difference) and choosing our examples at random, and with no particular bias in our choice, we will find that, for example:

1. 67 volumes of Oxyrhynchus papyri were published in 100 years, i.e. 1 volume each 1.5 years.
2. 4 volumes of Rylands papyri were published in 40 years, i.e. one volume every 10 years.
3. Neglecting longer works on papyrus (works which were much quicker and easier to publish) 7 volumes of the smaller British Museum papyri were published in 83 years, i.e. one volume every 12 years.
4. 15 volumes of the Berlin papyri were published in 90 years, i.e. one volume every 6 years.
5. 3 volumes of the Tebtunis papyri were published in 36 years, i.e. one volume every 12 years.
6. 14 volumes of the papyri of the Italian Papyrological Society were published in 40 years, i.e. one volume every 3 years.
7. 17 volumes of the Michigan papyri were published in 65 years, i.e. one volume every 3.8 years.

3. These counts may surprise some of my fellow symposiasts; thus one of them has opined that by 1977, '24 years after the establishment of de Vaux's editorial team, its members (had) produced only two out of the planned thirty volumes.' Strange, for by my reckoning in that period there were published, according as one includes or not a few volumes *hors série*, not two but between ten and twelve volumes. Does this difference arise from some of our colleagues' ignorance of many of our publications or from biased and willful neglect of them? Or are they merely mathematically 'challenged', as the Americans might say?

8. 6 volumes of the Strassburg papyri were published in 70 years, i.e. one volume every 12 years.

The average time of gestation of a volume seems to have been 7.2 years, the extremes being between one and twelve years. For Qumran, the comparable figures by 1990 were of 18 volumes published in 36 years, i.e. one volume every two years. Those who characterize our speed and performance as the greatest scandal of the century seem to be themselves scandalously ignorant of the standards prevailing in similar editorial projects. Hysteria and *cris à scandale* are really uncalled for, nor do they reflect any credit upon the knowledge or judgment of such critics.

Could then our rights of publication be abrogated, or should they be, by a decision of the owners of the manuscripts if they became persuaded that they should break their commitments to us on the ground that the team they had set up was inadequately large to publish the manuscripts, or too slow at its work? Governments of course can and will do what they like, but owners who are both public and private bodies, such as museums, libraries and the like, will require more rational discussions. In general, such arguments about the powers of and wider obligations to, the public and to scholarship, of museums and other owners it might be interesting for you to follow up, but in this case the facts appealed to are non-facts, however incessantly they are repeated. In fact, (a) the *size* of the editorial team was in the beginning as big as our financial resources permitted, while towards the end it was expanding rapidly under the careful supervision of the earlier nucleus of editors who selected new scholars to collaborate with them on this work or that—this expansion marks the work of the editors to this day, though it no longer always expresses the choice and control of the original editors; and (b) we worked at the same *pace* as do the editors of any similarly sized project, when confronted with fragments of similar difficulty—and there are over 100 years of experience with work on Greek papyri to establish what should be the norms of speed, size, and acceptable style. Setting our rate of publication beside that of other not-dissimilar projects, comparing the numbers of volumes or of manuscripts published in each year, and also comparing the number of editors involved, we were neither lazy nor a cartel, a closed circle of monopolists—of all the other series only the exemplary Oxyrhynchus volumes were published a little faster. In fact, some who know Greek papyrology have told me that they found our pace somewhat headlong.

4. *Addendum*

After reading the preceding contributions of Professors Carson and MacQueen and the Judgment of Judge Dorner (but before having knowledge of the decision of the Appeal against her judgment), I recognise that it would be beyond my skills to comment on most of the topics discussed by them, and not even that useful or helpful for me to correct the many but perhaps minor details in their accounts of the history of the editorial work on MMT done by Qimron and myself. Two points however, one very brief and one longer, might be of interest:

1. Would it not be useful to pay special attention to the numerous other books which publish editions of and commentaries on fragmentarily preserved works? As the copyright law of various countries has evolved in the last century or so, what was the interplay between it and scholarly practice in the case of such books?
2. I suspect that our legal colleagues may not have adequately understood and defined the several activities which made up our work in producing editions of such manuscripts; a better knowledge of the nature and parts of such activities might help them in judging whether our editorial work and the results obtained by it could be copyrighted, and what were the special features in our work of preparing our editions which show that creativity and originality needed for copyrighting.

In the case of several of these tasks, for example, (a) the cleaning of the fragments, (b) photographing them, (c) the identification by the use of a concordance of such fragments as were biblical, (d) the material joining together of several fragments as in a jigsaw puzzle, once it has been established that they could have been written by the same hand (but such material joins can usually be made with less than five per cent of those fragments which seem to belong to the same manuscript), and (e) the decipherment (for transcription) and partial translation of most of the surviving text of each fragment—all these components of our editorial activity, where the correctness or not of our results can usually be easily seen, are somewhat banausic, and few of us would claim copyright for any of them.

Other tasks, however, partake more of the nature of a combination of art and critical skill; for example, (a) for each non-biblical manuscript the identification, *on palaeographical grounds alone*, of the fragments which could be grouped together[4] (of course in the case of biblical manuscripts this was a much easier task), (b) the decipherment (and translation also, if possible) of the more badly damaged parts of the fragments, (c) the determining what sort of work these fragments implied, (d) the establishment of how each fragment of a manuscript could have been related to the others spatially, and (e)—the most important task, but also the most hypothetical—the conjecturing what emendations were needed and how the gaps in each line were to be filled in the light of considerations of the linguistic possibilities, of the probable sense, and of the literary genre. Unlike the other parts of our work which I described above as banausic, these phases were the ones where the results attained gave us a sense of achievement, pride and creativity, for which all our abilities had been especially called on and to propose which perhaps even from our birth we had been predestined!

It has been suggested that, in law, when such a reconstruction is a correct one it cannot be copyrighted: it could only be so if the reconstruction was erroneous! At least to one who spends his time practicing these noble arts, this seems perverse; the greatest creativity surely marks the brilliant, creative, and correct conjecture, not the brilliant and ingenious but wrong one; and in any case how can the Law say with any certainty which conjectures are the correct ones, and which the seductive but mistaken ones—to tell these apart is the proper task of the *critical* scholar, not its.

4. In the special case of the 4Q non-biblical fragments, we must perform this task on all the countless fragments from what were once more than 450 manuscripts. These fragments represent only part of each manuscript and can never be completely joined together; usually material joins can be made between only c. 5–10 per cent of the fragments from each manuscript.

Access to the Dead Sea Scrolls: Fifty Years of Personal Experience

Geza Vermes

Perhaps what I am going to say dates me, but when I started my University studies, I was presented with the ideal of a great republic of letters in which a brotherhood of scholars would happily share their insights and whole-heartedly devote themselves, not to self-promotion or the search of financial gain, but to the advancement of knowledge, understanding and learning. The discovery in 1947 of the Dead Sea Scrolls, hailed as the most important Hebrew manuscript find in history, soon allowed me to put this ideal to the test.

I have been hooked on the Scrolls ever since I first came across in 1948, in my undergraduate days in Louvain, of a headline in a Brussels daily about an *eleventh century BCE* biblical manuscript found on the shore of the *Black* Sea! With a paper published in 1949 I rank, to the best of my belief, as the senior Qumran scholar still active today. Here is then a brief account of half-a-century of personal experience during four-fifths of which direct access to unpublished sources was denied to all but a handful as against the situation during the 1990s with freedom of inquiry extended to all.

Let me start my short survey *in medias res*, in April 1977 in Scotland, at the University of Dundee, where I concluded the first of my Margaret Harris Lectures in Religion on *Qumran in Perspective* with a sound bite which was to become a battle cry in the following years:

> On this thirtieth anniversary of their coming to light the world is entitled to ask the authorities responsible for the publication of the Qumran Scrolls...what they intend to do... For unless drastic measures are taken at once, the greatest...of all Hebrew...manuscript discoveries is likely to become the academic scandal *par excellence* of the twentieth century

This outburst needs to be looked at in retrospect. The publication process of the Scrolls did not start badly. On the contrary. The seven rolls plus all the fragments yielded by Qumran Cave 1 were made available in print by 1956. In the spirit of the 'republic of letters' the American and Israeli editors of the Cave 1 manuscripts, in order to expedite publication, generously restricted themselves to issuing only photographs and transcriptions without translation and commentary. Likewise, scholars in charge of the Cave 1 fragments not only proceeded very fast with the more complicated editorial work (DJD 1 appeared in 1955), but shared information about them, as I personally can testify, with bona fide colleagues. The trouble started after the creation in 1953/54 by the first Editor-in-Chief, Fr Roland de Vaux, of a small editorial team to deal with the discovery of a mass of fragments in Cave 4. From then on, and once more I speak of personal experience, but not of mine alone, until 1990, requests for information were in general either refused or simply ignored. This aloofness was coupled with an increasingly slow rate of publication. By the time of my first Dundee lecture in 1977, 24 years after the establishment of de Vaux's editorial team, its members produced only two out of the planned thirty volumes. The outlook was extremely gloomy. Five years earlier, in 1972, I persuaded C.H. Roberts, the then Director of OUP, publishers of DJD, to urge the defaulting editors to specify in a signed undertaking the date by which they would deliver their finished work. Some gave such dates the latest of which expired by 1976 without any manuscript being sent to Oxford. Some are still awaited in 1999.

Dissatisfaction grew because the editors' procrastination hampered not only the work of Scrolls scholars, but also those researchers who were investigating issues indirectly touching on Qumran. Often one needed only a negative statement, namely that the unpublished Scrolls contained nothing that might affect conclusions arrived at from published Qumran manuscripts or from non-Qumran sources. It was rather tiresome to end every study of a Dead Sea text with the escape clause that the conclusions are valid provided that no unpublished Qumran fragments contain something to the contrary.

Understandably, public dissatisfaction was increasing and complaints began to multiply, but I waited another ten years until 1987, when at a conference in London marking the 40th anniversary of the Scrolls and attended by nearly all the editorial team still alive, I demanded in the name of all the frustrated researchers that the photographs of the still unpublished texts be released without delay. This request which would have left intact the assignment of the material to the original editors, was bluntly rejected by Editor-in-Chief number three without any explanation or justification.

While the battle over the Scrolls was raging, the possibility of a new opening arose when the Israel Antiquities Authority decided to provide the Oxford Centre for Hebrew and Jewish Studies, of which I was then one of the governors, with a full set of Scrolls' photographs. A ray of sunshine at last? Not quite. Unknown to me, at the request of the IAA the Centre signed an undertaking to reserve access to unpublished material only to persons nominated by the IAA, i.e. to the official editors.

In 1991, after four decades spent out in the cold, to my genuine delight, Editor-in-Chief number four, Emanuel Tov, invited me to take charge of the Cave 4 fragments of the important Community Rule. I immediately made it known that any *bona fide* researcher could consult the material allocated to me. Having become an insider of the editorial group, and being the person in charge of Qumran studies at the Hebrew Centre, I expected to have access for research and seminar purposes to all the photographs kept in the Qumran Room of the Centre, but a formal approach to this effect met with a cold rebuff from the Director of the IAA, who explicitly stated that unpublished photographs should be kept 'strictly beyond the reach of scholars' save those personally appointed by the IAA. This was intolerable and, in September 1991, I with a fellow governor planned to have a proper showdown at a special meeting of the board of the Oxford Centre, and should our views be accepted by the majority of the governors, we would confront the IAA. Our project was overtaken by events: the revolution broke out first in Washington, then in California. I shall not recount the details; suffice it to observe that by the end of October 1991 the embargo on the unpublished Dead Sea Scrolls was officially lifted by the IAA, and a new era of freedom in academic enquiry began.

How did this change affect the status of those in charge of unpublished text and the progress of research in general? Universal free access and free publication obviously brought to an end the monopolistic privilege of the appointed editorial team. The official *editio princeps* could from then on be preceded by any number of 'unofficial' editions. In fact, this did not turn out to be harmful in any way to the general interest; on the contrary, it may be said that it has been beneficial to scholarship. By November 1991, two volumes of a photographic edition were on the market at a very reasonable price. It was soon followed by a rather expensive microfiche edition and, in 1997, by a definitely overpriced CD-ROM edition, both of them published with the IAA's blessing. Moreover, most of the scholars charged with the preparation of the 'official' editions, realizing that the days of protected vested interest were over, and that any undue delay might result in their being beaten by enthusiastic rivals, have become much more active. Also, thanks to the gentle goading of a most competent and persuasive Editor-in-Chief, it is hoped that perhaps as many as 30 out of the 40 planned volumes of DJD will be published or in the press by the turn of the millennium, and the rest will follow in the opening years of the twenty-first century.

Not being a lawyer, I shall not be so foolish as to get involved in questions of intellectual property right and copyright law. Nevertheless I would like to end my reminiscences by listing a few 'historical' facts that may be relevant to legal issues and help future thinking on these matters.

I do not know whether public institutions intended for the dissemination of knowledge, such as museums and libraries, are legally entitled to refuse access to their holdings to qualified researchers. Be this as it may, restrictive practices of this sort are surely contrary to the spirit of free enquiry. Leaving the Scrolls aside, in my past experience in this country, I have come across only once a library, not one belonging to the top league, which prevented a student of mine from consulting a manuscript because a rather selfish, but locally influential scholar claimed that he was working on its publication. (He never managed to edit it.) In any case, in 1991, while I was collecting ammunition for our battle about the opening of the Qumran Room at the Oxford Centre, I sought information about the policy adopted by the Bodleian Library and the Ashmolean Museum in Oxford, and gathered from authoritative sources that neither the Bodleian nor the Ashmolean would keep any of their holdings under lock and key just because someone was engaged in editing it. Whatever its legal status, this liberal custom should serve as a universal model.

Again I disclaim any real knowledge of the law relating to intellectual property, especially as it affects the edition of an ancient text. But as an editor myself, I know that the purpose of my effort is to make a previously unpublished text available to all other scholars. My labour in deciphering, transcribing and restoring the text aims at helping future users. The text printed is not mine, but the ancient authors'. As for my hypothetical reconstructions, they are unlikely to be wholly correct. If correct, the authorship is once more that of the original writer; if erroneous, it belongs to me, but should preferably be forgotten. I gladly allow other scholars' *bona fide* use of my edition and would not dream of demanding that every user should specifically ask me for permission, though no doubt I would rather appreciate it if users would kindly acknowledge the source on which their work is based. We all belong to the same club, and should abide by the same unwritten rules.

Let me signal finally the extraordinary copyright notice which appears in vol. 10 of DJD, and compare it to the parallel notices printed in the other volumes of the series.

Back in 1955, Oxford University Press did not even bother to insert any copyright mark in vol. 1 of DJD. By contrast, the American Schools of Oriental Research and the Hebrew University customarily asserted their copyright in their respective Scrolls editions by Millar Burrows and his colleagues in 1950–51 on the one hand, and by E.L. Sukenik in 1954/1955 on the other.

From vol. 2 to vol. 9 (1961–92), the DJD series is simply copyrighted for Oxford University Press without any mention of the editors. Then with vol. 10 edited by Elisha Qimron and John Strugnell in consultation with Ya'akov Sussmann we witness a copyright notice, which for its length and tortuous complexity deserves a place in the *Guinness Book of Records*. It reads:

> © Elisha Qimron 1994, without derogating from any right vested in the Israel Antiquities Authority with regard to the Scrolls' fragments, photographs, and any other material which is in the possession of the authority, and which the authority has permitted Qimron to use for the purposes of the Work, and its inclusion therein.

There is also a double silence here which speaks loud and clear: neither the co-editor John Strugnell nor the consultant Ya'akov Sussmann are associated with the copyright statement, although Strugnell's contribution to the volume was substantial and Sussmann's highly significant.

After the DJD vol. X curiosity, OUP's copyright style reverted to the *ante Qimron* status except that in most volumes a special declaration acknowledges the copyright of the IAA to the photographs and of Stephen Pfann to the concordance compiled by him. Finally with vol. 25 published in 1998, Oxford University Press on their own initiative devised a new tripartite copyright formula naming the author(s) for the text, the IAA for the photographs and Pfann for the concordance. In other words, Oxford University Press is no longer the holder of the copyright, but its administrator on behalf of its holders. In fact, the matter is only of academic, not of financial, significance since royalties are not payable to the authors until the Press has recouped the production costs, but such a happy event has not yet materialized, as far as I know, in the 44-year-old history of DJD.

PS. I deliberately abstain from commenting on Professor John Strugnell's account and especially on his statistics, and am happy to leave it to the readers to judge.

THE PUBLICATION OF THE DEAD SEA SCROLLS

Emanuel Tov

When the so-called Dead Sea Scrolls were found, no one had the slightest idea that these Scrolls would preoccupy the minds of scholars and the general public alike to such a great extent. Ever since the 1950s, the interest has been widespread, and hundreds of books and thousands of articles have been written. There has been sensation and journalists spoke of scandals; according to some, these scandals still persist today. Probably some 50 conferences have been devoted to the Scrolls. Research on the Scrolls continues and journalists continue to write prolifically, often without any factual basis. Scholars, too, are often responsible for disseminating incorrect information about the Scrolls. Some impatiently write premature articles based on partial information, and prematurely publish texts and translations, often in an attempt to reap some of the fruits of the fame of writing on the Scrolls.

Between the years 1947 and 1956, literally thousands of large and small fragments of Scrolls were found in 11 caves at Qumran, predominantly in the so-called Caves 1, 4 and 11. Some of these fragments are sizable, in rare cases very sizable, even constituting complete Scrolls, while others are medium-sized or minute. Probably most fragments are of medium size, allowing for a reasonable investigation of their contents. These fragments belonged to what were once some 900 complete documents in Hebrew, Aramaic, and Greek, written in these languages as well as in two cryptic scripts. Among these were some two hundred Scrolls containing individual books of the Hebrew Bible. The name Dead Sea Scrolls actually encompasses more than the area of Qumran, since remnants of Scrolls and papyri were also found at other locations in the Judaean Desert south of Qumran in Naḥal Ḥever, Naḥal Ṣe'elim, Wadi Murabba'at, Wadi Sdeir, Wadi Mishmar, and on Masada. Recent finds in Jericho should be added to this list. Most of the interest has been directed at the manuscript finds of Qumran, by Bedouin and archaeologists, and when using the term 'Dead Sea Scrolls' we first of all think of Qumran.

It is very difficult to give an adequate description of the contents of the Dead Sea Scroll fragments as the discussion of their nature is ongoing, and furthermore no overall theory on Qumran origins will ever be accepted by all scholars. Almost all the fragments from Qumran are sections of literary works, and this fact has some implications for our understanding of this site. On the other hand, most of the fragments from the other sites in the Judaean Desert are what we call 'documentary texts', that is they contain such archival documents as receipts, wedding contracts, and lists of various kinds. As to the nature of Qumran, according to the widely accepted theory, a select group of Essenes lived at Qumran from about 120 BCE until 70 CE, and when moving to Qumran they brought with them Scrolls copied in various places in Palestine. At the same time, they also composed and copied Scrolls at Qumran itself. Many of these texts were biblical and they provide us with an excellent record of the transmission of the biblical text in the period between 300 BCE and 70 CE. That is, the oldest Scrolls were copied prior to the settlement in Qumran, and they were brought there by the settlers themselves. For our understanding of the Scrolls it does not really matter whether one accepts this majority view or another one, as most scholars agree that some or many of the Scrolls found at Qumran were copied elsewhere, while others were copied at Qumran itself. Beyond the biblical Scrolls, we now have a very good idea of the Jewish literature of this period, as the caves contained hundreds of literary works. The corpus of the compositions found at Qumran probably reflects the literary taste of the Qumran community, but even this is not certain. These Scrolls include compositions of diverse genres such as Wisdom literature, psalms, biblical interpretation, apocalyptic compositions, calendric documents, prayers, rewritten biblical books, and magical documents. Almost every single text found at Qumran expands our understanding of the larger group of texts to which it belonged. Many texts have been found in multiple copies, so that the interrelations between these copies can now be researched on the literary level and their textual transmission can be well illustrated.

Ever since the discovery of the Scrolls, an international team has been preparing the publication of the Dead Sea Scrolls. This work is now almost complete. At the same time, there is a small group of small and medium-size texts about which relatively little is known at this stage, although they are now included, without commentary, in the study edition by García Martínez and Tigchelaar.[1] Some of these texts may shed light on as yet unknown areas. For example, recently M. Broshi and E. Eshel released their analysis of a document named 4Q248 (4QHistorical Text A) which refers to a Greek king not known from other Qumran documents, probably Antiochus IV Epiphanes. Even though he is not mentioned by name, the description seems to fit him best. In another text, 4Q468e (4QHistorical Text F), Broshi recognized the name Potlais/Ptolaus. These new documents thus add to the small stock of historical figures that was known previously from the scrolls.[2] Taking this complex situation as our point of departure, we now turn to the decipherment and publication. Again other texts, to be published in 2000, will illustrate other aspects of the Qumran literature. The calendrical texts of the Qumran community are to be published in vol. 21 by S. Talmon with J. Ben-Dov, many still unknown Aramaic texts in vol. 31 by E. Puech, and the pseudo-Prophetical literature in vol. 30 by D. Dimant.

The history of the discovery and publication of the Scrolls is surrounded with bad fortune, mishaps, inexperience, and manifold mistakes, not to mention some scandals. At the same time, most of the members of the initial team were and remain major scholars in their fields, and were it not for their acumen, ingenuity, and devotion, the progress in the publication would not be where it is today.

However, it was simply bad fortune that the fragments were handed over to the scholars in complete disarray, often after having been maltreated by Bedouin. For example, according to Père Barthélemy, the Greek Minor Prophets scroll from Naḥal Ḥever was kept under the *kefiyyeh* of one of the Bedouin (see the Preface to DJD, 8), and according to Strugnell, one of the copies of 4Q416, the so-called 4QInstruction[a], was 'hidden under Kando's shirt and absorbed his perspiration, as he hid it there to prevent its discovery during a police search' (DJD, 34, p. 73). These external conditions did not improve the quality of the Scrolls, to say the least. Likewise, the Temple Scroll from Cave 11 was hidden for many years in a shoe box in Kando's garden in Bethlehem, and the present decay of the top part of that Scroll probably could have

1. F. García Martínez and E.J.C. Tigchelaar, *The Dead Sea Scrolls Study Edition* (2 vols.; Leiden: E.J. Brill, 1997–98).

2. Both texts have now been published in S.J. Pfann *et al.*, DJD, 36 (Oxford: Clarendon Press, 2000).

been prevented had it been stored in better conditions.

It was also unfortunate that the region in which the Scrolls were found from 1947 onwards was in political turmoil, so that all kinds of *ad hoc* solutions had to be devised. The fact that the Scrolls were found in Jordanian territory created a difficult situation. Thus, the authorities who were responsible for the Scrolls barred Israelis and Jews from immediate contact with them for several decades.

It was inexperience that caused the initial group of eight scholars to believe that they would be able to publish all these fragments themselves, without involving additional scholars. Had their approach been more open from the outset, many an outcry would have been avoided. It was also lack of experience which accompanied the first steps of the physical treatment of the Scrolls, which were pieced together with scotch tape. Two decades later, that scotch tape caused serious decay at the points where the fragments were joined.

Mistakes were made, and some of them continue to harm scholarship. Thus several archeological artefacts, such as coins and pieces of glassware, were mysteriously lost, rendering it impossible to complete certain investigations. Some of these artefacts are apparently to be found somewhere in Europe. Several fragments of Scrolls were taken out of the country in the 1950s, with or without the consent of the Jordanian authorities, and are now exhibited or stored in Paris, Heidelberg, and elsewhere. At the same time, the scholars themselves were very skilled, many of their initial identifications were ingenious, and from the outset very high standards were set for the publication.

It was fortunate that the Scrolls were found at all, but the circumstances in which they were found and handed over to the scholars were anything but favourable. It would have been helpful had the Scrolls been uncovered *in situ* by archaeologists, for in that case we would have been certain about the place of origin of each discovery and about its position in relation to other fragments. For the major treasure, Qumran Cave 4, only some 20 per cent of the texts were discovered *in situ* by archaeologists. The majority of the texts were removed from the caves by Bedouin. We are not even certain that some of the fragments which carry a certain identification, such as ‘Qumran Cave 4’, were indeed found at that site. Thus, there still is uncertainty about the documentary texts carrying the siglum ‘Qumran Cave 4’, but which probably derived from Naḥal Ḥever and Naḥal Ṣe’elim (see A. Yardeni in DJD, 27, pp. 281–317); most of the texts named Seiyal probably also derived from Naḥal Ḥever, because the Bedouin did not want to admit that they crossed the Israeli border to Naḥal Ḥever from where they retrieved these texts. Worst of all, the fragments were handed over by the Bedouin in a condition of total disarray. The members of the initial team succeeded in disentangling this chaos for the most part, but some of the remaining mysteries derive from this initial disorder.

When referring to the disarray of the fragments, we mean that piles of literally thousands of fragments were sold to scholars who then spent five years making the initial identifications. If a fragment was identified as containing, for example, a piece of the book of Isaiah, it would stand to reason that other fragments found in the vicinity would have belonged to the same Scroll. But as it was, scholars did not know where these fragments were found, so that the work of identification had to be repeated for each tiny fragment. This work placed an enormous burden on the shoulders of the original team. They placed the fragments under glass plates on several long tables in a room in the Rockefeller Museum which they named the Scrollery. At a second stage they combined all the fragments that presumably belonged to a given Scroll. These fragments were then rearranged in a tentative internal order on so-called Museum plates, each of which was photographed separately.

The identifications themselves were made on the basis of content, handwriting, the colour of the leather, and the shape of the fragments. These identifications were not without problems. Firstly, reliance upon handwriting is subjective, especially because of the rather formal style of the writing of most documents. For example, the fragments which F.M. Cross ascribed to a single Scroll, 4QJer^{b}, were subsequently ascribed to three different Scrolls on the basis of presumably different handwriting and scribal features (4QJer^{b,d,e}).[3] But neither of these views should be considered solid as the fragments are small. The implication of these two different views is that we either possess fragments of a single Scroll of Jeremiah or of three different Scrolls. This description implies that our overall knowledge of the number of Scrolls found at Qumran is very uncertain. In another case, two small fragments of Isaiah deriving from the beginning and end of the book, were ascribed to two different Scrolls. However, if the beginning of the

3. E. Tov, '4QJer^{b}', in E. Ulrich and others, *Qumran Cave 4.X: The Prophets* (DJD, 15; Oxford: Clarendon Press, 1997), pp. 71-176.

Scroll was written by one scribe, and the end by another one, the two fragments could have actually derived from a single Scroll, rather than two different ones. Situations like these illustrate the uncertainty regarding the overall number of Scrolls.

In the above-mentioned cases, the identification of the content is at least stable, as the biblical text is known. However, it is sometimes hard or even impossible to know whether a small fragment derived from a biblical Scroll or a so-called rewritten Bible composition. It is even more difficult to identify fragments of compositions which were unknown before the discovery of the Qumran Scrolls. To determine the sequence of fragments of an unknown composition is like working with a jigsaw puzzle for which we have no picture. Often we do not even know whether a given fragment belongs to composition *a* or composition *b*, copied by the same scribe. As a result, over the course of the initial identification and subsequent research, some fragments were shifted from one composition to another, even following their publication.

Problems of identification are also reflected in the names given to the compositions. In our set-up, the editor of the individual texts in the DJD series determines the official names of the composition. Consequently, some of the names are unusual, such as 4Q184, named by Allegro '4QWiles of the Wicked Woman'. Other names are problematical. The name given by J. Sanders to the large scroll of psalmic compositions from Cave 11, namely 11QPsalms[a], ascribes to this Scroll a canonical status. That is, this name presents the Scroll as a copy of the biblical book of Psalms, in this case also including non-canonical psalms, and this assumption has major implications for our understanding of the biblical book of Psalms. Accordingly, this is not an objective name, since most scholars do not consider this Scroll to contain a collection of biblical Psalms, but rather a secondary liturgical collection of both biblical and nonbiblical psalms. Likewise, the Scroll which S. White and I published as '4QReworked Pentateuch' (4Q364–367 [DJD, 13]), containing a non-canonical, that is nonbiblical, text rewriting the Bible, should according to some be renamed as '4QPentateuch', that is an actual biblical manuscript containing a deviating biblical text. The name which we have given to this composition, '4QReworked Pentateuch', is thus subjective, reflecting the nature of this text according to the best of our understanding. The most well-known problem connected with identification and nomenclature is probably that of the

Greek fragments from Cave 7 (7Q3–18), published as *fragments non identifiés*, but identified by J. O'Callaghan and C.P. Thiede as reflecting parts of the New Testament and identified by others as the LXX.[4]

The process of renaming is an ongoing activity. The scholar who publishes the text in DJD is entitled to determine the name of the composition, upon consultation with the Editor-in-Chief. Names assigned in this way may differ from those given in a preliminary edition, whether by the DJD editor or others who published or analyzed the text (in the DJD edition as well as in the published inventories such earlier names are always mentioned, but nevertheless some confusion may occur). Studies on the Qumran texts as well as the published translations, are not always up to date with regard to these name changes. Many of the alterations pertain to changes from generic to specific names. Thus a text which previously was named '4QSapiential Work' (4Q410) is now called '4QVision and Interpretation'. The general name '4QSapiential Work A' (4Q415–423) has become '4QInstruction', etc.

The work of decipherment and identification continues even today and will probably do so into the next generation as well. The initial identifications have been handed down to the present generation of editors, and only when the current editor of a text analyzes that composition in detail will he or she be able to assess the pertinence of all the fragments to the composition. At that point the presumed sequence is also determined, although often such a sequence is tenuous.

Going back some 40 years in time, the fragments were provisionally placed on plates in the Rockefeller Museum and subsequently photographed with infra-red photography, revealing details invisible to the naked eye. This process has been repeated three times following progress in the identifications. The results of these photography sessions were superb, due to the skills of the Museum photographer, Albino. As a rule, these early photographs still form the best sources for scholars, and the plates accompanying the DJD editions are usually composed of

4. J. O'Callaghan, *Los papiros griegos de la cueva 7 de Qumrân* (Biblioteca de autores christianos, 353; Madrid: Editorial Catolica, 1974); C.P. Thiede, *Die älteste Evangelien-Handschrift? Das Markus-Fragment von Qumran und die Anfänge der schriftlichen Überlieferung des Neuen Testaments* (Wuppertal: Brockhaus, 1986). Translated as: *The Earliest Gospel Manuscript? The Qumran Fragment 7Q5 and Its Significance for New Testament Studies* (Exeter: Paternoster Press, 1992).

segments cut out from these photographs taken in the 1950s and 1960s, rather than from new photographs. It is true that recently taken photographs by two California teams, infra-red on film, and multi-spectral imaging, with the use of computers, often provide greater detail than the older photographs. The ability for improved photography is there, but for several reasons such photographs have not been taken systematically of all the Scrolls. For one thing, in many cases the edges of the fragments have deteriorated over the course of five decades, rendering new photographs valuable only as sources of information for the centre sections of the fragments.

These older photographs, and in some cases newer ones, have served as the basis for most study of the Scrolls over the last 50 years, although scholars have also consulted the original fragments for select details.

The system used by the original team ensured that all the fragments were photographed. Each group of fragments assembled on a Museum plate was photographed on a PAM (Palestine Archaeological Museum) photograph. It is probable, but not entirely certain, that all the fragments have been assigned to scholars, and this aspect can only be verified by a detailed examination of the Museum holdings compared with the editions. Beyond this issue, another problem is encountered, that of the current incompatibility of the Museum Plates with the photographic records. At the outset, each Museum Plate (numbered 1–1100) was identical to a given PAM photograph. However, following insights gained by scholars subsequent to the photographing of the last series (43.000 and 44.000), the fragments were moved on the plates (without leaving a record), but they could not be changed any more on the PAM photographs. Furthermore, over the course of the years some mishaps have occurred; some fragments have been either mislaid or lost, and therefore cannot be consulted at this stage. In these cases, the photographs provide the only record of the fragments. Conversely, some fragments cannot be located on the PAM photographs. It is hard to assess all the details, as several fragments have fallen apart or have been combined with other ones.

All the fragments from the Judaean Desert have been given identification numbers according to their place of origin (e.g. 1Q1, that is, item 1 from Qumran, Cave 1) and their content (e.g. 1QGen[a]). Each fragment was thus assigned four numbers: one based on its origin and content, such as 1QGen[a], one denoting its inventory number (e.g. 1Q1), another referring to its location on a Museum Plate (1–1100), and the fourth pertaining to its photographic record (e.g. PAM 40.501). The identifications based on the content, such as 11QT^{a} (11QTemple Scroll, copy a) are the best known; the other sets of data being pertinent only to Qumran insiders. The official editions as well as some handbooks provide all the needed cross-references.

The Scrolls are known from photographs, text editions in the original languages, and from translations.[5] For several years now scholars can consult the Brill Microfiche edition,[6] and more recently also the CD-ROM of Brill/Oxford University Press containing digitized images of all the original negatives and the FARMS database containing almost all the Qumran texts together with digitized images.[7] A photographic facsimile edition was published in 1991.[8]

The increased accessibility of the photographs (including the microfiche edition) since 1991 and the electronic tools since 1997

5. There are now very good translations, some of them named 'authoritative' or 'complete', in a number of languages: four in English, and others in French, German, Spanish, Italian, Dutch, Polish, Finnish and Hungarian. T.H. Gaster, *The Dead Sea Scriptures* (3rd edn; Garden City, NY: Anchor/Doubleday, 1976); G. Vermes, *The Complete Dead Sea Scrolls in English* (London: Penguin, 1997); F. García Martínez, *The Dead Sea Scrolls Translated—The Qumran Texts in English, The Authoritative New Translation of the Dead Sea Scrolls Complete in One Volume* (trans. W.G.E. Watson; Leiden/New York/Cologne: E.J. Brill, 1994); M. Wise, M. Abegg, Jr, and E. Cook, *The Dead Sea Scrolls: A New Translation* (New York: HarperSanFrancisco, 1996); F. García Martínez, *Textos de Qumrán* (Madrid: Trotta, 1992); F. García Martínez and A.S. van der Woude, *De rollen van de Dode Zee* 1-2 (Kampen/Tielt: Kok, 1994–95); *idem*, *Texti de Qumran* (Brescia: Paideia, 1996); J. Maier, *Die Qumran-Essener: Die Texte vom Toten Meer* (3 vols.; Munich/Basel: Reinhardt, 1995–96); P. Muchowski, *Rekopisy znad morza martwego Qumran–Wadi Murabb'at–Masada Biblioteka zwojów tlo Nowego Testamentu* 5 (Kraków: Enigma, 1996).

6. E. Tov with the collaboration of S.J. Pfann, *The Dead Sea Scrolls on Microfiche—A Comprehensive Facsimile Edition of the Texts from the Judean Desert*, with a *Companion Volume* (Leiden: E.J. Brill and IDC, 1993, 1995).

7. Timothy H. Lim in consultation with P. Alexander, *The Dead Sea Scrolls—Electronic Reference Library* (Oxford/Leiden: Oxford University Press/E.J. Brill, 1997); E. Tov (ed.), *The Dead Sea Scrolls Database (Non-Biblical Texts)* (The Dead Sea Scrolls Electronic Reference Library, II; Prepared by the Foundation for Ancient Research and Mormon Studies [FARMS]; Leiden: E.J. Brill, 1999).

8. R.H. Eisenman and J.M. Robinson, *A Facsimile Edition of the Dead Sea Scrolls* (2 vols.; Washington DC: Biblical Archaeology Society, 1991).

could have heralded a new era in the history of the scholarship of the Scrolls, but it has failed to do so. Although everyone was then able to see all the relevant photographs in his or her study, few scholars actually turned to them. It needs to be borne in mind that without much preparation it is very hard for the uninitiated to read most of these photographs, or to make joins between any two fragments, especially if they are found on different negatives. It is equally difficult to know exactly where on the negatives the various fragments of a given composition were found. As a result, most scholars continue to depend on text editions based on the expertise of scholars who have studied these fragments for years, and to wait for the upcoming editions in the DJD series. Historians will therefore judge whether or not the heated discussion of the early 1990s on the accessibility of the photographs was a waste of energy (it should have occurred 20 years earlier). Some have said in the past year that the upheaval, which delayed the publication of the Scrolls by at least half a year, was pointless, while others consider it to have been an important event in the struggle to 'liberate' the Scrolls.

The main vehicle for the knowledge of the Scrolls remains text editions, which digest for the reader information also available on the photographs, but in a much easier way, and after study of years. Among these editions, the series *Discoveries in the Judaean Desert* (*of Jordan*) is considered the central place for the publication of the Dead Sea Scrolls, published by Oxford University Press (OUP). Individual volumes of texts are also published elsewhere by J. Charlesworth.[9] OUP probably did not realize the extent of the enterprise it was committing itself to when it agreed to publish the Scrolls in the DJD series. Indeed, the series turned out to be much more extensive than was planned initially. When trying to locate a Press willing to publish the Scrolls, G. Lankester Harding wrote to the Press that he was thinking in terms of 'altogether, perhaps, five volumes.'[10]

The pace of publication has accelerated in this decade, with the expansion of the original international team of eight scholars to some 80. This expansion occurred with the reorganization of the team, the

9. J.H. Charlesworth (ed.), *The Dead Sea Scrolls, Hebrew, Aramaic, and Greek Texts with English Translations* (4 vols.; Tübingen/Louisville: Mohr/Westminster/John Knox Press, 1994, 1995, 1999).

10. His letter is archived in Folder 1118 of the Palestine Archaeological Museum.

increased involvement of the Israel Antiquities Authority, and thanks to the personal enthusiasm and energy of its director, Amir Drori. Eight volumes of DJD were published by OUP between 1951 and 1990, while in the past ten years another 26 volumes have appeared. Altogether the DJD series is scheduled to contain 40 volumes, including an overall concordance.

The international team, entrusted since 1953 with the task of publishing the Scrolls found in the Judaean Desert, created the DJD series in which these texts are being published. The Editor-in-Chief of the international team has served at the same time as the general editor of this series, that is R. de Vaux (vols. 1–5), P. Benoit (vols. 6–7), J. Strugnell (vol. 8), and E. Tov (vols. 9ff.). Throughout, the series has been named *Discoveries in the Judaean Desert*, with a short interlude (1962–1968) during which vols. 3–5 were named *Discoveries in the Judaean Desert of Jordan*.

Most fragments and artefacts found in the Judaean Desert by archaeologists or purchased from Bedouin between 1947 and 1956, as well as the archaeological background of the sites have been published in the DJD series. These volumes thus cover most of the texts and artefacts found within the boundaries of the British Mandatory Palestine and the Hashemite Kingdom of Jordan during those years. Material found at Naḥal Ḥever, the one site within Israel's borders, was taken to Jordan and incorrectly labeled as 'Seiyal'.

The only scholars involved in the publication of the texts in the first volumes of DJD were members of the international team which convened in Jerusalem, Jordan, not long after the texts were found, and whose activities were centred in the Rockefeller Museum and the École Biblique. The initial group consisted of the following eight scholars (in alphabetical order): J.M. Allegro, F.M. Cross, C.-H. Hunzinger (subsequently replaced by M. Baillet), J.T. Milik, P.W. Skehan, J. Starcky, J. Strugnell, and R. de Vaux. In his description of the 'Travail d'édition' in vol. 6, pp. 6–8 (1960), R. de Vaux also mentioned M. Baillet; he did not include P. Benoit who took part in vol. 2 and who was to become Editor-in-Chief after him, nor D. Barthélemy who published the biblical texts of Cave 1 in vol. 1. Over the years, this international team has been expanded greatly.

It was the intention of the original team that the DJD series should contain the official publication of the texts in conjunction with a commentary, but not in all cases was this the *editio princeps*. Many texts were published preliminarily elsewhere, and in other cases, complete text editions were published in separate volumes.[11] The large texts from Cave 1 have been published long ago in separate editions, and were not scheduled to be republished in the DJD series, with the exception of the Isaiah Scrolls, to be included in vol. 32. The volumes of Wacholder and Abegg, which are based on the transcriptions and views of members of the international team in the 1950s and 1960s,[12] have now been superseded by the DJD volumes themselves.

As often occurs in the publication of a series, the volumes are not released sequentially, but, rather, according to their readiness for publication. Thus the first volume of material from Cave 4 (vol. 5) covered 4Q158-4Q186, although many may have expected to see the publication of 4Q1ff. (biblical texts) first (see the foreword of R. de Vaux to vol. 5).

The basic format of the individual volumes in the series, as determined in vol. I contains the following components:

1. general introduction;
2. transcription of the text(s);
3. translation of the nonbiblical fragments or sections;
4. short notes on the readings;
5. a commentary;
6. concordance or index of all the words occurring in the non-biblical texts;
7. plates and figures. The infra-red photographs presented in DJD are generally of high quality, and from 1996 onwards these plates are usually superior to the positives presented to OUP.

The general philosophy behind the DJD editions is to provide the

11. The major editions published outside the DJD series are: A. Grohmann, *Arabic Papyri from Hirbet el-Mird* (Bibliothèque du Muséon 52; Louvain: Publications Universitaires, 1963); J.T. Milik, *The Books of Enoch* (Oxford: Clarendon, 1976); D.N. Freedman and K.A. Mathews, *The Paleo-Hebrew Leviticus Scroll* (Winona Lake, IN: Eisenbrauns, 1985); Y. Yadin, *The Temple Scroll* (3 vols.; Jerusalem: IES, 1977) (Hebrew); *idem*, *The Temple Scroll* (3 vols.; Jerusalem: IES, 1983).

12. B.Z. Wacholder and M.G. Abegg, *A Preliminary Edition of the Unpublished Dead Sea Scrolls. The Hebrew and Aramaic Texts from Cave Four*, I–IV (Washington, DC: Biblical Archaeology Society, 1991–96).

scholarly public with a workable edition of the text, which, while presenting the best possible edition according to its editor, may be improved upon by subsequent generations of scholars. This idea is appropriately expressed by J.A. Sanders on p. viii of his preface to vol. 4: 'Search for truth is rooted in a fear of falsehood, and no man alone can find the one, or shun the other. Scholars will note, as I continue to see, further needs for improvement: and that is, as it should be, reason sufficient to go to press without further delay.' In accordance with this philosophy, many scholars provided a minimal commentary, to be improved by others or by themselves, while others provide a rather extensive commentary.

The first volume of DJD introduced a system of presentation of the texts which attempts to represent in the transcription all the elements of the text and leather as precisely as possible, including the exact position of the letters in the columns and fragments and the spaces between them, corrections, crossing out with a line, erasures, supralinear or intralinear additions, the existence of margins on all sides of the writing block, spaces within the line (*vacat*), marginal notations, dots between words in the palaeo-Hebrew script, letters or words in the palaeo-Hebrew script, numbers, etc. (the detailed description in vol. 1, pp. 44-48: 'Table des sigles' mentions most of these details). This system was used from vol. 1 onwards, and although scholars necessarily differ in their conception of the certainty ascribed to the preserved parts of letters, the system is used more or less consistently.

Most volumes have been published in English, while a smaller number (vols. 1, 2, 3, 6, 7, 25, 31 and 33) have been or are being published in French.

By far the greatest number of volumes is devoted to Qumran Cave 4 for which no less than 26 volumes have appeared or are scheduled to appear. Within these volumes the material is further subdivided according to a binary division of biblical and nonbiblical texts, when the appellation 'biblical' refers to the Hebrew Bible and Apocrypha.

The early DJD volumes of non-biblical texts were subdivided into literary genres, with the non-biblical texts from Cave 4 in vols. 13ff. reflecting single literary genres. The original intention of the international team was for each published volume to contain the texts allotted to individual scholars, which in themselves often reflected different literary genres. However, with the reorganization of the team in 1990, a different procedure was instituted for the Cave 4 material, resulting in the publication of the texts according to their literary character rather than the allotments to the members of the original team. Thus, in the new arrangement, volumes are co-authored by several scholars, such as the volumes containing the so-called 'parabiblical texts' (vols. 13, 19, 22, 30). Similar volumes contain sapiential texts (20, 34), poetical and liturgical texts (11, 29) and halakhic texts (35).

While most volumes contain publications of texts, several also publish archaeological data on the caves in which the Scrolls or artefacts were found, on the artefacts themselves, and on the archaeological missions (vols. 1, 2, 3, 6, 8, 24, 38).

Vols. 1–9 contain single-word indexes of the Hebrew, Aramaic (vols. 1, 2), Greek (vols. 2, 3, 8, 9), Latin (vol. 2), and Arabic (vol. 2) words of the nonbiblical texts or sections as well as signs (vol. 7). Using a different system, vols. 10ff. contain full keyword-in-context concordances of all the words in the nonbiblical texts.

A feature, which has been developed fully in recent volumes, is that of indicating parallel texts. It was used for the first time in the edition of 2QNew Jerusalem ar (vol. 3, p. 85), and this system was used ever since *inter alia* in the editions of 4QMMT (vol. 10), the Damascus Scroll (vol. 18) and of the *Serekh ha-Yaḥad* from Cave 4 (vol. 26), also involving the longer parallel texts, namely the mediaeval CD and the *Serekh ha-Yaḥad* text from Cave 1. Internal parallels on a less extensive scale are also denoted for other texts, such as the *Hodayot* (vol. 29).

The scholars who publish the scrolls are more or less equally spread among three regions: North America, Israel, and Europe.

During the course of the publishing enterprise, extensive inventorizing became necessary. A full inventory was made of all the Qumran compositions, photographs and fragments, and the results were published in 1993 and 1995 in a companion volume accompanying the microfiche edition.[13] An updated form of these lists is contained in the *Jubilee Volume,*[14] while the final form of that list will be included in the Introductory volume (vol. 39).

Vols. 1–7 and 9 were type-set in Oxford. The camera-ready manu-

13. E. Tov, *The Dead Sea Scrolls on Microfiche*.

14. 'A List of the Texts from the Judaean Desert', in P.W. Flint and J.C. VanderKam (eds.), *The Dead Sea Scrolls after Fifty Years—A Comprehensive Assessment* (2 vols.; Leiden: E.J. Brill, 1999).

scripts of vols. 9ff. were prepared in Jerusalem[15] for the non-biblical volumes (except for vol. 11 which was prepared in Notre Dame) and in Notre Dame for the biblical volumes (8, 12, 14, 15, 16). The preparation of these camera-ready manuscripts has made possible by generous annual contributions from the Oxford Centre for Hebrew and Jewish Studies, the Dead Sea Scrolls Foundation,[16] and the National Endowment for the Humanities, the latter contributing to the University of Notre Dame and to some individuals in the US.

15. The production was managed by Claire Pfann (1991–1996) and J. Karnis (1996–). Copy-editing and typing was performed by: Eva Ben-David, Miriam Berger, S. Ben-Or, S. Chavel, N. Gordon, Janice Karnis, Claire Pfann, Sarah Presant-Collins, and Valerie Carr Zakovitch. At various times S. Chavel, S. Holst, M. Morgenstern, and S. Pfann served as research assistants.

16. The Dead Sea Scrolls Foundation, with S. Paul as director and W. Fields as its executive director, receives donations from individuals and foundations, mainly for the purpose of the publication of the texts in the DJD series.

Part IV

SCHOLARLY ENTERPRISE AND INDIVIDUAL PROPERTY RIGHTS

TO PUBLISH OR NOT TO PUBLISH?
ANECDOTES FROM THE SECRET HISTORY OF EPIGRAPHY*

John Richardson

The papers in this volume are for the most part dealing with questions which arise over the ownership, both physical and intellectual, of documents from the ancient world, and in particular with the legal status of these forms of ownership. These questions are not, of course, peculiar to the Dead Sea Scrolls, though the importance attached to the Scrolls both by the scholarly world and by the popular press has meant that disputes concerning them have acquired more publicity than is usually the case. This paper deals with another area of scholarly endeavour which has given rise to a similar set of questions, the investigation of inscriptions in Greek and Latin from the ancient world. As the title suggests, it consists of a series of anecdotes about epigraphic research over the past half-century or so. I can vouch for the absolute accuracy of none of them, though I have closer acquaintance with the detail of some than of others; each presents a slightly different question as to what was the appropriate action or reaction, whether from a legal or from a scholarly point of view; and in some cases, colleagues have been at least threatened with legal proceedings following the decisions they have made regarding them. The parallels with the case of the Scrolls will be obvious, and I hope that these few reflections of my anecdotage, if not quite my dotage, may provide a little extra food for thought.

First, a little background. I am a historian of the Roman world, and specialise in Roman Spain, whence most of my examples will be drawn. It is not an exaggeration to say that our understanding of the history of the Romans in Spain has been substantially reshaped over

* I am grateful to several colleagues for assistance with this paper, and especially Professor Michael Crawford of University College London. The opinions expressed herein are entirely my own.

the past 25 years or so by the discovery of a surprising number of inscriptions on bronze tablets, some of which have been of very great significance indeed. Several copies, for instance, of the decree of the senate in 20 CE, following the suicide of Cn. Calpurnius Piso, who had been accused of the murder of Germanicus, the adopted son of the emperor Tiberius[1]; or a substantial part of the local regulations for the small town of Irni in Andalucia, originally on ten tablets, each some 58 cm high and 91 cm wide (about which, more below). The discovery of many of these inscriptions, and virtually all those which I shall be describing in what follows, owes less to the increasingly active prosecution of careful, scientific excavation in the Iberian peninsula than to the invention and widespread use of the metal detector. This, of course, is a tool which does not need an archaeologist to operate it, and both the *lex Irnitana* and the largest copy of the *sc de Cn. Pisone* were discovered by unofficial collectors at the same place, in the district of El Saucejo in the south of the province of Sevilla, in the 1980s.[2]

The problems raised by such sources of supply will be obvious to all; but they are exacerbated both by the vulnerability of inscriptions both on bronze and on stone, and by the long tradition of collecting such objects by private individuals. A glance at the magisterial collection of the *Corpus Inscriptionum Latinarum*, begun under the auspices of the Berlin Academy and the editorship of Theodore Mommsen in the second half of the last century, reveals the huge number of inscriptions recorded as in private possession. Moreover, many of these are now no longer in existence, or at least their whereabouts is unknown. In a conversation some fifteen years ago, one of the editors of the new edition of the second volume of *CIL* (which relates to the Iberian peninsula, and was originally complied by Emil Hübner in 1869, with a supplement in 1892) estimated that about half of the inscriptions recorded by Hübner were no longer visible, and that of those known to have been discovered since, approximately the same proportion survived. This situation, which relates to inscriptions long known as well as those recently discovered, is by no means confined to Spain. It raises a second set of questions, which relate not so much to the matter of ownership of property, intellectual or otherwise, but to the processes of

1. Fully published by W. Eck, A. Caballos and F. Fernández, *Das senatus consultum de Cn. Pisone patre* (Vestigia Band 48; Munich: C.H. Beck, 1996)

2. See Eck, Caballos and Fernández, *Das senatus consultum*, pp. 1-3.

epigraphic scholarship and the question of what it is that is being published.

But to my anecdotes: the first two form a pair, and are about two inscriptions, both of which I was responsible for republishing. The first is Italian, rather than Spanish. It is a fragment of a bronze tablet from Taranto in southern Italy, and contains the last section of a piece of a Roman statute, probably from the very end of the second century BCE. It was first published from the office of the local Sopritendenza in 1947, with a rather inadequate photograph and a text which proved to need a considerable amount of adjustment.[3] The reason I mention this inscription is that it had in fact been discovered underneath a Roman mosaic pavement in 1909, and had lain in the store of the Soprintendenza since that date.[4] Since the right to publish this important document belonged to the official office of the state and since other matters (including two World Wars) had distracted the attention of the Soprintendente, it did not appear until nearly 40 years later. The second case is that of a small bronze tablet, found in 1979 by an unofficial excavator with a metal detector at Bottorita, a site of a Celtiberian settlement on the edge of the Spanish *meseta*, just south of the valley of the river Ebro. The inscription records the settlement of a dispute about water rights, and is dated to 87 BCE. Its interest lies not least in the fact that the judgment is presented in the form of a legal formula, modelled directly on that which would have been used by the praetor in the court in Rome, and is the first, indeed the only surviving instance of such a formula used in a judicial context.[5] In this case, the inscription, thanks to the sage advice of a lawyer, found its way into the hands of Professor Guillermo Fatás of the University of Zaragoza, who published a first reading with exemplary speed, and subsequently produced a full publication, with excellent photographs.[6] In both these cases, despite

3. R. Bartoccini, 'Frammento di legge romana rinvenito a Taranto', *Epigraphica* 9 (1947), pp. 3-31 and 10 (1948), p. 158.

4. J.S. Richardson, in M.H. Crawford *et al.*, *Roman Statutes* 8 (London: Institute of Classical Studies, 1996), no. 8.

5. See J.S. Richardson, 'The tabula Contrebiensis', *JRS* 73 (1983), pp. 33-41; P. Birks, A. Rodger and J.S. Richardson, 'Further aspects of the tabula Contrebiensis', *JRS* 74 (1984), pp. 45-73.

6. G. Fatás, *Bolletino de la real Academia de la Historia* 176 (1980), p. 3; G. Fatás, *Contrebia Belaisca II: Tabula Contrebiensis* (Monografías arqueológicas, 23; Zaragoza: Universidad de Zaragoza, 1980).

the actual and potential vagaries of official and unofficial transmission, publication was achieved, and, equally if not more importantly, the inscriptions themselves are now in museums in Taranto and Zaragoza, where they can be inspected by interested scholars.

My second set of inscriptions presents a less happy story. This is a collection of decrees from the third century BCE from the site of Hellenised native settlement at Rocca di Entella in central Sicily. Excavations here had been begun by the Soprintendenza Archeologica di Palermo and the Scuola Normale Superiore of Pisa in the 1950s, but had not been completed. In the late 1970s and early 1980s the existence of eight decrees in Sicilian Doric Greek became known to the scholarly world, through transcriptions made by an anonymous anglophone correspondent (who produced six of them), a scholar based in the USA (who contributed another) and a French scholar, who had a text of an eighth. They were brought together in a publication by Professor Nenci of Pisa, with a full discussion, in 1982.[7] The sources of these copies of the decrees, which are of immense interest for the development of this obscure settlement and of both Sicilian and Roman involvement in the area, were ultimately the owners of the items and the dealers who obtained and sold them.[8] The inscriptions themselves have never been seen by the scholars who write on them, nor (to the best of my knowledge) are there any photographs available.[9]

My third and last case is that of the *lex Irnitana*, which I have already mentioned. This remarkable set of bronze tablets was discovered in 1981 by a group of men with metal detectors, hunting for Roman coins. These people then proceeded to sell the tablets to interested parties in Spain, which led to their dispersal throughout the country to collectors in Barcelona, Ronda, and elsewhere, and eventually to museums in Sevilla, Huelva and Madrid. Now, fortunately, all are together, displayed in a small but remarkable room in the Museo

7. G. Nenci *et al.*, *Annali della scuole normale superiore di Pisa* ser.3, 12 (1982), pp. 771-1103

8. See G. Daux, 'Un septième décret inédit d'Entella (Sicile)', *BCH* 106 (1982), pp. 307-308 and 527-28 (p. 308 n. 5).

9. Another decree (the ninth) was discovered separately from the other eight, and published with a photograph a few years later (V. Giustolini, *Nakone ed Entella alla luce degli antichi decreti recentemente apparsi e di un nuovo decreto inedito* [Sicilia archeologica che scompare, 7; Palermo: Centro di Documentazione e Ricerca per la Sicilia antica 'Paolo Orsi', 1985], pp. 16-24).

Arqueologico Nacional de Sevilla. For a time, none of the holders of the tablets knew of the existence of the others. Eventually, however, the truth emerged, and a group of scholars was formed to work, in great secrecy, on the new find. Photographs of the tablets, taken before extensive cleaning had taken place, were distributed to members of the group, and work on an exhaustive publication and commentary was commenced. It will be of no surprise to those who have taken part in collaborative enterprises of this sort to learn that progress was not rapid. Inevitably, before the projected edition was far advanced, articles began to appear, based on texts drawn from the photographs, including a Spanish translation of the whole.[10] Eventually one scholar, who had been establishing the text of the document, decided that it was time to produce a proper version, which consequently appeared in the *Journal of Roman Studies* in 1986.[11] The resentment that this caused was immense, but it is perhaps worth noticing that the eventual definitive publication of the inscription, without the intended commentary, did not take place until 1990, when it appeared with excellent photographs and a full account of the archaeological context, produced by the directors of the Sevilla Museum and of the Museum in Palencia,[12] and the full-scale study originally projected has in fact not appeared at all.

Of the three sets of anecdotes I have related, only the last presents issues of intellectual property of the type that is of interest to a lawyer, and even that instance is confused by further questions about the ownership of inscriptions as property of a more ordinary variety. In the case of the *lex Irnitana*, however, the matter that was at the heart of the

10. A. D'Ors, 'Litem suam facere', *SDHI* 48 (1982), pp. 368-84; 'La nueva copia irnitana de la 'lex Flavia municipalis'', *AHDE* 53 (1983), pp. 5-15; 'Nuevos datos de la ley Irnitana sobre jurisdiccíon municipal', *SDHI* 49 (1983), pp. 18-50; 'Una nueva lista de aciones infamantes', in V. Giuffrè (ed.), *Sodalitas: scritti in honore Antonio Guarino* (Napoli: Jovene, 1984), pp. 2575-90; 'De nuevo sobre la ley municipal', *SDHI* 50 (1984), pp. 535-73; 'La ley Flavia municipal', *AHDE* 54 (1984); T. Giménez Candela, 'La lex Irnitana: une nouvelle loi municipale de la Bétique', *RIDA* 30 (1983), pp. 125-40; 'Una contribuccíon al estudio de la ley Irnitana: la manumisión de esclavos municipales', *Iura* (1981, pub. 1984), pp. 37-56.

11. J. González, 'The *Lex Irnitana*: a new Flavian municipal law', *Journal of Roman Studies* 76 (1986), pp. 147-243.

12. F. Fernández Gómez and M. del Amo y la Herra, *La lex Irnitana y su contexto arqueologico* (Marchena, Sevilla: Museo Arqueologico de Marchena, 1990).

resentment engendered and of the legal proceedings that were threatened was not about ownership of the physical objects, but about ownership of the text, and the right to publish it. It must be said, and my division of my anecdotes into three categories rather gives this away, that my primary concern with these examples is not with the legal questions of ownership, but with what might be called the ethics of scholarship. From this standpoint, my three sections provide three different questions: the last is about the justification in presenting a text in which others have an interest in the publication, whether that is an interest that could be expressed in legal terms or relates to a less readily defined notion of the scholarly reputation of the interested parties; the first set (the inscriptions from Taranto and from Botorrita) raises the question of the justification in withholding publication because of a right (undisputed in the case of the Taranto fragment) of an institution or individual to be the first publisher; and the second (the Entella decrees), the somewhat different matter of the justification of the publication of inscriptions, which are not in principle accessible to other scholars.

Several of these matters are of particular interest to me because of my involvement in a recent project by an international group of epigraphists and historians to produce new texts, with translation and commentary, of all examples of Roman statutes from the earliest times to the mid-first century CE, a project that reached completion in the publication of two volumes, entitled *Roman Statutes*, in 1996.[13] In that case, it became clear that access to the original objects was essential in order both to establish a text and an improved understanding of that text, even though some of the inscriptions involved had been worked on by scholars of the highest repute for many centuries. For instance, in one case a join was noticed between two sections of an inscription, known since the sixteenth century, which led to a radical re-evaluation of two texts (one on each side of the bronze).[14] This was despite the fact that the fragments of this particular bronze were set in a sheet of metal and kept in a frame in the Archaeological Museum in Naples, which made identifying and confirming the join extremely difficult. The production of this collection also raised questions of ownership of texts and of interpretations, especially in the context of a co-operative undertaking, and the role of the person deputed to be the group's

13. M.H. Crawford *et al.*, *Roman Statutes* (London: Institute of Classical Studies, 1996).

14. M.H. Crawford, in Crawford *et al.*, *Roman Statutes*, pp. 45-51 and pl. I.1.

general editor. These are from my point of view primarily questions of the practice of the scholarly profession, and only secondarily, if at all, of rights under the law; but I am inclined to think, perhaps naïvely, that if the ethics of our own profession prove insufficient not only to protect, but to enable the academic work on which we are engaged, the processes of even the most sophisticated legislation are likely to prove a blunt and an unwieldy instrument for the purpose.

KENYON'S JERUSALEM EXCAVATION REPORTS

Kay Prag

1. *Introduction*

An archaeological training may be very broadly based, but can hardly be said to cover the legal parameters of intellectual property rights. The following paper summarizes the 'in field' solutions and pragmatic decisions which one archaeological expedition reached, and the rules which underpinned them. It does not pretend to be authoritative, or exhaustive. It is largely a personal view after 40 years experience as an archaeological excavator, researcher, publisher and editor working contextually in the Dead Sea environment. During that 40 years, many assumptions and processes have changed radically.

2. *The Joint Expedition*

The Joint Expedition to Jerusalem between the years 1961 and 1967 was led by Kathleen Kenyon, initially in partnership (1961–63) with Père Roland de Vaux and the École Biblique et Archéologique Français in Jerusalem, and mainly (1962–67) with Douglas Tushingham and the Royal Ontario Museum in Canada. The expedition was sponsored by the British School of Archaeology in Jerusalem (henceforth BSAJ, now merged in the Council for British Research in the Levant, henceforth CBRL), the British Academy and the Palestine Exploration Fund. The multinational staff included 102 people over the seven seasons; up to 500 local workmen were employed each season; trenches were excavated in 22 different locations in and around the city. In all, the expedition excavated approximately 26,367 cubic metres of cultural deposits. As well as the complex recording of stratigraphy and architecture, over 9000 objects were registered, drawn and photographed; plus nearly 4000 coins; approximately five tons of pottery and glass fragments were retained for study; the archive contains 1269 site photographs; and so on. In many respects the enterprise is comparable to the scale of the publication of the Dead Sea Scrolls. It has been estimated that archaeological post-excavation work requires 6 to 12 times as long as excavation, so the basic sum suggests between 8 and 16 years are required to complete the post-excavation analysis—but this sum requires a post-excavation team that would be commensurate with the size of the excavation and of the excavation team. Without doing more complicated sums, the length of time required to analyse the results of the expedition is far greater than is generally recognised. This may also strike a chord amongst Scroll scholars. Indeed, just as Jerusalem and Qumran have mutual themes in personnel, in history and in religious studies, so also modern political processes have played a role affecting the finds from both sites.

3. *Government Regulation*

Six seasons' work were completed in Jerusalem with the permission and under the regulations of the Department of Antiquities of Jordan; and the final season (which began in July 1967, immediately following the June War of 1967) with the permission and under the regulations of the Department of Antiquities of Israel, with the 'tacit consent' of Jordan. These regulations underlie the organization and process of the project, and are fundamental to it

The contemporary regulations of the Jordanian Department provided for a liberal division of finds. 'The Department will usually keep for its museums the unique and rare pieces, as well as a representative collection of other finds, and it will usually give a fair share of the finds to the excavation.' 'Concerning division, every project director' must state 'that his share of the division is going to his sponsoring institution(s)' (see Hashemite Kingdom of Jordan, Rules of Excavation, 1 January 1975: Section IV, which were broadly those applicable in the 1960s). Thus the Government's share of the division of the registered finds from Jerusalem for 1961–66 was deposited at the Jordanian Government store at the Palestine Archaeological Museum in Jerusalem (now the Rockefeller Museum), and in due course objects from the 1961, 1962, 1963 and 1965 seasons were transported to the stores of National Museum of Jordan in the Amman Citadel, where they were registered and are now curated. For unclear reasons, the finds from 1964 and 1966 remained in the Jerusalem store. Following the 1967 season, a division was made with the Israeli Department of Antiquities, on a slightly different basis, by which, for example, all Hebrew inscribed material was included in the Government's share. The Government's share from the 1967 season was deposited with the Israeli Department of Antiquities. Subsequently, the objects from 1964 and 1966 in the Jordanian store in the Palestine Archaeological Museum (the Rockefeller Museum) were added to the 1967 material, and all three seasons' finds are now housed and registered in the storehouse of the Israel Antiquities Authority. All the Expedition's share of the finds 1961–67 was, as stipulated in the Jordanian agreement, sent only to the public institutions which had provided financial support to the work (no excavated items are the property of private individuals; no excavation funds were personal funds). Thus these finds were distributed in the year of excavation to approximately 15 institutions world-wide, from Otago in New Zealand to St Andrews in Scotland (in recent years the St Andrews material was transferred to Edinburgh). The collections are located principally in the US and Britain. Jordanian liberality over the finds has meant accessible teaching collections, and has stimulated interest in Jordanian archaeology amongst a wide international audience.

It should be noted that the two governments have revised their Antiquities Laws over the years since; and various international agreements have related to the Treatment of Cultural Properties and Antiquities in Occupied Territories, as The Hague 1954, New Delhi, 5 December 1956, etc., which may or may not affect the ownership and rights relating to some of the Jerusalem material.

4. *Sponsorship*

Sponsors of expeditions working in Jordan and Israel should be guarantors of academic quality and of the agreements made between individual and institution, and between institution and government. Foreign expeditions working in Jordan and Israel are usually sponsored by archaeological institutions, or by the institution which employs the director of the project. In Israel, the same regulations that bind the site excavator (the 'licence holder') apply to the sponsor or joint sponsor of an excavation (Israel, Israel Antiquities Authority, Terms and Conditions to Conduct an Archaeological Excavation in Israel, as current in 1997). The immediate sponsor of the Joint Expedition was the BSAJ, and following Kenyon's death in 1978, the BSAJ (since 1998/99 the CBRL) in 1979 accepted responsibility for the scientific publication, but lacked funding to see the process to publication.

5. *The Funding*

The Joint Expedition was conducted with public, not personal funding, although research grants for the project were made to the director of the project, as well as to the project itself. The expedition funds were not personal taxable property, and the expedition funds were separately accounted. They were not adequate to meet the cost of post-excavation work.

6. *The Archive*

The archive consists of all the paper record, the images, both paper and photographic; the study collections of pottery, glass and other items. The archive (except for the photographs) was held by Kenyon at her home, and was moved to the Manchester Museum in 1980; the photographic archive remained at the Institute of Archaeology, University College London, until 1994, when it also joined the archive in Manchester. The CBRL retains copyright to site records, databases and photographs.

7. *The Publication Process*

The publication of the Jerusalem project is a large, complex undertaking; and the distinction between personal intellectual property and public enterprise is equally complex. The regulations of the national departments placed the responsibility for publication on the excavator, sometimes defining a time limit, and with penalty clauses for non-compliance ('the Department will not approve an application for a new or renewed permit to excavate' (see Hashemite Kingdom of Jordan, Rules of Excavation, 1 January 1975: Section IIIC). Similar rules apply in Israel. The excavator bears the responsibility for, and should play a key role in, the publication. The responsibility implies rights, and these rights are generally accepted in practice, whether attributed on the basis of 'the sweat of the brow', or through an unwritten 'academic trade union'.

8. *Personal Intellectual Property*

a. *The Rights of the Project Director*

The appropriate publication process involves both preliminary reports after each season (mandatory requirements for the excavator by both Jordanian and Israeli governments) and final reports (also mandatory). For the Jerusalem excavations, the preliminary reporting process was prompt (see Kenyon 1962, 1963, 1964, 1965, 1966, 1967a, 1968; de Vaux 1962a and b, 1963, 1964a and b). In the Wheeler tradition, Kenyon also believed in the importance of, and responsibility for, the dissemination of the findings to a wider public, and published several 'popular' books incorporating the main preliminary results (Kenyon 1967b, 1974). The writings of K.M. Kenyon are regarded as her personal copyright (this is in accord with current [1999] Association of University Teachers guidance in the UK). Kenyon was, during the years of the excavation, employed as a university teacher, and as the principal of an Oxford college. The partners in the enterprise also retained publication rights (e.g. de Vaux, as above); however, the École Biblique withdrew from the project in 1963, and transferred the Site J paper archive to the Joint Expedition for publication. The final report on this work should be published during 2002 (Prag, forthcoming); the Royal Ontario Museum published Dr Tushingham's (1985) final report.

K.M. Kenyon's intention, as at Jericho, was to produce a core stratigraphic and ceramic report, with multiple specialist reports. Kenyon had a phenomenal memory for site stratigraphy and was rarely absent from the site; no matter how detailed the notes (not using standardized record sheets, but a standard system), she had an irreplaceable overview of the site. This knowledge was more than mere intellectual copyright. In addition, her death in 1978 left the huge project rudderless, and without a defined publication team. However, publication rights can be transferred and delegated. This was the role of the BSAJ, the principal sponsor.

b. *Transfer of Publication Rights*

Publication rights to part of the material were transferred to Professor H.J. Franken in 1980 and three volumes have been published (Franken and Steiner 1990; Eshel and Prag 1995; Steiner 2001). Further volumes are projected. In these cases, the text has remained the copyright of the respective authors, but the original photographs, etc., which are held in the archive, remain the copyright of the CBRL.

The responsibility is for appropriate, full publication. Subsequent work has not been bound by Kenyon's planned publication process. Research is not static, and current approaches need to account for the many advances in knowledge and process between the 1960s and the twenty-first century. The personal intellectual property involved in the author's textual copyright recognizes the right of the author to advance beyond the routine processing of records, to synthesis and independent conclusions.

9. *Intellectual Property Rights of Expedition Members*

Accepted conventions of the 1960s were applied. Although the expedition offered at most a small honorarium and cost of travel to its core staff, and basic accommodation, training and invaluable experience to its volunteer staff, and not contractual employment, the copyright of the material generated by the Expedition remained the copyright of the Expedition, with appropriate acknowledgement. For example, in terms of the archive, there were at least six expedition photographers over the years of fieldwork. Peter Dorrell (one of the principal photographers) continued to process expedition photographs until 1994, when the negatives were placed with the archive in The Manchester Museum. Since his death, his personal negatives relating to Jerusalem have also been given to the archive.

10. *Copyright*

Generally speaking, copyright resides in the image and not the object; and the photographic archive and the drawings form basic elements in the Jerusalem archive's publication copyright. Many unpublished objects are, however, spread around the world, in the care of curators whose institutions now own the objects, and who are, therefore, free to photograph and publish them as items in their collections. The contextual data of many of these objects has been published, and they are fully and freely accessible to the public and academic worlds within these parameters. Although museums generally respect the publication rights of the excavator, the lack of contextual data for the unpublished objects does not prevent the publication of the objects themselves, it simply limits the presentation of contextual information. Most of the Jerusalem objects are important solely because they have a context: indeed, few rate as first class art historical objects and are often incomplete. Divorced from context, they are little more than minor antiquities, hardly comparable to what is bought on the antiquities market.

Museum curators of unpublished objects are subject to guidelines; they may retain the photographic rights and thus maintain copyright of all images; or before permitting photography, require the applicant to seek the permission of the excavator/donor.

11. *Access*

Access to published and unpublished material varies according to the rules of the institution, and may be governed by cost and accessibility. For the Jerusalem archive material, access to *bona fide* scholars is mainly governed by questions of curatorial availability and appropriate control for protection of artefacts from theft, damage or disarrangement. Some small collections are readily accessible, but the sherd material, bagged and boxed, is more difficult. Enquiries are met where possible.

12. *Summary*

In real terms, whatever the legal position (and time limits are, or were, defined in agreements in some instances), it is tacitly accepted that within the lifetime of the excavator the right of publication of site records remains primarily with the excavator, and secondarily with the sponsor(s); these rights can be transferred. This tends to be a *de facto* position, because the excavator normally controls the site archive, and the primary contextual data. Today there is much discussion over imposing contractual obligations on the excavator at the time research grants are conferred, with a fall back to the often reluctant sponsor. The accepted practices are usually governed by tacit rather than contractual agreements, and a process of 'fair-dealing', which recognizes scholarly input with generally liberal policies, but where pragmatic choices are often governed by cost and time. The breakdown of these processes is undoubtedly difficult to repair.

Appendix

THE SUPREME COURT JUDGMENT

IN THE SUPREME COURT SITTING AS THE APPELLATE COURT FOR CIVIL APPEALS*

C.A. 2790/93
C.A. 2811/93

Before:	**The Honorable Justice A. Barak** **The Honorable Justice Y. Türkel** **The Honorable Justice D. Beinish**
The Appellant in C.A. 2790/93 **And the Respondent in the Counter-Appeal:**	**Robert Eisenman**
The Appellants in C.A. 2811/93 **And the Respondents in the Counter-Appeal:**	**1. Hershel Shanks** **2. James M. Robinson** **3. Biblical Archaeology Society**

v.

The Respondent and the Appellant in the Counter-Appeal:	**Elisha Qimron**
	Appeals of the Judgment of the Jerusalem District Court in C.F. 641/92 [*sic*] of March 30, 1993 Given by the Honorable Judge D. Dorner
Date of Proceedings:	**19 Adar 5758 (March 17, 1998)**
For the Appellant in C.A. 2790/93 **And the Respondent in the Counter-Appeal:**	**Adv. A. Hausner**
For the Appellants in C.A. 2811/93 **And the Respondents in the Counter-Appeal:**	**Adv. D. Frimer and Adv. Y. Hoffman**
For the Respondent:	**Adv. Y. Meltzer**

* Translated by Yoninah Hoffman.

JUDGMENT

Justice Y. Türkel:

Background

1. The '*Miqṣat ma'aśe ha-torah*' scroll (hereinafter—the 'Scroll') is one of the Hidden Scrolls[1] that were found in the caves of Qumran in the Judaean Desert. The Scroll is written in a language that is earlier than the language of the Mishnah and is, apparently, a letter of the leader of the Judaean Desert sect to the leader of the people in Jerusalem. The fragments of the Scroll were discovered at the beginning of the fifties in 'cave no. 4' at Qumran, in which approximately 15,000 fragments of different scrolls were discovered. Professor John Strugnell of Harvard University (hereinafter—'Strugnell') was the first researcher who worked on joining the Scroll fragments to make one scroll and he was able to identify approximately 100 fragments of the Scroll, and also to join them—according to their shapes—to form approximately 67 fragments. The decipherment work of the Scroll required completion of the missing portions with the help of linguistic and *Halakhic*[2] knowledge that Strugnell did not have. Against this background Professor Elisha Qimron joined—he is the respondent in the appeals before us and the counter-appellant—(hereinafter—'Qimron') Strugnell in 1981 for the purpose of completing the decipherment of the Scroll. Qimron is a professor of Hebrew language at Ben Gurion University in Be'er Sheva, works on philological research and his expertise is in research of the scrolls found in the caves of Qumran. During the following eleven consecutive years Qimron worked on decipherment of the Scroll, most of the work was done by him, and he is the one who called it by the name '*Miqṣat ma'aśe ha-torah*' (in short, in English[3]—MMT). From the 67 fragments that he received from Strugnell he was able to construct a 121 line text (hereinafter—the 'Deciphered Text'), approximately 40 per cent of which are completions that are not found in the writing on the fragments.

During the course of the decipherment period Qimron and Strugnell passed on a number of copies of the draft Deciphered Text to a number of scholars in order to obtain their reactions. In 1990, towards the end of the decipherment work, a principle agreement was made between Qimron and Strugnell and the English Oxford publisher with respect to the publication of the Deciphered Text accompanied by photographs of the Scroll fragments and words of interpretation.

Mr Hershel Shanks (hereinafter—'Shanks')—the appellant no. 1 in C.A. 2811/93 and the respondent in the counter-appeal—is an attorney and the editor of an archaeological journal called *Biblical Archaeology Review* (hereinafter—'BAR'),

1. 'Hidden Scrolls' is the literal translation of the Hebrew '*ha-megilot ha-gnuzot*' commonly referred to in English as the Dead Sea Scrolls.

2. 'Halakhic' knowledge means knowledge of Jewish law.

3. The Hebrew word is '*la'az*' which literally means 'a foreign language'.

that reaches more than a half million readers in many countries, among them Israel. The Biblical Archaeology Society (hereinafter—'BAS') publishes the BAR. BAS is incorporated as a company in the United States and is the appellant no. 3 in C.A. 2811/93 and the respondent in the counter appeal. In November 1991, before Strugnell and Qimron published the Deciphered Text and without obtaining their consent, Shanks published in the United States, published by BAS, a book called 'A Facsimile Edition of the Dead Sea Scrolls' (hereinafter—the 'Book'), in which photographs of hundreds of fragments of the Hidden Scrolls and among them photographs of fragments of the Scroll were included. The editors of the Book were Dr James Robinson (hereinafter—'Robinson')—the appellant no. 2 in C.A. 2811/93 and the respondent in the counter-appeal—and Dr Robert Eisenman (hereinafter—'Eisenman')—the appellant in C.A. 2790/93 and the respondent in the counter-appeal (hereinafter—the 'Editors'). The Editors wrote an introduction to the Book and prepared an index of its photographs. The Book also included a 'Publisher's Foreword' that Shanks wrote. A number of appendices were attached to this Foreword, one of which is a copy of the draft of the Deciphered Text, without noting Qimron's name on the text (for the sake of brevity the 'draft of the Deciphered Text' will be referred to in the following as—the 'Deciphered Text').

2. On January 14, 1992 Qimron filed a complaint in the Jerusalem District Court in which he petitioned to order Shanks, BAS and the Editors (hereinafter—the 'Appellants') to refrain from distributing the Book so long as it includes the Deciphered Text of the Scroll and to compensate him for the violation of his copyright. Likewise he petitioned for temporary relief until the final resolution of his primary complaint. The District Court (the honourable Judge D. Dorner), in its decision from January 21, 1992, acceded to Qimron's request and instructed the Appellants to refrain from publicizing or distributing the Book in Israel or abroad, as long as it included the Deciphered Text. Likewise it permitted Qimron to serve the Appellants with the court papers out of bounds of the jurisdiction. A petition by the Appellants to cancel the service permit was denied. Until grant of the temporary injunction approximately 200–300 copies of the Book were sold, most of them in the United States and some of them even in Israel.

Judgment of the District Court

3. The District Court, in its judgment of March 30, 1993, held that the Appellants infringed Qimron's copyright pursuant to the Copyright Law, 1911 (hereinafter—the 'Law'), issued a permanent injunction as it was requested and obligated the Appellants to pay Qimron damages in the amount of 100,000 NIS: of these 20,000 NIS as statutory damages without proof of damage and 80,000 NIS for the mental anguish that was caused to him. It also obligated the Appellants to pay Qimron attorneys fees in the amount of 50,000 NIS.

The court held that the infringement occurred in the United States. At the same time, it decided the complaint according to prevailing Israeli law after finding that the presumption of the equality of laws applies to the matter. In its judgment it held that Qimron has copyright in the Deciphered Text; that Qimron's moral right was infringed as a result of publication of the text without noting his name; that in the circumstances under which the Appellants published the Deciphered Text they do not enjoy the *good faith* defence and that no policy considerations exist that are able to relieve the Appellants of liability. It also held that all of the Appellants are liable to Qimron jointly and severally for the infringement of his copyright and his moral right; however, since Shanks is the one who decided to publish the Deciphered Text and took upon himself full responsibility for its results, the court held that 'his relative liability as against the two [the Editors—Y.T.] is 100 per cent'.

4. In C.A. 2811/93 Shanks, Robinson and BAS petition to cancel the judgment of the District Court, including its remedies and the obligation for costs. In C.A. 2790/93 Eisenman petitions to cancel those portions of the judgment that relate to him. In his counter-appeal Qimron petitions to determine that he is entitled also to compensation for the pecuniary injuries that he claims were proven to have been caused to him and also to increase the amount of damages that were awarded to him. Discussion of the appeals was combined.

In the framework of the appeal proceedings a body named the 'Committee of Concerned Intellectual Property Educators' submitted a petition to allow it to join the proceeding in the status of a 'friend of the court' (*amicus curiae*) and to submit principal arguments.[4] Qimron opposed the petition. In our decision of 24 August, 1999 we denied the petition and our reasons will be detailed in the following (Section 31 hereinafter).

The Main Contentions of the Parties

5. The Appellants argue that there was no infringement of Qimron's rights in Israel, and therefore he has no cause of action according to prevailing Israeli law; that circumstances did not exist that justify the application of the presumption of the equality of laws; that Qimron's act of completing the text is but a reconstruction of an existing work and therefore the Deciphered Text is not a protected work pursuant to copyright laws; that the grant of protection to the act of reconstruction that Qimron performed harms academic research, provides Qimron with a property right in 'a part of the cultural heritage of the Jewish People', and is not reconcilable with proper legal policy; that the publication of the Deciphered Text, in the manner it was done, is in line with 'scholarly convention' accepted by academia, and therefore it is protected as 'fair dealing' with the work or as a publication done by virtue of Qimron's implied consent even though in fact Qimron did not give his consent to the publication; that the Deciphered Text was distributed by Qimron himself among scholars in academia without his name appearing thereon; therefore, there is no foundation for ruling that its publication without the notation of Qimron's name infringes his moral right. In any case, under the circumstances the Appellants fulfilled their duty in that they noted that the Deciphered Text was made by Strugnell 'together with another colleague'; that Qimron suffered no pecuniary injury for which compensation should be awarded; that the amount of the compensation

4. In Hebrew *'iqarei ti'un'*.

awarded to Qimron for mental anguish and the amount of attorneys fees awarded to him are exorbitant.

The Editors argue additionally that the part of the Book that includes the Foreword that Shanks wrote and the copy of the Deciphered Text was not included in their editorial area and that they did not have control over their inclusion in the Book; that they objected to the very addition of a foreword to the Book but Shanks ignored their objection; that they did not even know in advance that a copy of the Deciphered Text would be added to the Book; and that in any case, they did not commit any act that constitutes copyright infringement.

6. In his Counter-Appeal Qimron argues that the violation of his right to be the first publisher of the Deciphered Text caused him pecuniary injuries as well as non-pecuniary damages and therefore the court should have awarded him actual pecuniary damages and should not have been satisfied with statutory damages; that in spite of the difficulty of estimating his pecuniary injuries sufficient evidence was brought before the court to award him with pecuniary damages; that, alternatively, global pecuniary damages could have been awarded to him; and that the court ignored the fact that he requested also the remedy of the return of copies of the Book that remain in the Appellants hands, that he is entitled to under the provision of Section 7 of the Law.

Petitions to Submit Additional Evidence

7. The parties submitted petitions to add additional evidence in the framework of the appeal. We are speaking of evidence that did not exist at the time the complaint was heard in the District Court—they are primarily books and articles the most important of which are: Qimron and Strugnell's book that was published in 1994, other books about the same Scroll, a journalistic piece and articles that were published at a later date, and decisions in proceedings that were conducted against Qimron in the United States—and it had been impossible to submit them.

Since these pieces of evidence can shed light on the picture of matters before the court—without their being able to influence the results—I found it proper to accept them solely for this purpose.

Discussion of the Contentions

Application of Israeli Law

8. The District Court decided the lawsuit according to prevailing Israeli law, after it ruled that the presumption of the equality of laws applies to the matter. As it noted, 'all agree that the suit is governed by the law of the place of infringement, that is, the laws of the USA...It is also undisputed that this law has not been proved.' The Appellants dispute the application of the presumption of the equality of laws in the case before us and argue that since Qimron did not prove the law that applies in the place of the alleged infringement 'so he did not prove the facts that establish his cause of action'.

I am unable to accept the Appellants' argument and I agree with Qimron's claim that Israeli law applies to this matter without resorting to the presumption of the equality of laws. In this matter he relies upon the fact that copies of the Book were sent to readers in Israel and on the fact that a portion of the marketing efforts of the Book were done in Israel. In fact, from Shanks' testimony (*Protocol*, pp. 271-72) and the order forms that were submitted as evidence it appears that three copies of the Book were sent by BAS to readers in Israel. These copies were, it is true, ordered in the United States, and the consideration for them was paid there, but the fact that BAS sent them directly to readers in Israel is enough to find that it published the Deciphered Text in Israel. Since Qimron's cause of action is based upon the fact that his right to be the first to publish the Deciphered Text was denied, the copies distributed in Israel until the issuance of the injunction that brought about the cessation of the distribution—even if they were few—are sufficient for the application of Israeli law to this matter.

There are, therefore, no grounds for intervening in the court's conclusion according to which this matter must be decided according to prevailing Israeli law.

Does Qimron Have a Copyright in the Deciphered Text?

Preliminary Comment

9. Before we come to discuss the question does Qimron have a right in the Deciphered Text, it is proper to give some thought to some of the acts of research of the Hidden Scrolls found in the Qumran caves. The first scroll was discovered incidentally in 1947. In the following years a number of caves were discovered in Qumran and in them many additional scrolls were found. The Jordanian government, under whose control the region of Qumran was at the time, placed the scrolls—that were held at the Rockefeller Museum in Jerusalem—at the disposal of a small international team of scholars and only they were able to study the scrolls. As a result of the Six Day War the scrolls passed into the hands of the State of Israel and the Israeli Antiquities Authority continued the policy according to which the scrolls were studied only by a small international team of scholars, that expanded over the years. Qimron was a member of the team from the year 1980.

A bitter complaint about the 'monopoly' given to the international team of scholars, which prevented many scholars from studying the scrolls, is heard in the Appellants' arguments. In their opinion publication of the Book 'contributed to a great extent to the research of the Hidden Scrolls—if only in that it broke the monopoly that existed until that period'. On this point the District Court said that 'for many years Shanks has led from the pages of *BAR* an obstinate and polemical struggle to open up the study of the Dead Sea Scrolls to all who are interested… He testified that he served as the voice of all those who were left outside of the research cartel.' Shanks wrote similar things in the Foreword that he wrote for the Book:

> Surely we must admire the dedicated people who have devoted their professional lives to arranging and deciphering these seemingly impenetrable pieces of our common past. For the most part, the people who do this are not only dedicated but brilliant experts in what they are doing, conscientious to the nuances of their work. For this, all honour to them.

> But for their pride and greed—their unbending determination to keep exclusive control of these treasures for themselves, their heirs and their students—they must bear the shame.

I shall anticipate and say on this point that this debate is not set before us for resolution; nor is the justice of the reasons by virtue of which Qimron was given the right to work on research and decipherment of the Scroll or the justice of the reasons by virtue of which others were awarded this right. Also the justice of Shanks' public struggle—even if he saw publication of the Book as a part of this struggle—is not our concern, inasmuch as this matter deviates from the framework of the discussion of the copyright in the Deciphered Text.

What is the Object of the Right?

10. In order to decide the question of whether Qimron has a copyright in the Deciphered Text we must define what the object of Qimron's right is—what is the 'work' that Qimron created during the course of his work over eleven years? Here we must distinguish between two main components of the Deciphered Text. The first component, is the physical, the tangible, 'the raw material': the fragments of the Scroll that were created approximately 2000 years ago and were found at Qumran; the second component, is that which made the pile of fragments into a deciphered text by the physical attachment of the fragments, their arrangement, the decipherment of that which is written on them, to the extent that they required decipherment, and the completion of the missing portions between the fragments. In other words, the art of imbuing the fragments with the spirit and the soul that made them into a living and meaningful text. It is true, the Scroll fragments themselves are today in the public domain and may be used by all in the sense that anyone who wishes to attach them and to decipher them is permitted to do so. However, the fact that the 'building blocks', that were the material in the hands of the creator at work, are in the public domain, has nothing to do with the question of whether he has a copyright in his work. This court made this point when it said:

> it does not matter that the 'raw material' for construction of the tables is in the public domain—the question of whether there is an original work in the respondent's tables due to the thought, the effort or the expertise invested in them, must be decided by looking at the author's work as a whole (words of Judge [according to his title then] M. Landau in C.A. 136/71 *State of Israel v. Yitzchak Achiman*, P.D. 26[2]259 [hereinafter—the '*Achiman* Matter'], 261).

The question before us is whether Qimron has a copyright in the Deciphered Text by virtue of one or more of the things that he did: the physical attachment of the fragments, their arrangement, decipherment of that which is written on them and completion of that which is missing between the fragments. Does that 'spirit', that 'soul' that he imbued in the Scroll fragments, with the power of his knowledge and talent—that I suggest calling his 'inspiration' (in the sense of '*yitron haruach*'[5] according to one of the interpretations of the words in Malachi 2.15)—make the Deciphered Text as a whole a work protected by the Law?

When does Copyright in a Work Arise?

11. Section 35(1) of the Law provides that a 'literary work', that can be the object of copyright, includes, *inter alia*, also 'compilations' (in the original—'compilations'). As it has been said, by virtue of this provision 'copyright can apply to an editorial form or special design' provided that it includes an 'original work due to the thought, the effort or the expertise that were invested' (the *Achiman* Matter, at p. 261). So a 'literary work' will be entitled, as this term is used in the Law, to copyright protection only if it is an original work. (See paragraph 13 of my opinion in C.A. 8393/96 *Miphal Hapayis v. The Roy Export Establishment Company* [not yet published] [hereinafter—the '*Miphal Hapayis* Matter']; and T. Greenman Copyrights, Artists and Producers [5760] at pp. 25-26). As it has been said:

> The originality requirement was deleted for some reason from the official Hebrew translation of *The Laws of Israel*, but it appears in Section 1 of the English version of the law, that is the determinative version: 'every *original* literary, dramatic, musical, and artistic work…'. Copyright protection is not given for an abstract idea but for the tangible expression of an idea. This expression must be *original*.—The work does not have to be the expression of an original thought or invention. All that is necessary is, that the work not be copied from another work, but that its origin be in its creator, its author.—In order to test whether the work is deserving of protection one must view it in its entirety, as a single whole. If, despite the use the author made of an existing topic, he invested enough of his own independent effort and talent, that originate in him, the work will be protected (words of Justice S. Netanyahu in C.A. 360/83 *Strusky Ltd. v. Glidat Vitman Ltd.*, P.D. 40[3]340, 346) (my emphasis—Y.T.)

Originality is the main element and the investment of effort, time or talent is not sufficient to justify copyright protection. About this it has been said:

> In light of the purpose of copyright laws—it is clear that the conclusion is that effort alone is not sufficient in order to justify the grant of copyright protection to expression. This conclusion is supported both by the fact that copyright laws constitute a balance between competing social needs and in the extent of protection that the right holder is entitled to. *The balancing role* of the law derives from the fact that the grant of copyright in certain expression limits possible future expressions. An approach that views the right as deriving from the effort itself is not sensitive enough to this important balance that underlies copyright laws.

5. Literally, the 'advantage of the spirit'.

> It is true, the 'effort' approach is an acceptable approach for the justification of tangible property laws, and therefore there are those that view it as appropriate also for intellectual property laws—but it seems that the difference between the two areas does not permit its adoption in the area of intellectual property (words of the President M. Shamgar in C.A. 513/89 *Interlego A/S v. Exin-lines Bros. S.A.*, P.D. 48[4]133 [hereinafter—the 'Interlego Matter'], 165; see also M. Deutch *Property* [Vol 1, 5757] at pp. 78-79 [hereinafter—'*Deutch*']; compare with: *Feist Publications, Inc. v. Rural Telephone Service Company, Inc.* 499 US 340, 111 S. Ct. 1282 [1991]).

At the same time, it is important to note that there are those who contend that the investment of effort, time or talent by the author, in themselves, can testify to the existence of creativity (see the *Interlego* Matter, at p. 164). As for the amount of effort and creativity that is necessary it has been said:

> It is proper to note that according to all of the approaches we are talking of nothing but the most minimal tests, both with respect to the effort and the creativity that are necessary.—effort is expressed in the investment of any human resource: time, effort, talent, money, knowledge, judgment, development, pain or personal taste—it is required that the investment of the creator surpass a certain minimum, though that minimum is very low. It is necessary 'that it be possible to distinguish the independent contribution of the creator', or that 'the product be given to distinction from its building blocks' (the *Interlego* Matter, at p. 170).

Here thought must be given also to the crystallization process of the work in its final form and to what extent the creator contributed an original contribution of his own to this process:

> In testing originality there is no room for a comparison between the final work and other works, and the focus must be on the stage of crystallization of the work.—The proper test will focus on testing the considerations at the crystallization phase of the work and will check if these are taken from existing components or existing works, or that they contain something that is beyond this, from the original contribution of the creator. In other words, the original contribution is tested not in light of the final result but in light of its origin. Is the origin in the creator or alternatively someone existing and known. In this the purpose of copyrights is expressed (the *Interlego* Matter, at p. 171).

12. We have seen that compilation and editing may fall within the term 'literary work' as it is understood in the Law, and that the question whether copyright ensues in a work is tested by the extent of its originality. We have also seen that it is not enough that the creator invested his human resources but that an amount of originality is also required—not only in the work itself but also in the process of its creation—in order for the work to be entitled to protection.

From the Matter[6] *of Copyrights to the Scroll of 'Miqṣat ma'aśe ha-torah'*

13. The District Court held that Qimron has a copyright in the Deciphered Text after it found that the transcription of the writing and the completion of the missing portions from between the fragments were done based upon original Halakhic[7] and linguistic research. As it said:

> Certainly, according to the criteria which emerge in the case law, copying of an original, even if it is difficult and complex and requires skill, does not attract copyright. It is also true that in the case before me, the goal of the person who deciphers is to reconstruct the original Scroll. However, the original Scroll was not found intact. The tens of fragments which were discovered relate to different copies; there was no physical match between a considerable portion of the fragments, and even after assembling all of them together the missing portion amounts to about half of what had been written. As was said, it was not possible to join the fragments, one to another, and to fill in the gaps without research into the language and Halakha. There is no substantive similarity between the work of the Plaintiff, in which creative and original elements were found, and the cases under discussion in the case law upon which the Defendants depended, which concerned, as was said previously, the copying of a telephone book and of illustrations.
>
> From all that has been said, it appears that in editing the transcription and the combination of the fragments that are physically matched one to another no originality is required. In contrast to this, the assembly of the composite text depended upon Halakhic research and linguistic research from an original, and constitutes an original creation.

The Appellants reject the conclusions of the court with both hands. According to their argument, the completions of the missing portions by Qimron do not fall under the category of an original work but under the category of discovery and exposure of portions of the original text, as they were written two thousand years ago. There was here, therefore, only the discovery of facts, in the course of research of the scientific and historical reality, and as such it is not protected by copyright laws. Even if Qimron invested effort, time, knowledge and talent in the creation of the Deciphered Text, the Deciphered Text does not contain originality that entitles it to copyright. It is true, the original, complete and 'correct' version of the Scroll, is not in our hands so that one cannot compare between it and the Deciphered Text but, this does not make the Deciphered Text, in their words, 'from a factual work, that is not entitled to the protection of the law, to a work of fiction'. Since Qimron presented the Deciphered Text as a work that represents the 'true' version of the Scroll he is stopped from claiming that it is an original work. Also the completions that completed the missing portions are but the writing down on paper of ideas; even if the ideas were original they are not original expression deserving of protection.

6. The Hebrew word used for 'Matter' is '*Megillah*' which also means 'scroll'.
7. 'Halakhic' research means research in the area of Jewish Law.

Moreover, since the 'idea' that was embodied in the original version of the Scroll, it is possible to express in only one way—as Qimron expressed it in the Deciphered Text—there is no copyright in the idea and it is not protectable. This viewpoint is based upon the 'merger doctrine' (Merger), the source of which is in American law. The Appellants additionally brought various examples of situations in which no copyright protection is granted, from which, in their opinion, one can learn what the proper decision in our case should be. I am unable to accept their arguments.

14. We saw above that it is possible that he who compiled and arranged 'raw material', that was created by others a long time ago, will be entitled to copyright in his work provided that qualities of originality are found in it (the *Achiman* Matter that is discussed above). The Appellants try to create rules such as, 'it is not possible to acquire copyright in a reconstructed scroll', or 'it is not possible to acquire copyright in the product of scientific historical research', and to apply them to this matter, but this cannot help them. The resolution of the dispute before us more than it is anchored in rules is anchored in the specific circumstances of the matter, and in the principles that we noted above. The following makes this point well:

> In my opinion, one should not determine in advance when one is dealing with an idea and when one is dealing with its application, rather all is dependent upon the circumstances: the same fact pattern can be considered an idea for one matter and for another matter an application of the idea. Viewing the matter broadly no original thing exists rather every invention or 'idea' is a development of a previous invention or 'idea'; the question in each case is whether in actuality a person added something original of his own to a previous 'idea' or application (and then his work will be protected even though the foundations of his original work he drew from another source) or if he copied what another did and simply disguised it without having actually created anything original of his own (words of Justice [as his title was then] S. Levine in C.A. 23/81 *Hershko v. Orbach*, P.D. 42[3]749, 759).

The District Court thoroughly examined the process of Qimron's work, with the intent of examining the extent of originality in the process and not because it thought that a big effort is enough for purposes of acquiring copyright. This process at the end of which the bunch of fragments was a complete text, that has content and meaning included a number of levels of creation: construction of the fragments according to the way they fit together physically, the arrangement of the 'islands' of fragments that were constructed and their placement in the estimated framework of the parchment of the Scroll, the decipherment of the writing that is on the fragments, to the extent that such decipherment was necessary and the completion of the missing portions between the fragments. In the creation of each of these levels a different amount of originality and creativity is expressed and even so it is not appropriate to examine each level separately. In the case before us, the different levels of the work of creation are woven and bound to each other, dependent upon each other and influence each other. So the decipherment of the writing in a certain way influences the way in which the 'islands' of fragments are arranged; so the arrangement affects the possible meanings of the text, including its structure, its content and the way in which the missing portions are completed. One should not sever the levels of creation from each other and they should be seen as a single work of creation. Examination of the work, on all of its levels as a complete single work shows originality and creativity that are undoubtable. Qimron's work was not, therefore, technical work, 'mechanical', like simple manual labor the results of which are known in advance. His 'inspiration', the 'added soul' that he gave to the Scroll fragments, that transfigured the fragments into a living text, were not only confined to the investment of human resources, like 'sweat', in the sense of 'the sweat of man's brows'. These were the fruit of a process in which Qimron used his knowledge, expertise and imagination, exercised judgment and chose between different alternatives. On this matter the District Court brought examples that illustrate well Qimron's judgment and creativity:

> In any case, it was impossible to arrive at a uniform reconstruction, because the way of reconstructing and filling in the gaps depended upon the results of the research. These, for the most part, are not uniform, because disagreements arise among scholars. As an example of what I have said, the Plaintiff provided two disagreements between himself and Strugnell: (1) Strugnell believed that in particular fragments the sentences were nine lines long; and he therefore assembled them vertically. The Plaintiff arrived at the opinion, after research, that in the relevant fragment the sentence was of eighteen lines, and therefore it was necessary to assemble the fragments horizontally. Of course, the different assemblage has substantially affected the content of the Scroll (the Plaintiff, *Trial Transcript*, pp. 184-90); (2) one section is composed of six tiny fragments, and the Plaintiff explained that the entire method of relating them together is a speculation (*Trial Transcript*, p. 194). It depended upon the question of whether one missing letter should be filled by the letter *aleph*, as Strugnell thought, so that the word would read *orot* ('lights'), or should be completed by the letter *ayin*, so that the word would read *orot* ('hides'). After Halakhic research into the matter of purification of hides in the aforementioned period, the Plaintiff arrived at the opinion that the text is concerned with *orot* ('hides') (p. 181 of the *Trial Transcript*). He assembled the section depending upon this assumption, and of course the content was definitely different from the content which would have been accepted had he assembled the fragments on the basis of the assumption that the word under discussion was *orot* ('lights').

From all of these the picture of Qimron's original contribution is clearly seen. From this follows the conclusion that the 'inspiration', the 'added soul' that he imbued into the Scroll fragments by the force of his work make him the owner of copyright in the Deciphered Text.

Does Proper Legal Policy Justify the Denial of Protection by Virtue of Copyright Law?

15. The Appellants additionally argue that proper legal policy requires the conclusion that the Deciphered Text is not an original work and is not protected by copyright law. In their words, the ruling that Qimron has copyright in the Deciphered Text grants to Qimron a monopoly status over a document that has historical value, that is a part of the cultural heritage of the Jewish people. This status may deter other scholars of the Hidden Scrolls from examining and criticizing the reconstruction of the text and harm the research of the Hidden Scrolls in the future as well as the public interest. According to their claim, even if the feeling exists that 'an injustice was committed against the Respondent', copyright laws are not the proper source for the correction of this injustice. For these reasons the Appellants ask to rule that one cannot win copyright in the Deciphered Text and that in any case, Qimron does not have such a right.

There is nothing in these claims of the Appellants. We have made clear above that Qimron does not have a right in the 'raw material'—the fragments of the scrolls themselves—and he does not even request this. His copyright in the Deciphered Text does not prevent anyone from the possibility of researching the Scroll fragments, arranging them, deciphering the writing upon them and completing the missing portions between the fragments, in a manner different from that taken by Qimron, and to publish the results of his work and even receive copyright protection. As it were, before us is an equation of many 'variables' that all of those who come to solve it may try to place different 'values' in their places. The Appellants additionally argue that one must still fear that the copyright owner in the Deciphered Text will silence other scholars that come to criticize his work, based on the claim that they are infringing his copyright, and thus the freedom of academic research will be badly harmed. One must not take these claims lightly. In the past I remarked upon the importance that must be attached to the protection of academic freedom, while I noted that 'research, study and instruction in all areas of the human spirit, that do not have handcuffs on them, raise the individual within society and with him society as a whole. It is also the exercise of a basic human need' (see CR.A. 2831/95 *Elba v. The State of Israel*, P.D. 50[5]221, 335). It is true, we are dealing with a struggle between interests, that stand sometimes one against the other—the right of the individual to protection of the fruits of his creation against the right of society to continue to flourish upon the fertile ground of the past—between them one must balance. But in this case there is no need to discuss the proper balance since there is no reason to fear. As it was said:

> —The legislator did not ignore the significance of the extent of use and its purpose in shaping the right; certain uses under certain circumstances were removed from the areas of copyright protection for reasons of public policy. However, the qualification of these is possible only in the framework of the exceptions to the right (words of Judge Y. Maltz in P.C.A. 2687/92 *Geva v. Walt Disney Company*, P.D. 48[1]251, at

pp. 268-69 [hereinafter the '*Geva* Matter']; see also paragraph 21 of my opinion in the *Miphal Hapayis* Matter).

I am of the opinion that these exceptions in the Law are sufficient in order to ensure the freedom of academic research in spite of Qimron's copyright in the Deciphered Text. An example of this exception is set forth in Section 2(1) of the Law:

2. Infringement of Copyright

(1) Copyright in a work shall be deemed to be infringed by any person who, without the consent of the owner of the copyright, does anything the sole right to do which is by this Act conferred on the owner of the copyright: Provided that the following acts shall not constitute an infringement of copyright:

(1) Any fair dealing with any work for the purposes of private study, research, criticism, review or newspaper summary.'

From this, a scholar that comes to research the Deciphered Text or the manner of its creation, for the purposes set forth in the provision, shall be entitled to defend himself with the claim that his treatment of the work was 'fair dealing' likewise, he will also have at his disposal, as we will see as follows, other defences. The conclusion is that these reasons raised by the Appellants are not grounds for denying Qimron's copyright in the Deciphered Text.

Did the Appellants Infringe Qimron's Copyright?

The Infringement

16. In Section 1 of the Law it is said that:

1. Copyright

(1) —

(2) For the purposes of this Act, copyright means—if the work is unpublished, to publish the work or any substantial part thereof;—

(3) For the purposes of this Act, publication, in relation to any work, means the issue of copies of the work to the public—.

The act of publication of the work before the copyright owner published it and without his consent is an infringement of the right as mentioned in Section 2(1) of the Law that is quoted above. As aforementioned, the Deciphered Text was published in the Book before Qimron, the copyright owner, published it and without obtaining his consent. On this point there is no dispute. In this his copyright was infringed.

Do the Appellants Have a Defence Based upon 'Scholarly Convention'?

17. It was noted above that Qimron and Strugnell transmitted a number of copies of the Deciphered Text, before it was published, to a number of scholars, in

order to receive their reactions (Section 1 above). Apparently, one of the scholars passed a copy of the text that he received to others and in this way a copy of the text reached the hands of Dr Zdzislaw Kapera (hereinafter—'Kapera'), a Polish scholar from Krakow. In December 1990, before the Book was published, Kapera published the Deciphered Text in a journal entitled 'The Qumran Chronicle'. Beside the text he noted that the source of the text was anonymous and that readers are requested not to copy it or to transmit it to other people. Pursuant to Qimron's request the head of the Antiquities Authority sent on March 12, 1991 a warning letter to Kapera in which he noted that the publication violates the legal, moral and ethical rights of Strugnell and Qimron, and demanded to cease the distribution of the journal. Kapera responded to the head of the Antiquities Authority in a letter of apology, in which he explained that he distributed only a small number of copies of the journal and promised to stop the distribution. The Appellants argue that at the time of the publication of the Book, in November 1991, the Deciphered Text was, therefore, in the hands of the scholarly public and that therefore it was in the category of a 'published' text according to 'scholarly convention'. From here that one must view the publication of the Deciphered Text in the Book as if it were done by virtue of the 'implied consent' of Qimron, because one must not obligate the scholars, who see a text published in an academic journal, to check whether the publication was done with the consent of the copyright owner.

18. The arguments of the Appellants cannot stand up. The first reason for this is that in this case one cannot rely upon the accepted custom ('scholarly convention') with respect to the use of research material published by its author. As aforementioned the Appellants made use of material that was published without the author's name, with a specific request of the editor not to copy it and not to transmit it to additional people. This is enough to eliminate the basis of the argument. The second reason is that from the words of Shanks himself, in the Foreword that he wrote for the book, it is clear that he knew about the mentioned letter of the head of the Antiquities Authority to Kapera, that Shanks attached as an appendix to the Foreword, and that he knew that Kapera decided to stop the distribution of his journal and to destroy all of the copies. Under these circumstances it should be held that Shanks published the Deciphered Text even though he certainly knew that Qimron does not agree. Moreover, the District Court found as a fact that:

> Shanks, after deliberation, arrived at the conclusion that it was unlikely that he would be sued for an infringement of copyright, either by the illness-ridden Strugnell (and in this he was right), or by the diffident and modest Plaintiff [Qimron–Y.T.], not least because he lived in Israel.

We must reject, therefore, the argument that publication of the Deciphered Text was done in accordance with 'scholarly convention' or by virtue of Qimron's implied consent.

As an aside I would note that according to Section 8 of the Law an 'innocent infringer' is exempt from liability for payment of damages:

'Exemption of an innocent infringer from liability for monetary damages, etc.

8. Where proceedings are taken in respect of the infringement of the copyright in any work and the defendant in his defence alleges that he was not aware of the existence of the copyright in the work, the plaintiff shall not be entitled to any remedy other than an injunction or interdict in respect of the infringement he was not aware and had no reasonable grounds for suspecting that copyright subsisted in the work.

Shanks is not such an innocent infringer (and compare to *Deutch* at p. 191).

Are the Appellants Entitled to the Defense of 'Fair Dealing' with the Work?

19. We have seen that 'any fair dealing with any work for the purpose of private study, research, criticism, review, or newspaper summary' does not fall into the category of copyright infringement (Section 2(1) of the Law). The question whether there was 'fair dealing' with the work must be put to two tests: was the use fair? Was the use for one of the purposes mentioned in Section 2(1) of the Law? (see the *Geva* Matter at p. 270 as well as paragraph 22 of my opinion in the *Miphal Hapayis* Matter). According to the Appellants version publication of the Deciphered Text 'enabled scholars all over the world to access the text, to research it for their own purposes, and to criticize, as they wish, the claims and conclusions of the Respondent, as they were expressed in articles that he published over the years with respect to MMT'. According to their claim, publication of the Book, including the Deciphered Text, comes under the title of 'fair dealing' the purpose of which is research and criticism. They also argue that the publication is a 'newspaper summary', that brought 'news' to the attention of the public. At once, publication of the Deciphered Text was carried out in order to promote the public interest, while delay of the publication by Qimron harmed the public interest.

20. I cannot accept this argument. The Appellants published the Deciphered Text in its entirety, without noting Qimron's name and in this they knowingly violated his right to be the first to publicly publish the Deciphered Text. Likewise it is clear to all that the publication did not constitute 'fair dealing' with the work and was not intended for the purposes set forth in Section 2(1) of the Law. This is evident from the fact that the text 'is swallowed' among the appendices attached to the Foreword, including letters, without comment, explanation, criticism or any reference to its content. Likewise it follows from Shanks' words in the Foreword to the Book, as they were quoted above (Section 9) that the primary purpose was to publish the Deciphered Text in defiance of the research 'monopoly' given to the international team of scholars.

There is also nothing in the argument that the text was published as a 'newspaper summary'. Even if the term 'newspaper summary' suffers the meaning that the Appellants wish to give it—and with respect to this I am not expressing an opinion—the argument does not have any basis in the evidence. There is no statement or hint in the Book that the Deciphered Text included in it constitutes a piece of 'news' brought to the attention of the public or that there is an intention to bring it to the public as such. Furthermore, publication of the Deciphered Text *in its entirety*, as it was published, does not constitute a 'summary' and does not constitute 'the press'. Either way, even if we were dealing with a 'newspaper summary', the use of the Deciphered Text was not at all 'fair', since the text was not attributed to Qimron.

It follows from the above that the Appellants do not have a defense of 'fair dealing' with the work.

Did the Editors Infringe Qimron's Right?

21. The question whether the Editors infringed Qimron's copyright requires a separate discussion.

The Editors' names are stated in the Book's title page. The District Court held that they committed an act that violated Qimron's copyright. With this it held that 'his relative liability [of Shanks—Y.T.] as against to the two is 100 per cent' because Shanks is the one that decided to publish the Deciphered Text in the Book and also for the reason that Shanks took the responsibility for this upon himself. The Editors are appealing the court's ruling. According to their argument, their job consisted only of them receiving and sorting the photographs of the undeciphered scrolls fragments, they edited the index of the photographs of the fragments and wrote an introduction to the Book. They had no control over the writing of the publisher's Foreword, that Shanks wrote, and over its inclusion in the Book accompanied by appendices—one of which was the Deciphered Text—and therefore they are not liable for infringement of Qimron's copyright.

I will anticipate and say that after reviewing the Book and the evidence brought before the District Court I reached the conclusion, that it is the fate of the Editors' claim to be denied.

22. On the title page of the Book it was written that the Book was prepared by the Editors with an introduction and index:

A Facsimile Edition
of the
Dead Sea Scrolls
Prepared with
An Introduction
And Index
by
Robert Eisenman
and
James M. Robinson

Indeed, the Foreword that Shanks wrote, that was integrated in the body of the Book, was not mentioned in the title page, however, from the evidence brought before the District Court it is evident, that the Editors knew in advance of Shanks' intention to include the Foreword that he wrote in the Book, and he even produced the Foreword for the Editors' review at that time. In the Foreword it is also explicitly stated, that the text of the Scroll that was published by Kapera in 1990—that is the Deciphered Text—is attached as an appendix to the Foreword. Furthermore, the words of the Foreword testify to the fact that Shanks—and in that case also the Editors—were aware of the fact that the publication of the Deciphered Text constituted an infringement of Qimron's copyright. As stated above, the sequence of events that led to the cessation of distribution of the Deciphered Text by Kapera is described in the Foreword, including the quotation of a paragraph from the mentioned letter, that the head of the Antiquities Authority sent to Kapera, in which he insisted that the publication violates the rights of Strugnell and Qimron. It was also noted that this letter is also attached as an appendix to the Foreword (p. xvi of the Book). Nevertheless, the Editors were satisfied—as held by the District Court—with expressing their reservations regarding the *style* of the words of the Foreword and did not object to publication of the Deciphered Text in the Book. Once they agreed, under these circumstances, that their names be included in the Book as its editors—without disassociating themselves from the content of the Foreword or from the appendices attached thereto—this can be seen as implied consent to the act of copyright infringement.

Moreover I will note, that the liability of the Editors to Qimron may also be founded on an additional reason. In my opinion the notation of an editor's name on the title page of a book in and of itself establishes a presumption that all of the things that were published in the book are with his knowledge; unless it is explicitly written in the title page that it is not so. This presumption may be rebutted by the editor with evidence. In the case before us, it was written on the title page that the Book was prepared by the Editors with an introduction and index. This formulation, that describes the activity of the Editors, does not exclude the Foreword written by Shanks, with its appendices, from the bounds of their responsibility. Furthermore, in the introduction to the Book the Editors noted that not only did they assist in preparation of the edition but they also worked on the preparation of the introduction and the index (p. xi of the Book). These things strengthen the aforementioned conclusion.

As aforementioned, the Editors could have rebutted the above mentioned presumption by bringing rebuttal evidence, but this they also did not do. Review of the protocol of the hearing in the District Court teaches that they raised the claim that they are not responsible for the Foreword and its appendices in their pleadings, but they did not appear to testify in court. Also Shanks' testimony, pursuant to which he carries all responsibility for the Foreword that he wrote and also the testimony of the attorney William Cox who coordinated between the Editors and Shanks, cannot help them against Qimron, and they have relevance, at the most, on the level of their relations with Shanks.

Therefore, it is presumed about the Editors that all things published in the Book, including the Deciphered Text, were published with their consent.

Violation of the Moral Right

23. Besides the economic rights in the hands of the copyright owner he also has a personal-moral right (see Y. Weissman 'The Personal Right [*droit moral*] in copyright law', *Mechkarei Mishpat* 7 [1989], 51, 55). So it is said in Section 4A of the Copyright Ordinance (hereinafter—the 'Ordinance'):

> 4A.
> (1) The author shall have the right to have his name applied to the work in the accepted manner and to the accepted extent.
> —
> (3) The violation of a right under this section is a civil wrong, and the provisions of the Civil Wrongs Ordinance (New Version) shall apply thereto.
> (4) The right of the author under this section shall be independent of his economic right in the work and shall be available to him even after such right has been transferred to another, wholly or in part.

A man is entitled to have his name applied to the 'children of his spirit'. His spiritual connection to these is like, almost, his connection to those who come forth from his loins. Publication of a work without it being attributed to the name of its author 'in the accepted manner and to the accepted extent' is a violation of the author's moral right. The roots of this important principle are also delivered through Jewish law, that noted the greatness of the sin of a person who does not attribute his words to the person who said them. So it was said, among many things on this subject:

> Great is he who says something in the name of that person who said it and shall not steal the opinion of the person who said it, since such theft is more than the theft of money—and such is the greatness of this sin in my eyes, one who says the simple meaning of the writing in a book, or that he heard, and does not mention the name of the speaker or the writer (R. Yeshaya HaLevi Horowitz *Shnei Luchot Habrit*, Tractate Shavuot [Daf 183, p. B]; also see additional sources in N. Rakover *Zchut Hayotzrim BaMekorot Hayehudiyim* [5751], p. 35 and following).

As the District Court held, 'the fruit of the plaintiff's work, the Composite Text, was published without mention of his name, and thus his moral right was infringed.' The Appellants argue that under the circumstances that we noted, when Qimron's name was not noted on the Deciphered Text that Kapera published, one should not demand from the next publisher to check who the copyright owner is in the work. Furthermore, the Appellants argue that they fulfilled their obligation by attributing the Deciphered Text to Strugnell—who they claimed was the head of the research staff—and to an additional 'colleague'.

24. These arguments as well must be rejected. The court found unambiguously that Shanks knew that Qimron participated in the creation of the Deciphered Text:

> As for the Plaintiff's [Qimron–Y.T.] part in the assembly of the composite text, Shanks admitted that he knew that the Plaintiff had assisted Strugnell in the research of the Scroll (*Trial Transcript*, p. 259) and that in the context of this assistance he had participated in the reconstruction and that this possibly included also the filling in of the missing parts (*Trial Transcript*, p. 296). Not just this, but also Shanks' testimony on this matter of not having known the Plaintiff's part in the decipherment, is contradicted by objective evidence: Drori's [the head of the Antiquities Authority–Y.T.] letter to Kapera (Exhibit 5) which came into Shanks hands and which he published in the book Exhibit 14 (Figure 9). As previously noted, in this letter Drori stated that Strugnell and the Plaintiff were engaged for years in decipherment of the Scroll.

Shanks knowingly declined to note Qimron's name. There was not in this case an unknowing omission, or an omission as a result of not knowing the author's identity. Therefore in any case there is no relevance to the question whether one should impose an obligation to check the author's identity on the publisher of a work copied from a previous publication in which it was published without the author's name.

As for the argument that the Appellants fulfilled their obligation by mentioning Strugnell's name 'with another colleague', it must be rejected with both hands. In the Foreword to the Book is says that:

> with a colleague, Strugnell proceeded to write a 500-page commentary on this 120-line text. The commentary is still not published and no one knows when it will be.

The mention of a 'colleague' without noting his name, and without noting that here was an act of creation of the Deciphered Text is contempt and mockery of the poor. Such 'mention', including the argument that it is enough to fulfill the commandment of the Ordinance—if not the human-moral obligation—is more insulting than no mention at all. There is no need to add words with respect to the fact that the words that were quoted—that are two lines swallowed up within a Foreword of 11 pages, and far from the page on which the Deciphered Text was published, without the mention of a name—cannot fulfill the obligation to attribute the work to the author 'in the accepted manner and to the accepted extent'.

The conclusion is that the Appellants violated Qimron's moral right.

The Remedies for the Infringement

25. The District Court found that the pecuniary injury done to Qimron was not proven, and therefore awarded him compensation without proof of damages ('statutory damages') in the amount of 20,000 NIS, pursuant to Section 3A of the Ordinance. It also awarded him the amount of 80,000 NIS as compensation for the mental anguish caused to him because of the violation of his moral right.

The Appellants argue that there was no justification to award Qimron statutory damages. According to their argument, such damages can be awarded only when the existence of pecuniary injury was proven, but the scope of such damage was not proven. Therefore, since Qimron did not prove that any pecuniary injury had been caused to him, such damages should not be awarded to him. They further argue that Qimron did not sue for statutory damages but actual compensation for his injury, and therefore such damages should not be awarded to him. As for the damages for violation of his moral right, the Appellants argue that it was improper to award them in addition to the statutory damages, the purpose of which is to compensate the right owner for all of his injuries; moreover, according to their argument compensation for violation of the moral right should not be awarded when the violation is of the right of first publication, which is an economic right by nature. Likewise they criticize the amounts that were awarded. Against them Qimron claims that the evidence that he offered was sufficient in order to award him actual pecuniary damages in a higher amount and not only statutory damages. Alternatively he argues that the court should have awarded him global damages in a higher amount according to the court's estimation.

The Compensation for the Pecuniary Injury

26. In his claim for pecuniary damages Qimron claimed that by publication of the Deciphered Text in the Book, he was prevented from being the first to publish it, and because of this the level of sales of the book in which he published the Deciphered Text, together with Strugnell, at a later date, was damaged. This violation also injured his reputation and lowered his expected income from lectures.

The District Court found that 'it was proven that damage was caused to the plaintiff'; at the same time it found that 'minimal objective data, that would enable calculation of the damage according to some level of probability' was not brought before it. I have found no reason to intervene in these findings. As it is known, 'a factual finding made by the first instance shall not be easily invalidated by the appellate level, even if it would have decided differently if it had heard the witnesses itself. For so long as the determination of such a fact is based and rooted in the evidence the opinion of the judge who saw and heard the witnesses is that which is decisive' (see Y. Zussman, *Sidrei Hadin Haezrachi* [5755-1995], 856-57 and the citations there).

27. Once the court found, as aforementioned, that Qimron was unable to prove the amount of the pecuniary injury caused to him, it held that 'the plaintiff's matter falls under the category of cases in which the damage was not proven, in which the court is authorized by virtue of Section 3A of the Ordinance to award statutory damages'. With respect to this matter Section 3A of the Ordinance provides that:

> Where the damage caused by the infringement of a copyright has not been proved, the court may, on the application of the plaintiff, award, in respect of every infringement, compensation in an amount of not less than 10,000 New Shekels and not more than 20,000 New Shekels—.

Like the District Court I am also of the opinion that under these circumstances the court was permitted to award Qimron compensation without proof of damage pursuant to Section 3A of the Ordinance. The fact that from the beginning Qimron sued for actual compensation for his damages—and these were not awarded to him—does not deny him the right to have compensation without proof of damage awarded to him. It is further emphasized that in his complaint Qimron requested the alternative remedy of compensation without proof of damage, pursuant to Section 3A of the Ordinance. This also is sufficient to grant him his request after his attempts to prove the amount of pecuniary damage caused to him failed. Thus it has been held that:

> As aforementioned, Cheshev claims that one cannot choose statutory damages in a case in which the plaintiff attempted to prove his actual damages (or the profits of the infringer), but was unable to do so. The District Court correctly rejected this argument. The statutory damages are intended to assist creators, who in many cases cannot prove the actual damage caused to them as a result of the infringement—this purpose of the law would be frustrated if we accept Cheshev's position, pursuant to which a difficulty in proving the actual damage to the extent necessary for proof in a civil trial, removes the possibility of receiving statutory damages. One should not 'punish' a plaintiff who tries to prove his actual damages and deny him the possibility of receiving statutory damages, after he proved that his right was infringed (words of Justice T. Strasbourg-Cohen in C.A. 3616/92 *Dekel Sheirutei Machshev L'Handasa [1987] Ltd. v. Cheshev Hayechida Habein Kibbutzit L'Sheirutei Nihul Aguda Shitufit Chaklait Ltd.*, P.D. 51[5]337 [hereinafter—the '*Dekel* Matter', 350]).

I will add here from my own words in that matter, with respect to the amount of statutory damages that the court should award:

> —within the pretty narrow boundaries that the legislator set, I am of the opinion that we should be strict with the infringers and that without weighty circumstances in either direction it is proper to award the maximum amount, or an amount close to it. This, especially, for considerations of deterrence, the weight of which grows continually greater as the possibilities of infringing the intellectual property of another continue to grow with the sophistication of means of copying and reproduction (the *Dekel* Matter, at p. 353 and see also *Deutch* at p. 473).

The seriousness of the infringement of Qimron's copyright would justify the award of a very high amount, were this possible; certainly there is no place for lowering the amount of compensation without proof of damage. The court was correct, therefore, when it used the full force of the law against the Appellants and awarded Qimron the highest amount set forth in the law.

Damages for Infringement of the Moral Right

28. The award of damages for the pecuniary injury caused by copyright infringement, pursuant to Section 3A of the Ordinance, does not prevent an award of

damages for violation of the moral right, provided that a situation of double compensation for identical damage is not created (compare with Y. Engelard, A. Barak, M. Cheshin Dinei HaNezikin—Torat HaNezikin HaKlalit [G. Tadeski, Editor—5737] [hereinafter—'*Dinei HaNezikin*'], 573). In the matter before us damages were awarded to Qimron pursuant to Section 3A of the Ordinance for his pecuniary injury the amount of which was not proven. Likewise, he was awarded compensation for the violation of his moral right, that is a civil wrong pursuant to Section 4A(3) of the Ordinance. This compensation was awarded for the non-pecuniary damages caused to him, that does not overlap the damage for which the compensation was awarded pursuant to Section 3A of the Ordinance.

As for the amount of the compensation for non-pecuniary damages, the court held:

> There is no doubt that much mental anguish was caused to the Plaintiff [Qimron–Y.T.]. In his testimony the Plaintiff explained how he felt that his world had crumbled around him and his dream of gaining fame had vanished. As was previously said, the Defendants [the Appellants–Y.T.] violated the Plaintiff's moral right...and the Plaintiff is entitled to compensation for mental anguish...as was said, in this matter the court takes into account both the consideration of the compensation and the behaviour of the publisher...in this case, and considering the severity of the harm to the Plaintiff's feelings and Shank's behaviour, it seems to me that the suitable compensation for mental anguish is 80,000 NIS.

This compensation was awarded for the mental anguish that was caused to Qimron because of publication of the Deciphered Text in the Book without its attribution to him and it is not intended to compensate him for the pecuniary injury caused to him by infringement of his right to be the first to publish the Deciphered Text. On this point the court set the amount of compensation after it considered the evidence brought before it, and also took into account Shanks' behaviour (with respect to the matter of consideration of the wrong-doers behavior see *Dinei HaNezikin*, at p. 579). I looked at the Appellants arguments against the amount of compensation, that were awarded for the non-pecuniary damages, and I found no reason to intervene in the District Court's conclusion (compare with C.A. 685/79 Atrash v. Maalof, P.D. 36[1]626, 631).

Return Order

29. In the complaint and in his summation before the District Court Qimron petitioned for the remedy of a return order, pursuant to Section 7 of the Law:

> *Rights of owner against persons possessing or dealing with infringing copies, etc.*
>
> All infringing copies of any work in which copyright subsists, or of any substantial part thereof, and all plates used or intended to be used for the production of such infringing copies, shall be deemed to be the property

of the owner of the copyright, who accordingly may take proceedings for the recovery of the possession thereof or in respect of the conversion thereof.

In its judgment the District Court did not consider this remedy and did not award it to Qimron. The Appellants did not address this in their briefs. In this state of affairs, after it has been held that Qimron's copyright in the Deciphered Text was infringed, Qimron is entitled to receive the remedy of a return order as he requested.

Award of Costs

30. The District Court awarded attorneys fees in the amount of 50,000 NIS to Qimron. The Appellants argue that the sum of attorneys fees—its amount is half the entire amount of damages awarded to Qimron—is exorbitant and should be reduced.

It is precedent that the appellate court shall intervene in the first instance's award of costs only rarely, when a legal mistake, defect or flaw in the exercise of discretion is made in the award of costs. (see, for example, C.A. 378/78 *Mordechai Klinger v. Menahel Mas Halzavon*, P.D. 33[1]509, 510; C.A. 77/85 *Chevrat Chashmal Machoz Yerushalayim v. Chevrat Chashmal L'Yisrael Ltd.*, P.D. 39[2]592, 594). In light of the nature of the dispute and considering the complicated hearing one cannot find that there is a flaw in the award of costs that justifies our intervention. Therefore the obligation of attorneys fees shall remain as it was.

Petition to submit arguments on behalf of a 'friend of the court'

31. During the course of the appeal before us a body by the name of the 'Committee of Concerned Intellectual Property Educators' (hereinafter—the 'Petitioner') submitted a petition to permit it to join this proceeding in the status of a 'friend of the court' (*amicus curiae*) and to submit principal arguments. In our decision from 24 August, 1999 we denied the petition and here follow our reasons (see Section 4 above).

In its petition the Petitioner describes itself as an 'independent organization whose members are a respectable group of professors and lecturers in law faculties primarily in the United States, in the field of copyright. They number today approximately 60 members. Members of the organization have a professional interest to act for the attainment of a proper balance between the ownership right on the one hand, and the user's interest on the other, in the field of intellectual property—this organization acts not only throughout the United States but in every place in the world where there is a fear for violation or reduction of the copyright'. The Petitioner's attorney produced a power of attorney from Mr David Nimmer, who testified to the fact that he acts in the name of the Petitioner. Likewise, he produced a letter that sets forth the names of ten jurists with ties to universities in the United States, that he claims 'join in the petition'.

The Petitioner argues that 'at the base of this appeal lies the question whether copyright is limited to the territorial boundaries of a state or whether it is rather entitled to international protection. The decision of the Supreme Court on this matter may have significant ramifications for the understanding of copyright and its protection also outside the space of the State of Israel.—Because of the many ramifications of the subject of the appeal—the Petitioner requests the permission of the honourable court to bring before it the broadest possible information for the purpose of presenting a comprehensive and complete picture on the subject of copyright from the international perspective of the matter. This, in order to provide information that may assist the court in reaching the most appropriate decision that will accord with the international consensus in this area.'

Likewise the Petitioner recites considerations that guide the courts in the United States when granting the status of *amicus curiae*, like: the expected benefit to the court from the petitioner's brief; the existence of a special public interest that the petitioner is able to present; the ability of the parties to the proceeding to present their position before the court; the existence of an objection by the parties to the proceeding; timing of submission of the petition; and the ability of the petitioner to present legal issues in an objective manner.

32. Qimron objects to the Petitioner's petition, and relies in his objection upon procedural as well as substantive arguments. A summary of his procedural arguments is: the Petitioner is not a legal entity and therefore, the power of attorney that it submitted has no validity; the petition was submitted late, after the parties' written briefs were submitted; the Petitioner did not act openly and with integrity in that it did not disclose certain facts to the court that testify to a relationship between it and some of the Appellants and to the identity of those supporting the petition; the Petitioner did not support its petition with an affidavit, even though its petition is based upon facts, such as the identity of its members, their occupations, objectives and activities.

33. In a number of instances in the past this court discussed the question whether to join in a proceeding bodies that are not litigants in the status of 'a friend of the court' (see: C.F. 876/50 *A.B. v. M.B.*, P.M. 3' 263, 287; C.A. 173/84 *Ben Zion v. Gorney*, P.D. 39[3]757, 765; R.C.A. 2652/94 *Tendler v. La Club Méditerranéene* [Yisrael] Ltd. [not yet published]; R.C.A. 1185/97 *Izavon Milgram Hinda v. Mercaz Mishan* [not yet published]). In one instance, in which this court permitted the public defender to join the proceeding of a petition for a retrial in the status of 'friend of the court', the considerations that guide the court in these cases were set forth:

> Indeed, before the right will be given to a body or a person to express its position in a proceeding in which it is not an original party, the potential contribution of the offered position should be examined. One should examine its expertise, experience and the representation that it provides for the interest in the name of which it requests to join the proceeding. One should clarify the type of proceeding and the procedure that it follows. One should note the parties to the proceeding itself and the stage in which the petition to join was filed. One should be aware of the

> significance of the matter that is being decided. All of these are not exhaustive criteria. They cannot determine in advance when it would be correct to join a party in a proceeding as a 'friend of the court', and when it would not. At the same time, these criteria should be considered, among others, before it is decided to join as aforementioned (words of the President A. Barak in Retrial 7929/96 *Kozli v. the State of Israel* [not yet published]).

(See also CR.A. 111/99 *Arnold Schwartz v. the State of Israel* P.D. 54[2]241, 251-52 where it was decided to join the public defender in the status of 'friend of the court' in a proceeding the issue of which was the standards for examination of a petition for a stay of executing a prison sentence, and see the opposing opinion in this matter of Justice Y. Kedmi at pp. 287-88).

34. We have found no reason to grant the Petitioner's petition because of its procedural defects. There is therefore in any case no reason to discuss the petition substantively.

As aforementioned, the Petitioner did not support its petition with an affidavit. As a result of this the existence of the Petitioner and its nature were not proven. Likewise it was not proven that Mr David Nimmer is authorized to represent the Petitioner. The petition also does not present a sufficient factual basis on which one can consider: the expected benefit from the Petitioner's brief, the interest that it represents and its ability to faithfully represent the legal issues that are in dispute. It should be further said that the attorney's for the litigants spread a wide list of arguments before us and it seems that the submission of additional briefs by the Petitioner would not be able to contribute to the decision.

35. We decided, therefore, to deny the Petitioner's petition to join in the appeal in the status of 'friend of the court'.

Conclusion

36. The Appellants infringed Qimron's copyright in the Deciphered Text and violated his moral right. Therefore their appeals are denied. Qimron's counter-appeal is accepted in part in the sense that an order is hereby issued instructing the Appellants to deliver to Qimron all copies of the Book in which the Deciphered Text is included and all printing blocks and stencils in their hands used, or intended to be used, for the creation of copies.

Shanks and BAS shall pay Qimron attorneys fees in the amount of 40,000 NIS; each of the Editors shall pay him attorneys fees in the amount of 10,000 NIS.

(signature)
Judge

<u>President A. Barak:</u>

I agree.

(signature)
The President

<u>Justice D. Beinish</u>:

I agree.

(signature)
Judge

It was decided as aforementioned in the opinion of Justice Y. Türkel.

Given today, 29 Av 5760 (August 30, 2000).

(signature)	(signature)
	(signature)
The President	Judge
	Judge

<u>Copy true to the original</u>

Shmaryahu Cohen, Chief Administrator
M06.93028110

SELECT BIBLIOGRAPHY

Alter, R., *The Art of Biblical Narrative* (London: Allen & Unwin, 1981).

—*The Pleasures of Reading in an Ideological Age* (New York: Simon and Schuster, 1989).

Archaeological Sites in Europe: Conservation, Maintenance and Enhancement (1990: Conimbra, Portugal) (Architectural Heritage Series, 22; Strasbourg: Council of Europe, 1992).

Association of University Teachers, *Your Guide to Intellectual Property Rights* (London, 1999).

Baigent, M., and R. Leigh, *The Dead Sea Scrolls Deception* (London: Corgi Books, 1991).

Bartoccini, R., 'Frammento di legge romana rinvenito a Taranto', *Epigraphica* 9 (1947), pp. 3-31and 10 (1948), p. 158.

Betz, O., and R. Riesner, *Jesus, Qumran und der Vatikan: Klarstellungen* (Freiburg: Herder Verlag, 3rd edn, 1993).

Birks, P., A. Rodger and J.S. Richardson, 'Further aspects of the tabula Contrebiensis', *Journal of Roman Studies* 74 (1984), pp. 45-73.

Botsford, K., *Scrolls Better Dead Than Read?*, *The Independent* (12 October 1994).

Brooks, C., *The Well Wrought Urn: Studies in the Structure of Poetry* (New York: Reynal & Hitchcock, 1947).

Candela, T. Giménez, 'La lex Irnitana: une nouvelle loi municipale de la Bétique', *Revue Internationale des Droits de l'Antiquité* 30 (1983), pp. 125-40.

—'Una contribuccíon al estudio de la ley Irnitana: la manumisión de esclavos municipales', *Iura* (1984), pp. 37-56.

Carson, C.A., 'Raiders of the Lost Scrolls: The Right of Scholarly Access to the Content of Historic Documents', *Michigan Journal of International Law* 16 (1995), pp. 298-348.

Charlesworth, J.H. (ed.), *The Dead Sea Scrolls, Hebrew, Aramaic, and Greek Texts with English Translations* (3 vols.; Tübingen: J.C.B. Mohr; Louisville: Westminster/John Knox Press, 1994, 1995, 1997).

Cheshire, G.C., and P. North, *Cheshire and North's Private International Law* (London: Butterworth, 13th edn, 1999).

Cogswell, R., 'Copyright Law for Unpublished Manuscripts and Archival Collections', in R.M. Mersky (ed.), Law Library Information Report, No. 14, 1992.

Convention concerning the protection of the world cultural and natural heritage: adopted by the General Conference at its seventeenth session, Paris, 16 November 1972 (Paris: UNESCO, 1972).

Conventions and Recommendations of UNESCO Concerning the Protection of Cultural Heritage (rev. edn; Paris: UNESCO, 1983).

'Conventions on the Means of Prohibiting and Preventing the Illicit Import, Export and Transfer of Ownership of Cultural Property (Paris, 14 November 1970)', republished in *International Legal Materials* 10 (1971), pp. 289-94.

Cornish, G.P., *Copyright: Interpreting the Law for Libraries, Archives and Information Services* (London: Library Association, 3rd edn, 1999).

'Council Directive 93/7/EEC of 15 March 1993 on the Return of Cultural Objects Unlawfully Removed from the Territory of a Member State' in *Official Journal of the European Communities* No. L 74/74, 27. 3. 93

'Council Regulation (EEC) No 3911/92 of 9 December 1992 on the Export of Cultural Goods' in *Official Journal of the European Communities* No. L 395/1, 31. 12. 92.

Crawford, M.H. with a contribution by J.D. Cloud, *Roman Statutes* (2 vols.; London: Institute of Classical Studies, 1996).

Crewdson, R., 'Cultural Property: A Fourth Estate?', *Law Society Gazette* 18 (1984), pp. 126-29.

Daux, G., 'Un septième décret inédit d'Entella (Sicile)', *Bulletin de Correspondance Héllenique* 106 (1982), pp. 307-308 and 527-28.

Denicola, R.C., 'Copyright in Collections of Facts: A Theory for the Protection of Non-fiction Literary Works', *Columbia Law Review* 81 (1981), pp. 516-42.

Dickens, Charles, *Bleak House* (New York: Modern Library, 1985).

Dine, Jeffrey M., '"Authors" Moral Rights in Non-European Nations: International Agreements, Economics, Mannu Bhandari, and the Dead Sea Scrolls', *Michigan Journal of International Law* 16 (1995), pp. 545-82.

D'Ors, A., 'Litem suam facere', *Studia et Documenta Historiae Iuris* 48 (1982), pp. 368-84.

—'La nueva copia irnitana de la "lex Flavia municipalis"', *Anuario de Historia del Derecho Español* 53 (1983), pp. 5-15.

—'Nuevos datos de la ley Irnitana sobre jurisdiccíon municipal', *Studia et Documenta Historiae Iuris* 49 (1983), pp. 18-50.

—'Una nueva lista de aciones infamantes', in V. Giuffrè (ed.), *Sodalitas: scritti in honore Antonio Guarino* (Naples: Jovene, 1984), pp. 2575-90.

—'De nuevo sobre la ley municipal', *Studia et Documenta Historiae Iuris* 50 (1984), pp. 179-98.

—'La ley Flavia municipal', *Anuario de Historia del Derecho Español* 54 (1984), pp. 535-73.

Eck, W., A. Caballos and F. Fernández, *Das senatus consultum de Cn. Pisone patre* (Vestigia Band 48; Munich: C.H. Beck, 1996).

Eisenman, Robert H., and James M. Robinson (eds.), *A Facsimile of the Dead Sea Scrolls: Prepared with an Introduction and Index. With a Publisher's Foreword by Hershel Shanks* (2 vols.; Washington, DC: Biblical Archaeology Society, 1991).

Eisenstein, Elizabeth L., *The Printing Press as an Agent of Change: Communications and Cultural Transformations in Early Modern Europe*, I (Cambridge: Cambridge University Press, 1979).

Engstler, L.L., *Die territoriale Bindung von Kulturgütern im Rahmen des Völkerrechts* (Cologne: C. Heymann, 1964).

Epstein, Richard S., 'International News Service v. Associated Press: Custom and Law As Sources of Property Rights in News', *Virginia Law Review* 78 (1992), pp. 85-147.

Eshel, I., and. K. Prag (eds.), *Excavations by K.M. Kenyon in Jerusalem 1961–1967.* IV. *The Iron Age Cave Deposits on the South-east Hill and Isolated Burials and*

Cemeteries Elsewhere (British Academy Monographs in Archaeology, 6; Oxford: Oxford University Press, 1995).

European Convention on the Protection of the Archaeological Heritage (revised), Valletta, 16.1.1992 (European Treaty Series, 143; Strasbourg: Council of Europe, 1992).

Fatás, G., *Contrebia Belaisca II: Tabula Contrebiensis* (Monografías arqueológicas, 23; Zaragoza: Universidad de Zaragoza, 1980).

Faur, Jose, *Golden Doves With Silver Dots: Semiotics and Textuality in Rabbinic Tradition* (Bloomington, IN: Indiana University Press, 1986).

Fawcett, J., and P. Torremans, *Intellectual Property and Private International Law* (Oxford: Clarendon Press, 1998).

Fernández Gómez, F., and M. del Amo y la Herra, *La lex Irnitana y su contexto arqueologico* (Marchena [Sevilla]: Museo Arqueologico de Marchena, 1990).

Fitzmyer, J.M., *Responses to 101 Questions on the Dead Sea Scrolls* (New York: Paulist Press, 1992).

Francione, G.L., 'Facing the Nation: The Standards for Copyright Infringement and Fair Use of Factual Works', *University of Pennsylvania Law Review* 134 (1986), pp. 519-98.

Franken, H.J., and M.L. Steiner (eds.), *Excavations in Jerusalem 1961–1967.* II. *The Iron Age Extramural Quarter on the South-East Hill* (British Academy Monographs in Archaeology, 2; Oxford: Oxford University Press, 1990).

Freedman, D.N., and K.A. Mathews, *The Paleo-Hebrew Leviticus Scroll* (Winona Lake, IN: Eisenbrauns, 1985).

Frye, Northrop, *Anatomy of Criticism: Four Essays* (Princeton: Princeton University Press, 1957).

García Martínez, F., *Textos de Qumrán* (Madrid: Trotta, 1992).

—*The Dead Sea Scrolls Translated—The Qumran Texts in English, The Authoritative New Translation of the Dead Sea Scrolls Complete in One Volume* (trans. W.G.E. Watson; Leiden: E.J. Brill, 1994).

García Martínez, F., and A.S. van der Woude, *De rollen van de Dode Zee* I-II (Kampen/ Tielt: Kok, 1994–95).

García Martínez, F. and E.J.C. Tigchelaar, *The Dead Sea Scrolls Study Edition*, I-II (Leiden: E.J. Brill, 1997–98).

Garnett, K., J. Rayner James and G. Davies (eds.), *Copinger and Skone James on Copyright* (London: Sweet & Maxwell, 14th edn, 1999).

Gaster, T., *The Dead Sea Scriptures* (Garden City, NY: Anchor/Doubleday, 3rd edn, 1976).

Gerstenblith, P., 'Identity and Cultural Property: The Protection of Cultural Property in the United States', *Boston University Law Review* 75 (1995), pp. 559-688

Ginsburg, Jane C., 'Sabotaging and Reconstructing History: A Comment on the Scope of Copyright Protection in Works of History After Hoehling v. Universal City Studios', *Journal of the Copyright Society* 29 (1982), p. 647.

—'Colors in Conflict: Moral Rights and the Foreign Exploitation of US Motion Pictures', *Journal of the Copyright Society of the USA* 36 (1988–89), p. 81.

—'French Copyright Law: A Comparative Overview', *Journal of the Copyright Society of the USA* 36 (1988–89), pp. 269-81.

—'Creation and Commercial Value: Copyright Protection of Works of Information', *Columbia Law Review* 90 (1990), pp. 1865-1938.

—'Conflicts of Copyright Ownership Between Authors and Owners of Original Artworks:

An Essay in Comparative and International Private Law', *Columbia-VLA Journal of Law and the Arts* 17 (1993), p. 405.

Ginsburg, Jane C., and P. Sirinelli, 'Authors and Expliotations in International Private Law: the French Supreme Court and the Huston Film Colonization Controversy', *Columbia-VLA Journal of Law and the Arts* 15 (1991), pp. 135, 139.

—'Auteur, creation et adaptation en droit international privé', *RIDA* 150 (1991), p. 21.

Giustolini, V., *Nakone ed Entella alla luce degli antichi decreti recentemente apparsi e di un nuovo decreto inedito* (Sicilia archeologica che scompare, 7; Palermo: Centro di Documentazione e Ricerca per la Sicilia antica 'Paolo Orsi' [1985], pp. 16-24).

González, J., 'The *Lex Irnitana*: a new Flavian municipal law', *Journal of Roman Studies* 76 (1986), pp. 147-243.

Grady, Mark F., and Jay I. Alexander, 'Patent Law and Rent Dissipation', *Virginia Law Review* 78 (1992), pp. 305-50.

Greenawalt, K., 'Thinking in Terms of Law and Morality', *International Journal of Cultural Property* 7 (1998), pp. 7-20.

Grohmann, A., *Arabic Papyri from Hirbet el-Mird* (Bibliothèque du Muséon 52; Louvain, 1963).

Groner, J., 'Dispute Over Sacred Scrolls Lands', *US Court*, *Legal Times* (20 September 1993).

Gruenwald, Ithamar, 'Midrash and the 'Midrashic Condition: Preliminary Considerations', in Michael Fishbane (ed.), *The Midrashic Imagination: Jewish Exegesis, Thought and History* (Albany: State University of New York Press, 1993).

Halbertal, Moshe, *People of the Book: Canon, Meaning and Authority* (Cambridge, MA: Harvard University Press, 1997).

Hand, Learned, 'The Deficiencies of Trials to Reach the Heart of the Matter', in *Lectures on Legal Topics 1921–1922*, III (New York: The Macmillan Company, 1926), pp. 89-106.

Havelock, Eric A., *The Muse Learns To Write: Reflections On Orality And Literacy from Antiquity to the Present* (New Haven: Yale University Press, 1986).

Hewitt, David, 'General Introduction' to Walter Scott, *St Ronan's Well* (ed. Mark Weinstein; The Edinburgh Edition of the Waverley Novels; Edinburgh: Edinburgh University Press, 1995).

Hole, F., and R.F. Heizer, *Prehistoric Archaeology: A Brief Introduction* (New York: Holt, Rinehart & Winston, 1977).

Holyoak, J., and P. Torremans, *Holyoak and Torremans Intellectual Property Law* (London: Butterworth, 1998).

Hoving, Thomas, *Tutankhamun: The Untold Story* (New York: Simon & Schuster, 1978).

Jordan, Hashemite Kingdom, *Rules of Excavation* (Amman, 1975).

—*Regulations of Archaeological Excavations and Surveys in Accordance with the Provisions of the Law of Antiquities No. 21 for 1988* (Amman, 1988).

Julia, Dominique, 'Reading and the Counter-Reformation', *A History of Reading in the West* (eds. Guglielmo Cavallo and Roger Chartier; Polity Press, 1999).

Karjala, Dennis S., 'Copyright and Misappropriation', *Dayton Law Review* 17 (1992), pp. 885, 907 n. 80.

Kenyon, K.M., 'Excavations in Jerusalem, 1961', *Palestine Exploration Quarterly* 94 (1962), pp. 72-89.

—'Excavations in Jerusalem, 1962', *Palestine Exploration Quarterly* 95 (1963), pp. 7-21.

—'Excavations in Jerusalem, 1963', *Palestine Exploration Quarterly* 96 (1964), pp. 7-18.

—'Excavations in Jerusalem, 1964', *Palestine Exploration Quarterly* 97 (1965), pp. 1-12.

—'Excavations in Jerusalem, 1965', *Palestine Exploration Quarterly* 98 (1966), pp. 73-88.

—'Excavations in Jerusalem, 1966', *Palestine Exploration Quarterly* 99 (1967), pp. 65-71.

—'Excavations in Jerusalem, 1967', *Palestine Exploration Quarterly* 100 (1968), pp. 97-109.

—*Jerusalem. Excavating 3000 Years of History* (London: Thames & Hudson, 1967).

—*Digging Up Jerusalem* (London: Benn, 1974).

Kowalski, Wojciech, *Liquidation of the Effects of World War II in the Area of Culture* (Warsaw: Institute of Culture, 1994).

—*Art Treasures and War: A Study on the Restitution of Looted Cultural Property, Pursuant to Public International Law* (London: Institute of Art and Law, 1998).

—'Chapter A. At the Service of the Archaeological Heritage. Principle 1', *International Journal of Cultural Property* 7.1 (1998), pp. 223-30.

—'Cultural Tensions: The Case of Museums', *Art, Antiquity and Law* 3 (1998), pp. 101-102.

—'Conservation of Works of Art under Polish Copyright Law', *Art, Antiquity and Law* 4 (1999), pp. 101-102.

Kwall, Roberta Rosenthal, 'Copyright and the Moral Right: Is an American Marriage Possible?', *Vanderbilt Law Review* 38 (1985), p. 1.

Laddie, H., P. Prescott and M. Vitoria, *The Modern Law of Copyright and Designs* (London: Butterworth, 2nd edn, 1995).

Landau, Asher Felix, 'The Dead Sea Scrolls and the Recognized Rules of Copyright', *The Jerusalem Post* (11 April 1993).

The Law of the Sea: Official Text of the United Nations Convention on the Law of the Sea with Annexes and Index: Final Act of the Third United Nations Conference on the Law of the Sea: Introductory Material on the Convention and the Conference (New York: United Nations, 1983).

Lawrence, John S., 'Copyright Law, Fair Use, and the Academy', in John S. Lawrence and Bernard Timberg (eds.), *Fair Use and Free Inquiry* (New York: Ablex, 1980), pp. 3, 9.

Lim, Timothy H., in consultation with P. Alexander, *The Dead Sea Scrolls—Electronic Reference Library* (Oxford: Oxford University Press; Leiden: E.J. Brill, 1997).

Lucas, A., and H.J. Lucas, *Traité de la Propriété Littéraire et Artistique Litec* (Paris: Litec, 1994).

MacQueen, L. Hector, and B.G.M. Main (eds.), *Innovation, Incentive and Reward: Intellectual Property Law and Policy* (Hume Papers on Public Policy, 5.3; Edinburgh: Edinburgh University Press for the David Hume Institute, 1997), pp. 1-16.

Maier, J., *Die Qumran-Essener: Die Texte vom Toten Meer* (3 vols.; Munich/Basel: Reinhardt, 1995–96).

'The Marshall Files: The Complaints and the Library's Response', *The Washington Post* (27 May 1993).

Milik, J.T., *The Books of Enoch* (Oxford: Clarendon Press, 1976).

Muchowski, P., *Rekopisy znad morza martwego Qumran–Wadi Murabb'at–Masada Biblioteka zwojów tlo Nowego Testamentu* 5 (Kraków: Enigma, 1996).

Nenci, G. *et al.* [no title], Articles on the Entella decrees, *Annali della scuole normale superiore di Pisa* ser.3, 12 (1982), pp. 771-1103.

Nimmer, Melville B., and David Nimmer, *Nimmer on Copyright* (10 vols.; New York: Matthew Bender, 1997).

Nimmer, David, 'Adam and Bits: Of Jewish Kings and Copyrights', *Southern California Law Review* 71.2 (1998), pp. 219-45.

—'Copyright In the Dead Sea Scrolls', *Houston Law Review*, 38 (2001), pp. 1-236.

O'Callaghan, J., *Los papiros griegos de la cueva 7 de Qumrân* (Biblioteca de autores christianos 353; Madrid: Editorial Catolica, 1974).

O'Keefe, P.J., *Codes of Ethics: Form and Function in Cultural Heritage Management*, pp. 23-31.

Plucknett, T.F.T., *Early English Legal Literature* (Cambridge: Cambridge University Press, 1958).

Palmer, N.E., and E. McKendrick, *Interests in Goods* (London: Lloyds of London Press, 1993).

Prag, K., *Excavations by K.M. Kenyon in Jerusalem 1961–1967*, V.

Protection of Archaeological Heritage. Explanatory Report on the Revised Convention Opened for Signature on 16 January 1992 (Strasbourg: Council of Europe Press, 1992).

The Protection of Movable Cultural Property: A Compendium of Legislative Texts (Paris: UNESCO, 1984), I.

Prott, L.V., 'Restitution of Cultural Property', *University of British Columbia Law Review* Special Issue (1995), p. 45.

—'Symposium: The Native American Graves Protection and Repatriation Act of 1990 and State Repatriation related Legislation', *Arizona State Law Journal* 24 (1992), pp. 229-40

—*Commentary on the Unidroit Convention on Stolen and Illegally Exported Cultural Objects 1995* (Leicester: Institute of Art and Law, 1997).

Prott, L.V., and P.J. O'Keefe, *Law and the Cultural Heritage. Discovery and Excavation* (Abingdon: Professional Books, 1984), 1.

—'Cultural Heritage' or 'Cultural Property?', *International Journal of Cultural Property* 1 (1992), pp. 307-20.

Qimron, Elisha, and John Strugnell, *Discoveries in the Judean Desert*. X. *Qumran Cave 4*: V. *Miqṣat Ma'aśe Ha-Torah* (Oxford: Clarendon Press, 1994).

—'The Nature of the Reconstructed Composite Text of 4QMMT', *Reading 4QMMT: New Perspectives on Qumran Law and History* (eds. John Kampen and Moshe J. Bernstein; Atlanta: Scholars Press, 1996), pp. 9-14.

Rabinovich, A., 'Court Awards Dead Sea Scrolls Translator NIS 100,000', *The Jerusalem Post* (31 March 1993).

—'Court Hears Copyright Dispute on Dead Sea Scrolls', *The Jerusalem Post* (26 February 1993).

—'Dead Sea Scrolls Publisher Appeals Conviction for Copyright Violation', *The Jerusalem Post* (4 June 1993).

Regulations of Archaeological Excavations and Surveys in Accordance with the Provisions of the Law of Antiquities No. 21 for 1988 (Amman: Jordan, Hashemite Kingdom, 1988).

Richardson, J.S., 'The tabula Contrebiensis', *Journal of Roman Studies* 73 (1983), pp. 33-41.

—'Tarentum Fragment', in M.H. Crawford *et al.*, *Roman Statutes*, VIII (London: Institute of Classical Studies, 1996), pp. 209-18.

Rodota, S., 'The Art Trade. Report of the Committee on Culture and Education and Related Documents', *Council of Europe. Parliamentary Assembly*, Doc. 5834-E (Strasbourg: Council of Europe, 1988).

Rules of Excavation (Amman: Jordan, Hashemite Kingdom, 1975).

Schricker, G., *Urheberrecht Kommentar* (Munich: C.H. Beck, 2nd edn, 1999).

Shanks, Hershel, 'Qimron is Author of MMT Reconstruction, Jerusalem Court Holds', *Biblical Archaeology Review* (May–June 1993), p. 69.

—'MMT as the Maltese Falcon', *Biblical Archaeology Review* (November–December, 1994).

—'Qimron Defends His Lawsuit—"No Threat to Intellectual Freedom" ', *Biblical Archaeology Review* (March–April, 1993), pp. 68-71.

—*Jerusalem: An Archaeological Biography* (New York: Random House, 1995).

—*The Mystery and Meaning of the Dead Sea Scrolls* (New York: Random House, 1998).

Shanks, H. (ed.), *Understanding the Dead Sea Scrolls* (Washington, DC: Biblical Archaeo logy Society, 1993).

Sherwood-Edwards, M., 'The Redundancy of Originality', *International Review of Industrial Property and Copyright* 25 (1994), pp. 658-89.

Stearns, Laurie, 'Copy Wrong: Plagiarism, Process, Property, and the Law', *California Law Review* 80 (1992), pp. 513-53.

Stegemann, Hartmut, 'How to Connect Dead Sea Scrolls Fragments', in Shanks (ed.), *Understanding the Dead Sea Scrolls*, pp. 245-55.

Steiner, M.L., *Excavations in Jerusalem 1961–1967*. III. *The Settlement of the Bronze and Iron Ages* (Sheffield: Sheffield Academic Press, 2001).

Stoppard, Tom, *The Invention of Love* (London: Faber, 1997).

Strati, Anastasia, 'Deep Seabed Cultural Property and the Common Heritage of Mankind', *International and Comparative Law Quarterly* 40 (1991), pp. 859-94.

—*The Protection of the Underwater Cultural Heritage: An Emerging Objective of the Contemporary Law of the Sea* (The Hague: Martinus Nijhoff, 1995).

Summer, R. 'The Dead Sea Scrolls', *Publishers Weekly* (10 January 1994).

—*Terms and Conditions to Conduct an Archaeological Excavation in Israel* (Jerusalem: Israel Antiquities Authority, 1997).

Thiede, C.P., *Die älteste Evangelien-Handschrift? Das Markus-Fragment von Qumran und die Anfänge der schriftlichen Überlieferung des Neuen Testaments* (Wuppertal: Brockhaus, 1986); ET *The Earliest Gospel Manuscript? The Qumran Fragment 7Q5 and Its Significance for New Testament Studies* (London: Paternoster Press, 1992).

Tov, E., '4QJer^{b}', in E. Ulrich *et al.*, *Qumran Cave 4.X: The Prophets* (DJD, 15; Oxford: Clarendon Press, 1997), pp. 71-176.

—'A List of the Texts from the Judaean Desert', in P.W. Flint and J.C. VanderKam (eds.), *The Dead Sea Scrolls after Fifty Years—A Comprehensive Assessment* (Leiden: E.J. Brill, 1999), II, pp. 2ff.

Tov, E. (ed.), *The Dead Sea Scrolls Database (Non-Biblical Texts)*, in *The Dead Sea Scrolls Electronic Reference Library*. II. *Prepared by the Foundation for Ancient Research and Mormon Studies (FARMS)* (Leiden: E.J. Brill, 1999).

Tov, E., with the collaboration of S.J. Pfann, *The Dead Sea Scrolls on Microfiche—A Comprehensive Facsimile Edition of the Texts from the Judean Desert, with a Companion Volume* (Leiden: E.J. Brill and IDC, 1993, 1995).

Trever, J.C., *The Dead Sea Scrolls: A Personal Account* (Grand Rapids, MI: Eerdmans, 1977).

Tushingham, A.D., *Excavations in Jerusalem 1961–1967*, I (Toronto: Royal Ontario Museum; Leiden: E.J. Brill, 1985).

Ulmer, E., *Intellectual Property Rights and the Conflict of Laws: A Study Carried Out for the Commission of the European Communities, Directorate-General for the Internal Market and Industrial Affairs* (Deventer: Kluwer, 1978).

UNESCO, Records of the General Conference, 29th Session, 1997, Resolutions, 1 (Paris: UNESCO, 1998).

United Nations Conference on Succession of States in Respect of State Property, Archives and Debts : Vienna, 1 March–8 April 1983 (New York: United Nations, 1995).

Vaux, R. de, 'Jérusalem', in 'Chronique Archéologique', *Revue Biblique* 69 (1962), pp. 80-82.

—'Jérusalem (Ophel)' in 'Chronique Archéologique', *Revue Biblique* 69 (1962), pp. 98-100.

—'Jérusalem', in 'Chronique Archéologique', *Revue Biblique* 70 (1963), pp. 416-19.

—'Jérusalem', in 'Chronique Archéologique', *Revue Biblique* 71 (1964), pp. 253-58.

—'Les Hôpitaux de Justinien à Jérusalem, d'après les dernières fouilles', *Compte Rendus de l'Académie des Inscriptions et Belles-Lettres* (1964), pp. 202-207.

Vermes, Geza, Timothy H. Lim and Robert P. Gordon, 'The Oxford Forum for Qumran Research: Seminar on the Rule of War (4Q285)', *Journal of Jewish Studies* 43 (1992), pp. 85-92.

Vermes, Geza, *The Dead Sea Scrolls: Qumran in Perspective* (London: SCM Press, 1994).

—*The Complete Dead Sea Scrolls in English* (London: Penguin Press, 1997).

Visscher, C. de, 'La protection internationale des objets d'art et des monuments historiques', *Revue de Droit International et de Législation Comparée*, 11.1-2 (1935), pp. 32-74 and 246-88.

Wacholder, B.Z., and M.G. Abegg, *A Preliminary Edition of the Unpublished Dead Sea Scrolls: The Hebrew and Aramaic Texts from Cave Four*; *Biblical Archaeological Society*, I–IV (Washington: Biblical Archaeology Society, 1991–1996).

Weinstein, Lisa M., 'Ancient Works, Modern Dilemmas: The Dead Sea Scrolls Copyright Case', *American University Law Review* 43 (1994), pp. 1637, 1649-51.

Williams, Sharon A., *The International and National Protection of Movable Cultural Property: A Comparative Study* (Dobbs Ferry: Oceana, 1978).

Wilson, Edmund, *The Dead Sea Scrolls: 1947–1969* (Glasgow: Collins, 1969).

Wise, M., M. Abegg, Jr, and E. Cook, *The Dead Sea Scrolls: A New Translation* (New York: HarperSanFrancisco, 1996).

Wood, Daniel, 'Library That "Freed" the Scrolls Hears a Jericho-like Blast of Support', *Christian Science Monitor* (8 October 1991).

Yadin, Yigael, *The Temple Scroll* (3 vols.; Jerusalem: Israel Exploration Society, 1977) (Hebrew); Translated as *The Temple Scroll* (3 vols.; Jerusalem: Israel Exploration Society, 1983).

Your Guide to Intellectual Property Rights (London: Association of University Teachers, 1999).

INDEX OF AUTHORS

JOURNAL FOR THE STUDY OF THE PSEUDEPIGRAPHA SUPPLEMENT SERIES

1 John R. Levison, *Portraits of Adam in Early Judaism: From Sirach to 2 Baruch*

2 Per Bilde, *Flavius Josephus between Jerusalem and Rome: His Life, his Works, and their Importance*

3 Philip R. Callaway, *The History of the Qumran Community: An Investigation*

4 Tom W. Willet, *Eschatology in the Theodicies of 2 Baruch and 4 Ezra*

5 James R. Mueller, *The Five Fragments of the Apocryphon of Ezekiel: A Critical Study*

6 Robert G. Hall, *Revealed Histories: Techniques for Ancient Jewish and Christian Historiography*

7 George J. Brooke (ed.), *Temple Scroll Studies: Papers Presented at the International Symposium on the Temple Scroll (Manchester, 1987)*

8 Lawrence H. Schiffman (ed.), *Archaeology and History in the Dead Sea Scrolls: The New York University Conference in Memory of Yigael Yadin*

9 John J. Collins and James H. Charlesworth (eds.), *Mysteries and Revelations: Apocalyptic Studies since the Uppsala Colloquium*

10 Shemaryahu Talmon (ed.), *Jewish Civilization in the Hellenistic-Roman Period*

11 Maxwell J. Davidson, *Angels at Qumran: A Comparative Study of 1 Enoch 1–36, 72–108 and Sectarian Writings from Qumran*

12 David Bryan, *Cosmos, Chaos and the Kosher Mentality*

13 Gordon M. Zerbe, *Non-Retaliation in Early Jewish and New Testament Texts: Ethical Themes in Social Contexts*

14 James H. Charlesworth and Craig A. Evans (eds.), *The Pseudepigrapha and Early Biblical Interpretation*

15 Michael Owen Wise, *Thunder in Gemini, and Other Essays on the History, Language and Literature of Second Temple Palestine*

16 Randall D. Chesnutt, *From Death to Life: Conversion in Joseph and Aseneth*

17 Edith McEwan Humphrey, *The Ladies and the Cities: Transformation and Apocalyptic Identity in Joseph and Aseneth, 4 Ezra, the Apocalypse and The Shepherd of Hermas*

18 Jonathan Knight, *Disciples of the Beloved One: The Christology, Social Setting and Theological Context of the Ascension of Isaiah*

19 Ida Fröhlich, *Time and Times and Half a Time: Historical Consciousness in the Jewish Literature of the Persian and Hellenistic Eras*

20 Paolo Sacchi, *Jewish Apocalyptic and Its History*

21 Isaiah M. Gafni, *Land, Center and Diaspora: Jewish Constructs in Late Antiquity*

22 James H. Charlesworth, *Critical Reflections on the Odes of Solomon,*

Volume 1: Literary Setting, Textual Studies, Gnosticism, the Dead Sea Scrolls and the Gospel of John

23 Samuel Cheon, *The Exodus Story in the Wisdom of Solomon: A Study in Biblical Interpretation*

24 Doron Mendels, *Identity, Religion and Historiography: Studies in Hellenistic History*

25 Michael Chyutin, *The New Jerusalem Scroll from Qumran: A Comprehensive Reconstruction*

26 Stanley E. Porter and Craig A. Evans (eds.), *The Scrolls and the Scriptures: Qumran Fifty Years After*

27 Gerbern S. Oegema, *The Anointed and his People: Messianic Expectations from the Maccabees to Bar Kochba*

28 Phillip B. Munoa, III, *Four Powers in Heaven: The Interpretation of Daniel 7 in the Testament of Abraham*

29 James S. McLaren, *Turbulent Times? Josephus and Scholarship on Judaea in the First Century* CE

30 Nikos Kokkinos, *The Herodian Dynasty: Origins, Role in Society and Eclipse*

31 Siân Jones and Sarah Pearce (eds.), *Jewish Local Patriotism and Self-Identification in the Graeco-Roman Period*

32 Steve Mason (ed.), *Understanding Josephus: Seven Perspectives*

33 Craig A. Evans (ed.), *The Interpretation of Scripture in Early Judaism and Christianity: Studies in Language and Tradition*

34 Paulson Pulikottil, *Transmission of Biblical Texts in Qumran: The Case of the Large Isaiah Scroll (1QIsa^{a})*

36 Magen Broshi, *Bread, Wine, Walls and Scrolls*

37 Bruce N. Fisk, *Do You Not Remember? Exegetical Appropriations of Biblical Narrative in Pseudo-Philo*

38 Timothy H. Lim, Hector MacQueen and Calum Carmichael (eds.), *On Scrolls, Artefacts and Intellectual Property*

39 Lorenzo DiTommaso, *A Bibliography of Pseudepigrapha Research 1850–1999*